WRITING THE MEAL: DINNER IN THE FICTION OF
EARLY TWENTIETH-CENTURY WOMEN WRITERS

DIANE McGEE

Writing the Meal:
Dinner in the Fiction of Early Twentieth-Century Women Writers

UNIVERSITY OF TORONTO PRESS
Toronto Buffalo London

© University of Toronto Press Incorporated 2001
Toronto Buffalo London
Printed in Canada

ISBN 0-8020-3541-8

Printed on acid-free paper

National Library of Canada Cataloguing in Publication Data

McGee, Diane E.
Writing the meal : dinner in the fiction of early twentieth-century women
writers

Includes bibliographical references and index.
ISBN 0-8020-3541-8

1. Dinners and dining in literature.   2. Wharton, Edith, 1862–1937 –
Criticism and interpretation.   3. Mansfield, Katherine, 1888–1923 –
Criticism and interpretation.   4. Woolf, Virginia, 1882–1941 – Criticism and
interpretation.   5. Chopin, Kate, 1851–1904 – Criticism and interpretation.
6. American fiction – Women authors – History and criticism.   7. American
fiction – 20th century – History and criticism.   8. English fiction – Women
authors – History and criticism.   9. English fiction – 20th century – History
and criticism. I. Title.

PR888.F65 M34 2001   823'.91209355   C2001-930197-9

An earlier version of part of chapter 7 appeared as 'The Structure of
Meals in Kate Chopin's *The Awakening*' in *Proteus: A Journal of Ideas* 17: 1
(Spring 2000).

University of Toronto Press acknowledges the financial assistance to its
publishing program of the Canada Council for the Arts and the Ontario
Arts Council.

This book has been published with the help of a grant from the Humanities
and Social Sciences Federation of Canada, using funds provided by the
Social Sciences and Humanities Research Council of Canada.

University of Toronto Press acknowledges the financial support for its
publishing activities of the Government of Canada through the Book
Publishing Industry Development Program (BPIDP).

In memory of my parents, Lillian and Donald,
and for my son Matthew

Contents

viii   Contents

7 The Art of Domesticity   147

Conclusion   182

WRITING THE MEAL

Introduction:
'A Time to Eat'

A pleasant simple habitual and tyrannical and authorised and educated and
resumed and articulate separation. This is not tardy.

Gertrude Stein, *Tender Buttons*

This study explores the role of dinner in fiction by Edith Wharton,
Katherine Mansfield, Virginia Woolf, and Kate Chopin, as well as other
early twentieth-century women writers. The meals in the works discussed here range from two people sharing simple food to formal
dinners and parties. The dinner or dinner party is crucial not only in
defining the characters, their world, and their relationship to that world,
but also in structuring the novel or the story and, for the reader, in
understanding the author's relationship to her own world and her own
historical times. Certainly, some male writers of the period also describe dinners; however, I will argue that meals have particular resonance in the writing of women. When Leopold Bloom cooks a kidney
for his breakfast and makes tea and toast for his wife in *Ulysses*, it is
striking, unusual. For women, on the other hand, even across class
lines, some aspect of getting the meal on the table is generally a major
daily preoccupation, so much assumed, perhaps, that earlier generations of women writers would rarely have included details of breakfast
in their fiction.

Although I will also look at other meals, dinner is – both actually and
in the cultural imagination – the main meal of the day, the most social-
ized, the most likely to be ritualized. Conceptually, dinner is the weighti-
est meal, not only in terms of its menu, but also in the social expectations
and importance that surround it. I am not concerned merely with the

physical details of serving and of eating dinner, although a particular meal can be of great culinary, aesthetic, and symbolic importance, but also with larger issues that emanate from dinners in these novels and stories. An exploration of a fictional dinner leads into questions about the larger domestic role of women, about the representation of mothering and nurturing, about the political, economic, and class situations that underlie a particular meal, about philosophical issues, about time and death. In other words, this discussion will treat dinner as resonant, potent, full of meaning, an occasion and a source for understanding more than the table itself. It is important to note that it is often not only difficult but perhaps inappropriate to separate the discussion of dinner from discussions of food, the raw material of a meal. Issues surrounding foodstuffs obviously have a major impact on the literary presentation of dinners. For instance, the fact that some works of fiction describe only raw food *rather than* dinner is in itself significant.

On a very basic level, it makes sense that meals should be important in literature; food is as fundamental to human beings as to any other living organism. And more so, perhaps: anthropologist Sidney Mintz comments that 'food and eating afford us a remarkable arena in which to watch how the human species invests a basic activity with social meaning – indeed, with so much meaning that the activity itself can almost be lost sight of' (*Tasting Food* 7). Works of fiction have a close connection to the everyday; whether a writer attempts to reflect accurately the social world of ordinary life or deliberately to distort or ignore it, she is confronting it in one way or another. But the portrayal of meals plays a more important role than merely reproducing reality; because eating is important to us socially, emotionally, psychologically, and erotically, the fictional depiction of meals implies a rich potential for various levels of meaning. Some of the rules, rituals, and associations that surround the act of eating may repress or negate its physical nature, but may also enhance the meaning of the meal, giving it a social, a religious, even a mythic quality that is at least as important as its nourishment value. Moreover, meals are potent conveyers of larger social and economic issues, issues arising both within the text itself and in the larger historical context in which the work of art was produced.

Since the Greek *symposium*, the dinner or banquet has been an occasion for speech, and, since Plato, it has been portrayed in literature as such. In fiction, a gathering of people around the dinner table allows the plot to develop as confrontations occur and connections are forged. Whether in the setting of an intimate dinner or a large party, eating together means that human interactions occur: important issues are discussed, revelations made, intimacies exchanged, and seductions attempted. A fictional dinner may serve to elucidate or disclose the individual relationships of the people attending the dinner or party, but it can also do more than that. For instance, through the yearly ritual of Christmas dinner, James Joyce's 'The Dead' freely explores the entire range of social connotations that a dinner party brings to the fore: from the individual relationships of marriage, kinship, and friendship to the larger political and cultural context of Ireland as a whole. Dinners can also structure the novel. In Kate Chopin's *The Awakening*, for example, dinners mark the progress of Edna Pontellier's awakening, culminating in the extravagant dinner party which she hosts to mark her changed life and ending with a dinner that she orders but never intends to eat. In Zora Neale Hurston's *Their Eyes Were Watching God*, the whole novel turns on dinner: that is, the heroine tells her story after eating the dinner which her friend has cooked. In Virginia Woolf's *Mrs. Dalloway*, the entire novel builds up to and defines Clarissa's party. Within the fictional world, then, a dinner may be not only an occasion of speech but the impetus for the entire novel. In a larger sense, the novel itself can be viewed as a banquet served by the writer to the reader.

What is most fundamental to this study, however, is the fact that in most cultures – and certainly in the period under discussion – dinner is in one way or another a woman's affair. The failure or success of the meal is her responsibility. The dinner can be an expression of creativity or a mere chore – and is often a combination of both. The woman's abilities as a hostess may mean social, political, or financial success; a dinner might lead to the rise or fall of the family fortunes. A woman may be judged as a woman based on her dinners; the way she handles her role either as a provider of nourishment or as a social convener may be viewed by herself and others as indicative of her womanhood, her femininity. As the cook or the supervisor of servants, she creates the domestic community of the table, and, in so doing, holds the family together. As a hostess, she endorses social customs, social values; in giving a dinner party, she may wield a formidable amount of power in her social set.

But not always. The dinner may involve either an active, powerful, and perhaps creative role for women or a passive, largely powerless one. The woman is the cook, the organizer, and/or the server of the meal, but the implications of these roles vary greatly with the context. When a woman is a guest, more may be expected of her than merely to share a meal and dinner-table conversation; her own enjoyment of the food and the company is frequently secondary to larger social demands. At the beginning of the twentieth century, when traditional forms of domesticity and domestic models were no longer necessarily taken for granted, actual choices about this part of life may have been more possible, for some women, than in previous periods. Yet, at the same time, culture is strong and habits die hard. In the context of the meal, this study explores the contradictions between, on the one hand, the apparent changes signalled by modernity and, on the other, constraining factors such as tradition, custom, ritual, social definitions and pressures, poverty, fear, and repression – all of which inhibited possibilities for personal liberation and a transformation of social and family structures. In the literature of the early twentieth century, and especially in that literature written by women, individual perspectives on and responses to dinners can signify a more general attitude toward society: whether alienation, insecurity, rebellion, challenge, passivity, or complacency.

The first chapter of this study sets the groundwork for a reading of literary texts by exploring, from an anthropological and sociological perspective, the notion of the meal itself as a communicative text, as well as the fundamental connections between dining and culture, and the even more basic links between food and language. In the relationship of food to dining can be found the basis or the essence of culture, just as in the transformation of speech to text, literature emerges. Bearing in mind the profound cultural importance of food preparation and the rituals of the table, chapter 2 looks at popular trends in cuisine, dining, and social life in the turn-of-the-century period, and at the production of non-literary texts that reflect those trends. This period of social change was characterized by an anxiety about areas of domestic life that had formerly been accepted as given, an unease expressed on the level of popular culture and popular media by the proliferation of cookbooks and other manuals for housekeeping and entertaining.

Opening with a discussion of the far-reaching importance of manners, chapter 3 looks at the social ritual of fictional meals, a manifestation of the manners and customs which define a society. For the characters in a novel, such manners and customs may present a way of understanding – and sometimes of deliberately reinterpreting or revising – social relations and everyday experience. For the reader, the mealtime culture portrayed in a literary work provides an important access both to the fictional world and to the author's perspective on that world. In *The Age of Innocence*, Edith Wharton, writing in the 1920s, views retrospectively the highly mannered existence of late nineteenth-century upper-class New York, the conventions of which were subtly, perhaps, but firmly upheld – chiefly by women – in order to solidify society and maintain its conservative social and economic values. The rituals and rules surrounding dinner and, by extension, social life in general form a textual overlay of society and social life which is most evident in this novel, but is also crucial in other works of fiction.

A woman can be the guest at a dinner as well as the hostess. Chapter 4 looks at those who find themselves outside or on the margins of the traditional social world, hoping for invitations. In the role of guests, the female protagonists in Wharton's *The House of Mirth* and *The Custom of the Country* pose often unconscious but inherently critical questions about social life and about the society they belong to or wish to enter. Through their relationship to the dinner table, and the larger domestic and social struggles that the dinner table represents, these characters present a challenge to the accepted world of the novel and demonstrate that this world is on the cusp of change.

The alienated, solitary diner is one manifestation of the modern reaction to the highly structured, mannered, ritualized dinner and the traditional domestic role of women. For many of Katherine Mansfield's heroines discussed in chapter 5, the apparent relaxation of nineteenth-century social structures just means loneliness, even if it is a loneliness embraced resolutely. The sometimes oppressive mealtime tradition has been replaced by a vacuum which may appear to offer the possibility of freedom; however, such freedom may be without either direction or content, and finally desired only for its own sake. Hunger becomes the standard condition; basic needs may be fulfilled, but, in much of Mansfield's work, desire gnaws both at the text, and, body and soul, at the characters.

Tracing an architectural metaphor through Mansfield's 'Bliss' and some of her New Zealand stories, as well as Woolf's *Mrs. Dalloway* and *To the Lighthouse*, chapter 6 focuses on the traditional female role within the family, taught to girls at an early age, and on the woman who lives some version of that role within the structure of the house and the framework of domesticity. Women may be trapped and rendered powerless by their place in the home. In both Mansfield and Woolf, however, women's traditional position as cook or organizer of dinner is also depicted positively and, in some cases, even honoured, although not without authorial misgivings. It is not only in the old world of *The Age of Innocence* that a woman can be happy as a hostess. In 'Prelude' and *To the Lighthouse*, for instance, some women inhabit the dining-room rather comfortably, women whom the work of fiction completely identifies with their domestic role, women to whom the author gives no first name and for whom 'Mrs' is a sort of job title.

Women's role as organizers and servers of meals, then, can be celebrated, albeit with reservations, because of its inherently creative quality. Chapter 7 explores the link between the creativity of serving a meal and that of producing a work of literature or art. A number of modernist women writers use a dinner or dinners as a structuring device for an entire work of fiction, presenting the story or novel as if it were a meal offered to the reader. As well, some works of fiction demonstrate profound links between dinner and the woman artist. If *The Awakening*, structured around a series of meals, demonstrates the difficulty of being both an artist and a traditional wife, other works suggest the possibility of a more positive correlation between the two. Focusing on Woolf and other writers, chapter 7 revisits the connections between language, creativity, and food, arguing not only that the server of dinner may serve as a model and an inspiration for the artist, but also that the meal itself, through its literary presentation, may actually be transformed into a work of art.

If both the biological nature and the transformative power of eating remain more or less constant through history, the particular habits surrounding meals are linked to social and historical change. At the beginning of the twentieth century, dining customs were at the crux of changes which included perceptible shifts in gender roles, new attitudes toward the home, the loss of the past and tradition and their gradual replacement by a brand new world of consumerism and advertising. New and experimental forms of literature and art were another kind of response to changes in everyday life. For the writers discussed in this study, the dinner is not just the metaphorical centre of their work; it is, rather, what change is about for them, and it defines them as writers and as women. Overall, the complex sets of roles and rules that define women as hostesses, cooks, and guests emerge in fictional texts as indications of twentieth-century social change, cultural fragmentation, and personal anxiety. Some women characters reject or are excluded by these roles and their accompanying ideology, but a new way of living is difficult to achieve and has a cost; women who react against the status quo are in a certain sense still ruled by it. Nevertheless, in some fiction, the serving of food is linked – both metaphorically and literally – to women's creative potential. As women writers emerge from the kitchen or dining-room at the beginning of the century, their domestic experience may in fact supply them with a voice, and thus a creative bridge to their art. Indeed, if, as some argue, cooking is the primary creative experience of humankind, the literature of the twentieth century is enriched by writers who have lived that experience, either themselves or through their foremothers. In the literature discussed here, it is important that the meal and the text are delivered and controlled by the same gender.

1

Hors d'Oeuvres: Food, Culture, and Language

Meals and the customs surrounding food are important texts of a culture, with many inherent levels of significance and signification. In most cultures, the transformation of food into meals has been largely women's business: planning, preparing, presenting, serving, cleaning up; in general working with the raw ingredients that the woman herself may quite possibly have purchased, gathered, or planted and harvested. The customs and rituals surrounding all of these activities have also been practised, protected, and maintained by women, even though, in many cultures, the larger religious signification of food has historically been the provenance of men – rabbis, priests, shamans – who oversee the women's work. Yet sometimes food has been treated as if it were a rather abstract notion having little or no relationship to someone's labour. This approach has changed in recent years, with more specific study of actual details of food customs and their manifestation in daily habits. Still, in exploring different theories of food and food customs, one must bear in mind that it is through human *work* that foodstuffs are transformed into something meaningful, indeed of fundamental and enormous significance to entire cultures and social systems. And that work is basically women's.

Since food is important to us in so many different ways, it can be studied from a variety of perspectives. Meals, with their accompanying habits and rituals, are crucial not only biologically and psychologically, but also in establishing the identity of a culture and in defining social relationships. 'One could say that an entire "world" (social environment) is present in and signified by food' (Barthes 170). The choice of food, the preparation of food, the taboos and rituals surrounding food are all important aspects of cultural definition. The sharing of food both facilitates and defines social intercourse, social intimacy. Moreover, it both mediates between social groups and accentuates as well as symbolizes the differences between groups. Food is frequently a component of rituals and may in fact lead to the creation of rituals. Food and food customs are thus intimately intertwined with religion: from a certain perspective it is ironic that the satisfaction of the most physical of needs, constituting humankind's closest connection with the rest of nature, also creates, becomes a metaphor for, and fulfils spiritual needs. A prime example is, of course, the powerful Christian symbol of the Eucharist. The central mystery of this sacrament is that food, the manifestation of human mortality, should not only represent the deity, but also confer immortality on the consumer.

The various approaches of anthropology, sociology, and history to the links between dining and culture can form a foundation for understanding the role of food and meals in literature and in the historical and cultural contexts that give birth to literary texts. Norbert Elias's view of history and sociology as processes insists that, just as social mores and customs are not universal, neither are they static; rather, they are reflections and manifestations of the complex of forces at work in a society at any given time. Applied to the works of literature considered in this study, Elias's perspective suggests that the representation of dining customs in fiction is significant not only in terms of the world created in the novel or short story but also as an expression of the world in which the writer is writing and by which her work is influenced. In this conjunction between the real and the fictional worlds lies an important access to the text.

For all cultures, food and diet have functioned as conveyers of meaning both to those within the group and to outsiders. In this sense, the meal itself can be treated as a text: communicating its context, as well as its specific meaning, it gives us a reading of more than itself. As Roland Barthes observes, '[Food] is not only a collection of products that can be used for statistical or nutritional studies. It is also, and at the same time, a system of communication, a body of images, a protocol of usages, situations, and behavior' (167). Thus, food items or prepared dishes can never be viewed as isolated from the larger social and cultural network in which they are situated. To an anthropologist, the food system includes domestic space and organization, food-related artifacts, sources of fuel, technologies, kinship relationships, gender roles, sexual and marital customs, economic values, class, exchange systems, even war and peace – in short, the choice, preparation and presentation of food signify a good deal more than merely the available or customary diet of a people. The culture determines what is eaten, by whom, when, and under what circumstances, as well as how and by whom meals are prepared and served. At the same time, these food practices are manifestations of that culture. Historians argue that food issues – for instance the political economy of food production and distribution, or the demographic impact of a certain sort of food – may be crucial to an understanding of other aspects of history. For example, Sidney Mintz, in *Sweetness and Power*, demonstrates the interrelationship of sugar with European history: its significant, even pre-eminent impact on economics, politics, and historical movements. It is in this sense, then, that a meal can be considered a text: more than just signifying itself, it represents the larger domestic life, which is, in turn, indicative of many aspects of culture and of history.

Thus the study of food and 'foodways' has become, in recent years, a major topic of interest in the social sciences, and a substantial corpus of work in the sociology and anthropology of food and dining has emerged.[1] Mennell, Murcott, and van Otterloo note that, although '[f]ood and eating have not until very recently generally merited a "sociology of" to themselves,' their status has changed because 'the choice of food as a focus makes possible a very wide range of intellectual connections' (118). Food is of interest not only because it can be approached in so many different ways but also because it resonates in so many parts of our lives. Food is a crucial component of what anthropologist Christopher Tilley calls 'material culture.' While not, strictly speaking, an artifact in an archaeological sense – that is, it is perishable, rather than enduring – food defines a culture, leaving its stamp on articles made and used by a people, and determining intangibles such as customs, social hierarchies, economic systems, and forms and divisions of labour. Thus, the customs surrounding food are indeed enduring: the practices or habits of serving food are major components in what creates a continuous culture over a number of generations. Food and food habits, then, are perhaps unique from an anthropological perspective: developed and sustained at the intersection of 'biological needs and cultural values' (Wood 42),[2] they play a major role not only in defining but in creating a culture.

Claude Lévi-Strauss is generally 'regarded as the principal author of contemporary interest in food and eating' (Wood 8). In his theory of the early stages of societies, the moment of cooking becomes the civilizing moment. Lévi-Strauss's notion of the raw and the cooked posits that one – perhaps *the* – major distinction between the animal and the human is the ability to transform foodstuffs into a meal. Raw food can be eaten by animals; the preparation of food is key to the formation of human society. In this sense, food defines not only a particular culture but humanity as a whole, because its preparation denotes civilization, the profound characteristic of the human species. What is particularly significant for Lévi-Strauss is the double opposition 'entre cru et cuit d'une part, entre frais et corrompu de l'autre. L'axe qui unit le cru et le cuit est caractéristique de la culture, celui qui unit le frais et le pourri, de la nature, puisque la cuisson accomplit la transformation culturelle du cru, comme la putréfaction en est la transformation naturelle' (152). Food, in Lévi-Strauss's theory, is basic to the mythology of most cultures. Particularly important are myths on the origins of the cooking fire and the discovery of various foods, because they recount a version of the moment when civilization and culture begin. Thus the roots of storytelling, art, and religion are linked to cooking. I would posit as a corollary to Lévi-Strauss's argument that cooking and artistic representation are linked in another way, too, for they may both be viewed as acts of conservation. Just as an experience, a fleeting impression, or an idea is given a certain permanence when it is told or written, so fresh food is transformed through cooking or preserving for enjoyment at a future meal. A sense of history and of inheritance – of both the past and the future – is implied in both processes.

Moreover, for Lévi-Strauss, the raw and the cooked are two of the dynamic opposites[3] – like life and death, male and female, sky and earth that he sees as fundamental to human perceptions and systems of thought: 'des catégories empiriques, telles que celles de cru et de cuit, de frais et de pourri, de mouillé et de brûlé, etc., définissables avec précision par la seule observation ethnographique et chaque fois en se plaçant au point de vue d'une culture particulière, peuvent ... servir d'outils conceptuels pour dégager des notions abstraites et les enchaîner en propositions' (9). The meal, then, civilizes, categorizes, and hierarchizes the raw. Through this process of ordering and transforming the world, cooking can be viewed as the basis of thought. In Louis Marin's terms, 'all cookery involves a theological, ideological, political, and economic operation by the means of which a nonsignified edible foodstuff is transformed into a sign/body that is eaten' (121). In other words, cooking food, serving meals, and ritualizing the basic biological process which, in itself, would have no meaning beyond mere physical necessity are key to many aspects of culture; in that they *create* meaning, these activities are fundamental to thought and to language.[4]

If, arguably, the preparation of food defines humanity, so, on a smaller scale, food habits define both individual and group characteristics. Sidney W. Mintz postulates that this is something we all know intuitively: 'Our awareness that food and eating are foci of habit, taste, and deep feeling must be as old as those occasions in the history of our species when human beings first saw other humans eating unfamiliar foods. Like languages and all other socially acquired group habits, food systems dramatically demonstrate the infraspecific variability of humankind' (*Sweetness* 3). Food is obviously important to the individual: it allows us to live; physically, it makes all other activity possible. In her 1932 book *Hunger and Work in a Savage Tribe*, anthropologist Audrey Richards points out 'that the need to eat is the most basic need we human beings know, far exceeding in importance and urgency the sexual "drive"' (paraphrased by Mintz, *Tasting Food* 35). To use Maslow's categories, food is the most basic need; until it is satisfied, no further interaction with the world, let alone a sense of self-actualization or fulfilment, is possible (ch. 4). Even in the case of deliberate fasting, the individual is still oriented to food. The conscious effort *not* to eat, to resist the natural impulse of the organism, may become another kind of obsession with food. Human beings are more complicated than animals in this regard: if hunger is a biological urge, appetite is a psychological and social construct (Mennell 21). In the human being, need becomes desire; hunger – the manifestation of a need – becomes the desire for food, which is more than merely an urge to satisfy hunger. It seems obvious that eating is pleasurable, but, as is apparent in some literary works, this pleasure in eating is frequently denied, repressed, or diverted by the individual, the society, or both. Dinner organizes, perhaps defers, and sometimes satisfies desire, but always within rules.

For babies, of course, eating means being nurtured as well as satisfying desire, an association that has profound psycho-sexual effects throughout life. But eating also establishes a connection with the world; it is the link to the social universe, first through the mother, then through other family members and the larger social group. It has been pointed out that adults always have a nostalgia for childhood food; the first foods often remain the favourite (Pasquier). Moreover, food and food-related preferences may emerge early and form part of one's fundamental sense of identity: 'What we like, what we eat, how we eat it, and how we feel about it are phenomenologically interrelated matters; together, they speak eloquently to the question of how we perceive ourselves in relation to others' (Mintz, *Sweetness* 4). Food, then, is important in establishing and maintaining the individual not only as a biological entity but as a social entity as well: it allows the individual entry into the group. If food has 'affective significance,' it is also 'a means for validating existing social relations' (Mintz, *Sweetness* 5). Anthropologists have recorded the tremendous importance given by a society to the inculcation of food habits as demarcations between groups: 'Food choices and eating habits reveal distinctions of age, sex, status, culture, and even occupation. These distinctions are immensely important adornments on an inescapable necessity' (Mintz, *Sweetness* 3).

Distinctions between what is edible and what is not are cultural decisions: 'many of the substances which human beings do not eat are items which are perfectly edible from a biological standpoint' (Harris 13). Conversely, in some cultures, potentially poisonous substances are eaten. The choice of what is acceptable to eat plays a major role in defining the culture – whether of a nation, a tribe, a class, or a family. Thus one of the first things that the child learns is what is eaten in the group(s) to which he or she belongs. Accepting these strictures as absolute is a formative experience in childhood, both in terms of the development of the individual and of that individual's membership in the group. Indeed what is *not* eaten is considered non-food, and these distinctions may be impossible to break, even under extreme duress later in life; people may starve to death because they cannot bring themselves to eat food that they find repugnant. Nations and other groups may express the 'otherness' of their neighbours by naming them according to their diet.[5] Farb and Armelagos point out that in *Macbeth* the strangeness of the three witches is underlined by what they have simmering in their cauldron (165). Used by outsiders to define a group, food is also a key part of a group's self-definition. And more than the choice of food itself is important: the rites, rituals, and taboos surrounding the harvesting or slaughtering and the preparation, serving, and eating of food are particularly significant parts of this self-definition (Simoons). Societies which practise cannibalism – the biggest food taboo for our society and for many others – have very diverse but particularly strong taboos about food. These involve questions of who may or must become food, how they are to be killed, how eaten, and by whom (Farb and Armelagos 135–44; Harris ch. 10; Visser 8–17). People assert and confirm their civilized state by respecting their culture's taboos. The importance attached to doing so may indicate our unconscious awareness of the fragility of civilization.

Children, then, learn more at the table than merely what is good to eat. For one thing, they learn the manners that are acceptable in their

group: 'Mealtimes are occasions when social groups are normally together and therefore provide opportunities for the uninitiated – particularly the young – to observe what is acceptable in terms of
food-related behaviour' (Wood 48). For example, '[c]hildren today are
admonished not to snatch whatever they want from the table, and not
to scratch themselves or touch their noses, ears, eyes, or other parts of
their bodies at table. The child is instructed not to speak or drink with a
full mouth, or to sprawl on the table, and so on' (Elias 141). Thus Kezia,
in Katherine Mansfield's 'At the Bay,' is chided for playing with her
porridge. But more than a code of table manners is learned at the table:
'Mealtimes offer children opportunities to observe the roles played by
adults – roles of cook and server, roles of main consumer, the role of
"washer-up"' (Wood 48). Surrounding Kezia at the breakfast table are
various family dynamics and unexamined assumptions: values about
tidiness and about being grown-up; views on the proper place and
behaviour of children; competition among siblings to be seen as 'the
good girl.' Among the adults, Aunt Beryl, the single woman in the
domestic circle, is trying to make her presence felt; Stanley, the bread-
winner, is issuing orders; and all the women in the family are waiting
on and deferring to him as he heads off to work.

More widely yet, the way in which the ritual of eating is enacted
extends beyond the dinner itself to reflect the mores and customs of the
larger society and of subgroups within that society; it encompasses the
history of the culture within which it is situated. Thus Norbert Elias
sees the standard Euro-American system of manners, including those
which determine behaviour at the table, as symptomatic and descrip-
tive of the civilization that has evolved more or less steadily and consistently over the centuries in the post-Roman West with relatively
minor variations determined by such factors as geography, class, and
gender. This system of manners is generally assumed and rigorously
enforced. 'Each society's culture is transmitted to children through
eating with the family, a setting in which individual personalities develop, kinship obligations emerge, and the customs of the group are
reinforced' (Farb and Armelagos 5). In the opening pages of *To the
Lighthouse*, it is at a family dinner-table scene that Virginia Woolf describes the imposition of traditional gender roles on the Ramsay daughters. Mrs Ramsay wants her daughters to become, like herself, good
mothers, wives, and hostesses. Their inchoate questioning of these
roles encompasses a resistance to all the values of their class and of
England: 'Prue, Nancy, Rose ... sport[ed] with infidel ideas which they

had brewed for themselves of a life different from hers; in Paris, perhaps; a wilder life; not always taking care of some man or other; for there was in all their minds a mute questioning of deference and chivalry, of the Bank of England and the Indian Empire, of ringed fingers and lace' (14). It is interesting that the word 'brewed,' used to describe their rebellion, still maintains a food connection – and a very English one, at that. Food generates even the expression of resistance to its rituals and to what those rituals represent.

Attention to the act of eating *together*, then, is an essential component of any discussion of the social meaning of food: 'We use eating as a medium for social relationships: satisfaction of the most individual of needs becomes a means of creating community' (Visser ix).[6] Although in some societies people do not traditionally eat together (Farb and Armelagos 81), generally they do. Thus the choice of dining companions is crucial; the coming together to share a meal both represents and creates larger personal and social ties: 'Sharing food is held to signify "togetherness," an equivalence among a group that defines and reaffirms insiders as socially similar. Feasts cement agreements, treaties and alliances; reconciliations, patching up quarrels, or at least agreeing to differ are sealed in a shared meal – visiting heads of state continually entertain one another at banquets' (Mennell, Murcott, and van Otterloo 115). Being barred from the table is a punishment – like being banished or exiled. Beyond its functions in the family, the dinner distinguishes between the known and the foreign, the friend and the enemy; in its adherence to traditions, the dinner links the living and the dead (Chaline and Vincent 254). Murdering a dinner guest is one of the most horrifying of crimes because it breaches conventions of civility which are almost universal.

Sharing a meal also lends a certain intensity to personal relationships and interaction. Alain Lemenorel says, 'Le repas, c'est la rencontre, la communication, l'échange, le partage, voire la confrontation des passions.' However, he notes a very significant change in the twentieth century: 'Le mangeur social fait place au mangeur individuel, et le commensal au grignoteur isolé ... la table perd sa fonction sociale. Le taylorisme alimentaire tue la commensalité' (363). Because of the increased incidence of the solitary diner – like those in Katherine Mansfield's stories discussed in chapter 5 – the family meal takes on a new importance in the twentieth century. No longer merely assumed or habitual, as in, let us say, the novels of Balzac or Dickens, it becomes even more significant by virtue of its potential or actual absence. Thus

Joyce's *Dubliners*, for instance, is marked by several dinners *manqués*. The drunken uncle's arriving late for dinner in 'Araby,' the dinner shared by transient strangers in 'The Boarding House,' the battle over grocery money in 'Eveline,' and the solitary restaurant dinner in 'A Painful Case' create a sense of unease about mealtime and give more value to the celebration of family, friends, and tradition in 'The Dead,' the final story of the collection.

In addition to structuring the social milieu and the individual's position in that milieu, the consumption of food structures time. Marin points out that in Perrault's 'Sleeping Beauty' the cooking process stops as time does:

> Thus, 'with a single stroke of her magic wand,' [the good fairy] puts to sleep 'everything that was in the castle ... right down to the spits over the fire which were stuffed, to the point of overflowing, with partridges and pheasant. Even the fire dozed off.' ... The whole process of cooking is literally suspended. The dishes being prepared ... and the courses in the processes of being cooked ... are all suspended in a time that is fixed and immobile from then on: the culinary processes are brought to a standstill, and the culinary activities that transform wild meats into edible roasts 'doze off' into the permanence of a single, monotonous, and interminable moment. (136)

Perrault's emphasis on the suspension of cooking not only underlines the integral connection of this activity to human life, but also defines it as a marker of time. If time is, in one sense, a subjective construct which reflects the human life span, meals are one way in which human beings organize and give meaning to time. This function of meals to mark the passage of time is, of course, used frequently as a structuring device in fiction as well.

Indeed, eating is important to both the individual and the group in its very repetitive dailiness. Patterns of drinking and eating organize our time and distinguish the different functions of the day, the week, the year (Gusfield 73), as well as marking significant turning points in our lives. As something recurring, even ritualistic, within a small group or a family circle, the meal provides a structure in our lives. Hemingway's 'Big Two-Hearted River' describes in meticulous detail Nick Adams's making coffee and heating up the contents of cans. This simple version of cooking a meal is – along with pitching a tent and fishing – part of

Adams's attempt to ground himself in a series of small everyday activities and thereby to return to some kind of normal reality after the war.

Changes in meal patterns are disruptive. Wood argues that '[t]he patterning of food ... performs a regulatory function, encouraging family stability' (52). Sociologists have pointed out that even when people eat alone, they may try to retain a structure and a uniformity in their meals, in terms of the menu as well as the schedule and the ritual. Certainly, foods recently introduced to mainstream England, Canada, and the United States have changed contemporary tastes, but, once accepted as a staple, an 'ethnic' cuisine, like curry in England, Mexican dishes in the United States, and Chinese food in all three countries, is brought into the existing pattern of fast-food and take-out meals. In restaurants, the invariability of both the menu and the structure of the meal has been noted frequently by sociologists. McDonald's is certainly aware that people want a stable menu and familiar surroundings. The corporation's mass-produced meals and identical restaurants are the key to its profits. As well, even expensive restaurants demonstrate an appreciable degree of standardization in menu, décor, service, and presentation of dishes.

Larger political, economic, and class structures are also manifested in food habits and elucidated by a reading of the dinner table. For example, rank or status is regularly expressed through the dining rituals of a society. The traditional banquet is 'la mise en scène du repas hiérarchique, où chacun a la part et la place qui conviennent à son rang, [et qui] exprime, le plus souvent de façon spectaculaire, les structures hiérarchiques et les relations de pouvoir, en même temps qu'elle est ostention des richesses' (Thelamon 12). Such meals are events which, through time-honoured ritual, reinforce rank and hence the structure of society. Whatever the particular form the banquet takes, it is a serious matter when such rituals are violated. In *Macbeth*, for instance, the breaking of the banquet ritual is a key point in the disintegration of Macbeth's personality and in his political downfall. Macbeth astonishes his guests at the table not only by apparently seeing and speaking to a ghost, but also by behaving as neither a host nor a king should (Jeanneret 47). His wife's dismissing the group quickly and without regard to rank – 'At once, good night. / Stand not upon the order of your going, / But go at once' (III.iv.118–20) – accentuates the seriousness of the Macbeths' breaches of the custom and hierarchy through which the world of the play defines civilized human nature. Moreover, the play suggests that, without a sound basis in custom, the kingdom is unstable and in danger of collapse.

It can, in fact, be argued that rank is a creation of food. Oswyn Murray, in a study of the symposium throughout history, cites Engels's notion of agricultural surplus as a keystone of culture: 'In order to survive, a society must produce a sufficiency; in order to create a culture, it must produce a surplus' (3). This surplus may be used to create a social structure comprising a hierarchy of classes, including non-productive classes, and a culture which includes rituals such as banquets: 'The modes of commensality, the distribution of food and drink publicly or to groups of retainers, sacrifice, and the potlatch are some of the ways in which society is structured through the use of its surplus. Often these uses have direct and obvious functional justifications, in terms of the creation and maintenance of groups essential to the survival of society, for military, political, or religious reasons' (4). A surplus gives room for signs not tied to necessity; ultimately, however, these signs themselves come to be considered essential demarcators within the class system. Edith Wharton's novels provide a particularly good example of this tendency. In Wharton's New York, lavish dinners, carefully orchestrated to indicate hierarchy and supported by certain correct accompaniments – beautiful and stylish dresses, elegant possessions, homes decorated in a certain taste – become a mark of membership in a certain social group, and a test of would-be newcomers to that group. The food served at a meal may itself elucidate economic relations; for instance, in Wharton's *The Age of Innocence*, May Archer can afford to offer her dinner guests asparagus from Florida and other choice dishes. As sociologist Mary Douglas observes, 'It is disingenuous to pretend that food is not one of the media of social exclusion' (*Food in the Social Order* 36).

Indeed, food is part of a larger economic system, and, although the influence of economics on a meal may seem to be mediated by taboos, customs, and tastes, these cultural indicators may themselves be based on economic factors. Some economic pressures are expressed at the family level: for example, sociologists and social historians have observed that, at the dinner table, scarce food is often given first to the wage-earner(s), usually men. However, family dynamics and individual table habits are influenced, if not controlled, by much larger forces, often international economic and political forces which drive and direct custom and taste. For instance, Mintz documents how the British taste for tea and for sugar, as well as the cultural importance of these products, was created, determined, and maintained by the slave trade, by the plantation system in the Caribbean, by Britain's international political role, and by the evolving factory system in England. Conversely, once in place, the British market for these items in turn helped to maintain these larger systems.

Even though the historian or economist may recognize the link between a particular dinner table and such larger influences, the diner may not be fully aware of the reasons for the prevailing taste, preference, or choice of food, nor the hostess of the potent cultural and historical connotations of the dietary habits and customs to which she adheres. From their perspective, certain dishes are prepared, served, and eaten in a certain way because that is just how things are done. However, if, as Marin says, 'power' inheres in the meal as a sign (xvii), the meaning of this sign may be or may once have been imposed by distant forces. In the words of anthropologist Eric Wolf, '"Meanings are not imprinted into things by nature; they are developed and imposed by human beings ... The ability to bestow meanings – to "name" things, acts and ideas – is a source of power"' (qtd in Mintz, *Tasting Food* 30). Mintz adds that those who ultimately determine the meaning of food are 'the purveyors of the foods, the givers of employment, the servants of the state who exercised the power that made the foods available' (31). Obviously, the ascendancy of advertising in the twentieth century lends a new dimension to the notion of a distant wielder of power determining individual food habits and the mealtime customs of a society, as well as the meaning inherent in those habits and customs.

Finally – and perhaps the key concept underlying the notion of the meal as a representation of culture – meals are particularly significant texts because food is, itself, in its essence, closely related to language. To return to Lévi-Strauss's point, the use of symbolic language and the ritualization of eating are linked as the two most important distinguishing features of humanity. It is obvious, but nevertheless important, to point out that what Marin calls the 'ambivalent' (36) mouth is the primary organ associated both with speaking and with food. This connection is so basic that it is assumed, and goes largely unnoticed, except, perhaps, by young children. Marin argues that table manners are so important precisely because of the potential ambiguity arising from the conjunction of these two functions (36). The fact that both speaking and eating are oral activities may be one reason that dinner is particularly constituted as an occasion for speech: the word 'speech' denoting both the basic ability to speak and the formal public address which aims to create or celebrate community. In contemporary life, the format of various standard meals – for instance, the family dinner, the dinner date, the business lunch, the political fundraising dinner – includes, in each case, some kind of discourse. If we speak during and after a meal, it is as if we are, first, giving thanks for food – in a sense giving back the food as an offering – and second, demonstrating that food has been successfully transformed into a celebration of community: in other words, that it produces culture. Mere nourishment transcends itself through the use of words.

Going beyond the anthropological argument of Lévi-Strauss, Marin posits further that eating inherently – not only through the stimulation of the dinner table – induces and even creates thought. The transformation of raw food into dinner both parallels and permits the transformation of lived experience into language. Using as an example the archetype of the Eucharist and the sacramental statement, 'This is my body,' Marin proposes that, in the transformation of biological need into desire and of bread into a body, the word is born. This transformation involves a mortal body – for in eating, we transform food into our own flesh – but also the body politic and the deity: both 'a real socio-historical body and a mystical, divine body' (xix). The sacrament of the Eucharist is conceptualized as a meal; the faithful come together as a social group to the communion table, and really do ingest God, simply because a few words have been spoken. The signification and thus the reality of the food is changed: 'What is eaten at the end of the formula is not the edible thing of the beginning; what is eaten is both a sign and a body, a body as sign and a sign as body' (Marin 121). The need to satisfy desire demands the intervention of a transformatory statement and thus the creation of the word. 'The relationship between the body and discourse' (Marin 218), then, is a complex and potent one, suggesting that the combination of words and food is transformatory, magical: things are bound to happen at dinner – in literature and in life.

In summary, the basic physical necessity and the sensual pleasure of eating give meals and mealtime rituals a fundamental importance in all cultures. Although eating is, at its basic level, the satisfaction of a biological need, dining is much more than that. Marin argues that, at least symbolically, dinner is linked not only to words, but to the desire for the divine: 'This desire operates on the borders between Logos – the word and utterance – and Eros – pleasure and love – between a need for preservation, which is satisfied by food, and a desire realized through the pleasures offered by a dish or a meal' (Marin xix). In Barthes's terms, meals have a dual nature: 'People may very well continue to believe that food is an immediate reality (necessity or pleasure), but this does not prevent it from carrying a system of communication: it would not be the first thing that people continue to experience as a simple function at the very moment when they constitute it into a sign' (Barthes 168). Thus, in a complex of ways, food and the systems surrounding it make up an important text, one by which we – consciously or unconsciously – live our lives, and one that the writer can use to evoke the dynamics of the fictional world.

Dinners in literary works resonate with the kind of historical, social, psychological, religious, and linguistic issues raised in the preceding discussion. Thus, a text's exploration of these larger issues may emanate from the central event of dinner. From another perspective, food can be seen metaphorically as the content or the raw material of a book; the process of preparing and serving the meal corresponds to the literary or artistic treatment. Because of the historical association of women and meals, the women writers considered in the coming chapters are in a particularly good place to live this metaphor.

2

The Angel in the Kitchen:
Early Twentieth-Century Trends
in Dining

The focus on meals in the writing of early twentieth-century women reflects a general concern with domesticity in the light of changing cultural values. The late nineteenth- and early twentieth-century period was marked by new perceptions of food, meals, and the structures and systems surrounding them. If not necessarily a direct influence on writers, these current popular attitudes formed part of the context or background of literary production. Thus, before turning to an analysis of dining in early twentieth-century fiction, it is worth noting that other kinds of contemporary writing by and for women also responded to these changes. Food habits are interpreted on the most everyday level by texts *about* food: texts such as recipe books, cookbooks, and manuals on entertaining and etiquette, which mediate the crucial transition between food and dining, between 'the "what" of food and the "how" of cooking' (Marin 127), as well as the 'how' of serving, presenting, and eating the meal. Because of the cultural significance of meals, these texts can be read for an understanding of more general concerns as well: cookbooks, for example, 'have often gone beyond the mere presentation of instructions for preparing dishes; they have also consistently reflected historic foodways, general customs, and ways of thinking' (Williams 18).

Louis Marin postulates that cooking is like speaking or writing: 'the art of cooking is structured like language and obeys the same structural and functional constraints' (118). But Marin neglects to ask who is speaking. That cooking has been the language of women is perhaps self-evident, yet oddly understated. It is partly as a response to this neglect, perhaps, that women's domestic experience became a point of some importance to Virginia Woolf, Katherine Mansfield, and other twentieth-century women writers.[1] If the preparation of meals is the purview of women, then the social change which marked the early part of the twentieth century would have been felt, expressed, and interpreted by women in the realm of the kitchen – in changing roles and expectations, changing formats for serving dinner, and so forth. Because women are in charge of providing meals, it was deemed both appropriate and permissible for women to write about food, to publish cookbooks, etiquette books, and other domestic and social manuals.[2] As the authors of cookbooks, women were, literally, both servers and writers of food. Beginning in the late nineteenth century, and increasing in the first two decades of the twentieth century, there was a strong impetus not only to rationalize and regiment domestic life, but also to codify and organize instruction about domestic skills into school curricula, adult courses, books, and features in popular magazines – a movement which can also be read as a response to social change. Women may have turned to the experts in schools and mass-market publications in an attempt to understand and control, at least within their own kitchens, the changes happening around them. Texts about food would normally be classified as non-fiction; novels as fiction. Yet, at the start of the twentieth century, it may have been more likely for literature to reflect life as it was actually experienced, while cookbooks and other manuals for the housewife and the hostess depicted a view of life as it could only be fantasized.

The early twentieth century set in motion trends in food and dining habits that have continued until the present. For instance, the decline of the family meal and the growing trend toward eating alone were mentioned in the previous chapter. There were a number of reasons for this change: single people leading a solitary life, unattached to an extended family; changes in the structure of the work day; travel; and, in response to these other factors, the increasing numbers of restaurants and cafés, and the growing acceptability, even for women, of eating out. In the period immediately before and after the First World War, the structure of the family was changing, as was the role of women. The technological revolution in the home, with appliances and other electrical kitchen devices ever more readily available, had a huge impact. The rise of advertising was creating a new kind of consumer culture. And overall, of course, the First World War had an enormous effect on the way people viewed the world and their place in it. This effect was felt in every area of life. As Eric Hobsbawm says in *The Age of Empire*, it is not only that 1914 is seen today, nearly one hundred years later, as a break in history; it was felt to be so at the time as well.[3]

Women's role was also evolving from the earlier years of the Victo-

rian era, when, in both England and the United States, rapid technological and economic development progressed hand in hand with the
evolving notion of the 'angel in the house.' During the nineteenth
century, with much domestic production moving from the home to the
factory, women's work came to be viewed as marginal to the economic
order. Even in families whose livelihood remained the same, the role of
women may have changed. Jane Rendall traces the history of women
who were actively involved in running the family business in the late
eighteenth century, but whose nineteenth-century daughters and daugh-
ters-in-law were not (49–50). In all classes, the assumption that 'the
male worker should aim to support his wife and family was beginning
to undermine, in aspiration if not in practice, the older pattern of the
family economy to which all members contributed' (Rendall 57). At the
same time, 'the sentimental value of home expanded proportionately'
(Shapiro 13).

Nevertheless, by the late nineteenth century, there were a fair number
of women who were literate and of a class which permitted them
enough leisure time to become involved in activities outside the home.
Many women expanded their role as moral guardian of the home into
the wider world by taking part in various radical or reform movements:
in mid-century, the abolitionist movement in the United States; later the
suffrage movement in both England and the United States, as well as
the temperance movement and various causes that championed the
rights of the poor. 'Philanthropy could be seen as an extension of the
domestic world and therefore an activity permitted to women' (Rendall
47). The impetus was almost evangelical. Thus, in *To the Lighthouse*, Mrs
Ramsay takes food to the poor and concerns herself about efficiency
and sanitation in the dairy industry. Her activities are somewhat more
limited than those of her model, Julia Stephen, who, by all accounts,
exhausted herself nursing the sick; still, the fact that Mrs Ramsey's
interests are food-oriented identifies them as an extension of her role at
home.

Linked to work with the poor in both Great Britain and the United
States, as well as in continental Europe, was an attempt to reform the
home by improving the state of cooking and of housekeeping in general. To this end, cooking schools were established in the United States,
first in the 1870s in New York and Boston, and then in other cities
throughout the country. The immediate aim was to raise the level of
nutrition among the poor and working classes. It was believed that
nutritious meals not only were conducive to improved health, but were

the antidote to everything from labour unions to crime, drunkenness, and general immorality (Shapiro). As Mennell notes, however, '[t]he broad impulse to reform, however altruistic its conscious motivation, reflected the closer interdependence of social classes in the emerging urban-industrial societies' (230). In other words, since girls from these target classes also worked as cooks and servants in the houses of the wealthy and middle classes, improved cooking skills would not only help them to find and keep work but also ultimately increase the number of trained cooks and raise the quality of meals in the homes of the reformers. The opportunity at the school to use more and different utensils and a more varied supply of ingredients than was available in their own homes also introduced working-class students to middle-class standards (Mennell 231) and aspirations, and presumably gave them both a critical perspective on their mothers' dinners and a greater desire to climb the social ladder themselves.

In addition, as the twentieth century began, women and girls of the reformers' own social class increasingly demanded lessons for them-selves. Ostensibly the demand was there because mistresses wanted to be able to supervise their cooks, and to ensure that they followed the most modern nutritional recommendations. As the number of middle-class families keeping servants declined, however, the cooking skills taught were more and more frequently required by the lady of the house herself.[4] Although French cuisine was introduced to the British and American upper classes in the nineteenth century, middle-class families could not afford to hire servants trained in French cooking, and therefore headed in another direction, 'with the result that by the 1920's the American middle classes were taking the lead in inaugurating a modern era where status would derive from ingesting much smaller amounts of food in much simpler form. This new middle class cuisine would in turn become the standard for all classes, forming the back-bone of American foodways down to the present' (Levenstein 127).

The Boston Cooking School was the most influential of these institu-tions. Its recipes and menus ranged from the dull to the bizarre. The attitudes toward meals verged on the puritanical: enjoyment of food was not an issue, except in so far as it was considered necessary to tempt people to eat. Nevertheless, menus were often determined by a certain kind of aesthetic sense: for instance, luncheons or dinners where dishes were chosen to create a particular colour scheme were quite popular. (Green and white, the school colours, were served up at Bos-ton Cooking School graduation luncheons.) The meal itself was not prepared in particularly innovative ways. Indeed, it was quite bland: a plain white sauce was used indiscriminately in almost any dish and there was a heavy emphasis on traditional New England fare such as 'baked beans, brown bread, fish balls, doughnuts, and Indian pudding' (Shapiro 63). Cooking school cuisine was similarly uninteresting in England. Collections of recipes used in schools in Liverpool, Manchester, and London 'represent food very much in line with what one would expect from accounts of lower middle-class food ... It is very English, with almost no sign of the French influence prevalent in the higher reaches of society. Cooking methods are very simple – boiling, roasting, frying, stewing. There are lots of pies, puddings and cakes. Leftover recipes are prominent' (Mennell 231). Mennell also notes that as the cooking schools developed during the twentieth century, the focus tended increasingly toward kitchen sanitation and 'the prevention of food poisoning' rather than the pleasure of either cooking or eating (232).

The theoretical underpinnings of these schools were supposedly scientific. In fact, Ellen Richards, one of the founders and leaders of the domestic science movement, was the first female student at the Massachusetts Institute of Technology. Admitted in 1870 as a special student, she was responsible for setting up facilities for women to take chemistry courses at that institution beginning in 1876, some eight years before women were finally admitted as regular students (Shapiro 37–8). Her approach, advocated both in her training of other teachers and in her book *The Chemistry of Cooking and Cleaning*, was to create 'a household that ran as quietly and productively as a machine, under the guidance of a benevolent technician' (Shapiro 41). Richards and her followers emphasized that chemistry, anatomy, and other academic disciplines were involved in good cooking and that women were as capable as men of learning these disciplines, although in their own proper sphere (Shapiro 142). Indeed, although the students seem to have been most interested in cooking, by the 1890s there were many other courses included as part of the six-month program of studies at the Boston Cooking School: 'Psychology, Physiology and Hygiene, Bacteriology, Foods, Laundry Work, and the Chemistry of Soap, Bluing, and Starch,' as well as an elective course in Household Sanitation (Shapiro 65).

Working-class mothers, especially immigrants, were not capable of teaching their daughters these 'modern' American ways. Thus, the discipline of home economics was born. The subject was gradually introduced into public schools, beginning in 1885 in Boston: '"Our young women, ignorant of the value of home training, persist in fitting themselves for business rather than household life," complained the president of the National Household Economic Association – and [domestic science] quickly took its place as the standard female counterpart to industrial education' (Shapiro 140). Similar trends occurred in Europe as well: domestic science was introduced in French schools in 1882 (Mennell 231), and gradually into English schools during the same period. Domestic science also crept into American universities. Some recently founded women's colleges – Bryn Mawr, Vassar, Wellesley – refused to establish a department of home economics (Shapiro 179), much to the reformers' chagrin, but others did: Smith, for example (Mennell 231), as well as the University of Illinois and a number of other state universities. By 1914 a BA in Home Economics was available at 250 American institutions, and a PhD at the University of Chicago (Shapiro 185). Underlying the founding of these degree programs was the increasing demand for equal educational opportunities for women. However, the development of the field of home economics – for women only – certainly suggests a rather segregationist view of equality and a ghettoization of women within the university.[5]

As well as borrowing from the traditional scientific disciplines, the household reform movement adopted from the industrial world the principles of scientific management, which it applied to household tasks. Siegfried Giedion sees Catharine Beecher as the initiator of the quest to organize the work process, particularly in her arrangement of the kitchen for maximum efficiency. As early as 1841, Beecher had published her *Treatise on Domestic Economy for the Use of Young Ladies at Home and at School*. In 1869 it was followed by *The American Women's Home: or Principles of Domestic Science*, written in collaboration with her well-known sister Harriet Beecher Stowe. These manuals addressed not only cooking but all aspects of household management, from taking care of children to constructing houses and arranging furniture. Beecher's point was to impose a system of rational order on all aspects of the household. There were a number of similar manuals: for instance, Maria Parloa's *Home Economics* (1898), and, most notably, Mrs Isabella Beeton's much-reprinted *Book of Household Management*, first published in England in 1861.

Following Beecher, reformers of the early twentieth century sought to improve the efficiency of the kitchen and the rest of the home by applying directly the principles and methods of Frederick Taylor. In 1912, Christine Frederick performed time and motion studies, inspired by Frank Gilbreth's work in factories, counting and measuring the number of steps or physical movements involved in simple kitchen tasks – beating an egg, for instance – and tried to rationalize the activity so as to use only the minimum amount of human energy required. It was seen that a well-organized kitchen could reduce the physical effort and time needed for everyday chores. Frederick's book *Household Engineering: Scientific Management in the Home*, billed as 'a correspondence course' because at the end of each chapter readers were asked to apply the book's principles to their own home, went through several printings between 1915 and 1923. Frederick specifically makes business analogies throughout her text, calling the housewife at various times a 'purchasing agent' (315) and the 'executive head' of the household (380). She also defines the modern housewife as a consumer rather than a producer, and maintains that '[t]o become a trained consumer is ... one of the most important demands made on the housekeeper of today' (317; emphasis in original). These ideas were picked up and exploited by advertisers, who appealed at the same time to modernity and conservatism. Marchand reports that, in the 1920s and 1930s, 'copywriters constantly congratulated women for their presumed new capacities for management. But the proper field for these managerial talents remained the home.' The wife was cast as the 'general purchasing agent' of the family, 'and thus analogous to a business executive of modest power,' the husband 'as the home's "treasurer" or its "president"' (168–70).

Originally, many of the early reformers saw the future lying in communal kitchens: the expansion of the family into a community, which, by pooling resources, would lessen the load of housework and especially of cooking in each individual family. In fact, in 1889, *Good Housekeeping* magazine carried an article by Edward Bellamy encouraging this idea: 'The editors ... sensed correctly that while the bulk of their middle class readership would hardly sympathize with his socialism they would find his ideas on solving the "servant problem" of great interest' (Levenstein 130). However, the idea of cooperative kitchens never caught on. In fact, as noted earlier, the trend in the twentieth century has been in the opposite direction: toward eating alone.[6] Certainly advertising has played a role in this trend by targeting individual needs and thus bolstering a sense of life which runs counter to the notion of community.[7] This emphasis on the individual is only partly mitigated by the advertisers' image of the perfect nuclear family – a family made up of individual consumers.

If the woman of the family was destined, then, to cook every meal alone, early domestic scientists like Ellen Richards were very much in favour of improving kitchen technology in the interest of efficiency. Appliance manufacturers, seeing the possibility of sales, encouraged the further application of scientific management studies to housework. For instance, in the early 1930s, Lillian Gilbreth was hired by a gas company to study the efficiency of American kitchens.[8] There is a subtle but interesting shift, however, from Richards's valorization of housework – especially when linked to modern technological advances – as a noble, important, and scientific occupation, to the early twentieth-century emphasis on housework as inherently a form of drudgery that could be alleviated by the use of up-to-date equipment. An advertisement for S.O.S. steel wool pads, reproduced in Marchand's *Advertising the American Dream*, aptly demonstrates the modern woman's attitude to housework. A young woman – standing – is talking to a seated man: 'You think I'm a flapper but I *can* keep house. If we get married, I'll keep my house better than mother does hers. But I'm not going to turn into a slave. You *men*! You think drudgery is a sign of good housekeeping' (355). There are a number of interesting aspects to this advertisement: first, the notion that housework is not interesting in itself, but something to be done efficiently to leave time for other activities; second, the implication that there is nothing to be learned from mother. Moreover, although a modernist break with the past is suggested in this example, it is clear that being a good housekeeper is still considered one of the most desirable qualities in a wife.

The advertising campaigns for new kitchen appliances enticed the consumer with words and expressions like 'modern' and 'time-saving.' In the 1920s, advertisements for refrigerators and other appliances often showed well-dressed, relaxed women, sometimes in the company of party guests, suggesting that the appliance would make the housewife a hostess and bestow upon her a life of elegance and leisure (Marchand 270–4). Marchand points out that there is a religious aura about many of these scenes, with groups gathered reverently around the appliance and sometimes a mysterious light emanating from either the appliance or an unknown source. A woman on her own or in the company of friends is portrayed as brisk and efficient, but when women are shown with their families, there is usually a soft light cast over the scene (244). The lighting, the spatial structure, and the visual content of these family-oriented advertisements affirm the roles and power relations of individual family members and the social role of the family.

The notion of the 'new woman' is apparent in advertising, but underneath, the traditional stereotypes do not actually change.

The application of efficiency systems to the home, a central goal from the start of the home economics movement, was ostensibly intended to save women time, to create more leisure for outside activities, and, especially in the early years, to accord work in the home the same degree of status as outside work. Changes in the economy, in education, and in technology could and should have made cooking and other housework more efficient, yet many have recognized that, although the type of work changed, the amount of work did not necessarily lessen. As Ewen says, '[r]ather than viewing the transformations in housework as *labor-saving*, it is perhaps more useful to view them as *labor-changing*' (163). Yet these transformations signalled significant changes both in attitudes toward housework and in the home itself. These are perhaps most clear in the spatial and functional reorganization of the kitchen: 'The room that for three centuries had provided Americans with warmth, evening light, food, pleasant cooking odors, and an agreeable meeting place now began to lose many of these characteristics, especially in the cities, and became increasingly a laboratory presided over by a housewife-technician. The size of the kitchen shrank as its uses declined and, in urban areas, as escalating land values took their toll' (Hooker 211). Despite the nostalgic, perhaps sentimental tone of the above passage, Hooker has a point. The changes in the kitchen signify changes in the family as well, which were perhaps not always for the best. The overall impact of emulating industrial models in the home is that the housewife becomes like a factory worker (Ewen 164), or at best a foreman or manager, as capitalism enters the private as well as the public sphere. Ultimately, whatever possibility might have existed for exercising imagination or creativity in cooking and keeping house was lessened; in the new model, women cede their authority to outside experts selling new products and giving advice (Ewen 169). In the kitchen, moreover, when efficiency and image are the major aims, the emotional, sensual, pleasurable, ritualistic aspects of both cooking and eating are somehow lost.

A similar trend occurred in recipes and food products. The cooking reformers' ultimate goal was homogeneity: the same results every time. Thus, more 'scientific' and exact measurements were incorporated into recipes, with Fannie Farmer, the most celebrated principal of the Boston Cooking School and author of *The Boston Cooking-School Cook Book* – first published in 1896 – leading the way. Home economists interested in precision and guaranteed results in the kitchen applauded the growth of industrial standardization, believing that it would help achieve their goal of the 'scientific' kitchen. In the United States, this quest for standardization meant eliminating, appropriating, or homogenizing regional cooking styles and the cuisine of immigrants. As noted earlier, there was a clear prejudice in favour of the American (i.e., New England) way, defined as blandly as possible. Prepared foods were seen not only as more 'standard,' but as time-saving and sanitary. Shapiro reports that some women who taught at or directed cooking schools and lectured around the country ended up working for food-processing companies, often endorsing consumer products: baking powder, for example, or Crisco shortening. More and more, food became merely an industrial product, not necessarily pleasurable or appealing to the senses, and not even particularly nutritious: 'With the Crisco white sauce, scientific cookery arrived at a food substance from which virtually everything had been stripped except a certain number of nutrients and the color white. Only a cuisine molded by technology could prosper on such developments, and it prospered very well' (Shapiro 215). With a recipe for Crisco white sauce, the cook can make a dish that has no colour, no texture, no taste left. It is easy to see a certain vision of society here as well. Shapiro says, perhaps unkindly, 'When Fannie Farmer at last set down her measuring spoons ... she left behind a kitchen she had helped, crucially, to redirect toward social homogeneity and American cheese' (126).

Mennell, writing mostly about England, sees this trend emphasized by recipe columns in women's magazines, which had begun to address middle-class women in the mid-Victorian period (234), and had grown enormously in the last two decades of the nineteenth century and the beginning of the twentieth. These magazines may in fact have influenced more women than cookbooks did. He decries the lack of a 'sensual quality' (245) in the description of food, and notes that '[e]ach recipe is presented in isolation, with little sense that the dish, its ingredients, and the techniques it requires are interconnected with other dishes, ingredients and techniques – a sense of interconnectedness that can be found within an inherited tradition' (246). In fact, the guarantees of 'experts' in the magazines replace the inherited wisdom of a mother or a grandmother; since all recipes are supposed to have been tested by magazine personnel or by the manufacturers of the ingredients, women can consider the dishes foolproof and need not worry about failure. It is also worth noting that, as magazines counted more and more on advertising for financial support, the distinction between advertisements and articles became less and less clear, a trend that continues today in most women's magazines.

Ultimately, then, the reformers reinforced the role of women in the home and particularly in the kitchen, although modified ideologically with the rhetoric of equal but separate spheres, and despite the fact that they themselves were often absent from home pursuing successful careers as home economists/domestic scientists. Moreover, they reinforced the economic system, not only by extolling the stable home and, in the United States, implying the rightness of American middle-class ideology, but also by encouraging women's desire for modernity and status, and preying on their insecurity about measuring up to the model of the twentieth-century homemaker. Thus the domestic reformers helped to mould women into willing consumers of whatever the latest product might be. Early domestic scientists wanted to validate the woman's role in the home, yet, under the influence of manufacturers in the twentieth century, it was ultimately minimalized and downgraded.

As the twentieth century progressed, and more appliances, processed foods, and other household products became available and were advertised with women in mind, the home became 'an arena primarily of consumption' (Ewen 135–6), a notion, as I mentioned earlier, strongly endorsed by home economists such as Christine Frederick. For the upwardly mobile – then, as now – there was a clear link between consumerism and status, a connection which is particularly evident in Wharton's *The Custom of the Country*: Undine Spragg, newly arrived in New York City from a small town, wants not so much to own what the wealthy own as to buy whatever she believes the fashionable crowd is buying. (Red stationery and white ink, one example of her inept purchases, give a clear indication about her attitude toward the written word.) In Nella Larsen's *Passing*, published in 1929, possessions are important to Irene, the middle-class African-American protagonist, as a confirmation of her own class status. The novel, told largely from Irene's point of view, thus frequently calls attention to details of meals and of domestic items, both in Irene's home and elsewhere. The following description of a tea party in the hotel room of Irene's girlhood friend – who is passing for white – is a good example: 'The tea things had been placed on a low table at Clare's side. She gave them her attention now, pouring the rich amber fluid from the tall glass pitcher into stately slim glasses, which she handed to her guests, and then offered them lemon or cream and tiny sandwiches or cakes' (197). This is a world where every object, every gesture is important and suggestive. Such adjective-laden descriptions, which suggest an illustration in a women's magazine, often have symbolic overtones; here, the tea things evoke associations with race and with feminine beauty. But, more important, the writing itself, in evoking Clare's careful attention to detail and Irene's attribution of meaning to minor objects, underlines the two women's insecurity and wariness, and emphasizes the constant vigilance necessary, in Clare's case to 'pass' successfully,[9] and in Irene's, to assure herself of her middle-class identity. Although race makes the cases of these women extreme, advertisers preyed upon similar insecurity in the female population at large.

This insecurity was acute in the general area of social life. As can be seen in *Passing*, for instance, women expended a good deal of energy – and worry – on socializing and entertaining. In addition to their new scientific approach to cooking and domestic work, cookbooks at the turn of the century paid considerable attention to inviting guests to dinner. Beyond providing recipes for individual scientifically prepared dishes, cookbooks situated their recipes not just in the context of the family meal, but also as part of a socially acceptable and attractive package for entertaining the right people. Titles such as *Dinners, Ceremonious and Unceremonious and the Modern Methods of Serving Them* (1890) suggest a concern with the correct social formalities, and the presentation as well as the preparation of the meal. Many books on entertaining were also published in the turn-of-the-century period, including such titles as *Party-giving on every Scale: or the Cost of Entertainments with the Fashionable Modes of Arrangement* (1880), and, simply, *The Art of Entertaining* (1897).[10]

These manuals for hostesses have their complement in books of etiquette for guests. In the United States alone, the sheer number of etiquette manuals published in the late nineteenth and early twentieth centuries is astounding (Schlesinger 18). Increased literacy was certainly one of the factors contributing to their proliferation; a second was that people had to look outside the family unit for information and instruction about appropriate behaviour. In a situation of increasing social mobility, adults who, like the main characters in William Dean Howells's *The Rise of Silas Lapham*, rather suddenly found themselves rich, needed to learn quickly. Parents certainly did not have adequate knowledge to teach their children how to integrate into a higher class. This interest in etiquette is a pragmatic, one, then; moreover, as described in Wharton's novels and reflected in the popular texts of the day, it also suggests a particularly American concern for image. The lower and middle classes could follow high-class etiquette at their own poorer tables, perhaps in preparation for future success, but at the very least to differentiate themselves from their peers by setting a better table and taking on the manner of the class to which they aspired. Lessons on etiquette were accessible to all: magazines and newspapers – particularly, although by no means solely, women's magazines – also included advice on etiquette. Such instructions nearly always imply the practicality of the advice given and the eminent feasibility of carrying it out. It is worthy of note that many titles include words such as 'all,' 'everyday,' 'for everyone,' reinforcing the American ideology that there is really no such thing as class and that anyone can achieve success.[11] The 1901 guide, *Encyclopedia of Etiquette: What to Write, What to Do, What to Wear, What to Say: a Book of Manners for Everyday Use*, like Emily Post's *Etiquette in Society, in Business, in Politics and at Home*, first published in 1922, went through a number of editions over a period of years. The purpose of all this advice, as well as the blandness of what is expected or desired, is suggested in the title *The Art of Being Agreeable* (1897).[12] However, the titles also suggest an anxiety that permeated every aspect of life. Like the cookbooks described earlier in this chapter, the etiquette manuals reassuringly suggest that success is merely a question of following the right recipe, yet at the same time encourage insecurity by implying that there is only one correct way, and that experts know better than the ordinary person what that way is.

It is natural that table manners and the protocol of dinner parties were a major component of the books on etiquette written during this period. It was expected that those who had achieved wealth would flaunt it at the table, while those who were not wealthy would, of course, wish to emulate the rich. Indeed, the social importance of dinner parties was expanding. In England, socializing and entertaining in the home increased during the nineteenth century (Davidoff); in the United States as well, despite the 'servant problem,' from approximately the 1870s, 'dinner parties at home for friends, acquaintances, and important personages were ... becoming central aspects of middle class social life. On these occasions, not only was the food expected to impress, but so was the table. Flower-bedecked, linen-clad, and glittering with china, silver, and cut glass, it was expected to reflect the creativity and inventiveness of the hostess' (Levenstein 129–30). The dinner party provided 'a magnificent opportunity to show off the material possessions of the host' (Burnett 193). The dining-room itself was an indicator of status.[13] A nineteenth-century innovation (Hooker), it became a symbol of middle-class respectability: 'The possession of a well-furnished dining room indicated that the owner of a house had the wealth, the time, and the social knowledge to devote special effort to meal preparation and consumption' (Clark 149).

Sociability may not, however, always have indicated profound or meaningful ties. Charlotte Perkins Gilman, writing in 1903, argues that the home should be for private life, and not for display, and that women should undertake more meaningful pursuits than entertaining. She notes that real contact may not even happen at a party: 'Your friend may be at the same dinner ... the same reception, the same tea, the same luncheon – but you do not meet. As the "society" hand is gloved that there be no touching of real flesh and blood, so is the society soul dressed and defended for the fray in smooth phrase and glossy smile – a well-oiled system, without which the ceaseless press and friction would wear us raw, but within which we do anything but "meet"' (204). That a good deal of entertaining was being done is emphasized by the very fact of its being criticized. Gilman's dissenting voice is just one indication that, at the turn of the twentieth century, a preoccupation with serving dinner was a major part of the social and economic – as well as the domestic – landscape.

The literature of the period also demonstrates that people were indeed eating together, if under increasingly alienating circumstances. If cookbooks, magazine articles, guidebooks on entertaining, and etiquette manuals attest to modern anxiety about change in the home – while ostensibly dishing out recipes to allay it – modernist women writers depict and express this uneasiness around their own fictional dining-room tables. In the following chapters' exploration of various versions of dinner in turn-of-the-century fiction, I will argue that, although works of fiction do not give recipes and advice, the meals that are central to these texts are also expressions of uneasy shifts in everyday life.

3

In with the In-Crowd:
Edith Wharton and the Dinner Tables
of Old New York

Manners and Social Change

As described in the novels of Edith Wharton, the dining customs of the wealthy in the turn-of-the-century period are manifestations of a larger code of manners and social ritual which represented tradition, but also responded to economic and social change. It is significant that Edith Wharton, like and through her character Newland Archer, refers to upper-class New York society as a tribe: the people within a tribe, precisely because tribal life is their only reality, cannot imagine any other existence and do not see the relativity of their own customs and rituals. Nearly all of Wharton's New Yorkers are complacent about their way of life. Yet Wharton's work depicts a society whose mannered conventions may have become more prescriptive for the very reason that the world they represent is in the process of being destroyed.

If 'the custom of festive gatherings probably originated in motives of conviviality and religion' (Veblen 65), Wharton's novels demonstrate that dinner parties and other forms of socializing are also opportunities for the upper classes to show off wealth, to give evidence of 'conspicuous consumption.' According to Veblen, writing at approximately the same time as Wharton, a display of luxury goods and the 'consumption of choice articles of food' (61) became not only the prerogative but even the responsibility of the leisure class; moreover, the display of good breeding and manners showed that a person had enough leisure time to cultivate these qualities. In the late nineteenth and early twentieth centuries, dinners and the rituals and customs surrounding dining helped to define elite society both for its inner circle and for those who were outside. The effect on the latter was to emphasize to them that they were excluded. The effect on the former was a validation of the group itself and of the individual's place in both the group and the hierarchy within the group.

The notion of manners is a rather slippery one to define; it is difficult to delineate its parameters. Most people today, as in earlier periods, would likely see manners as synonymous with etiquette – a superficial veneer on social behaviour. The code of manners is usually viewed as prescriptive. Indeed, for centuries, dating back to Erasmus's very influential *De civilitate morum puerilium*, books on manners have helped to define the culture's norms of behaviour, and have been particularly instrumental in teaching the young. However, although it is almost impossible to avoid the denotation of prescriptive etiquette, the notion of manners goes far beyond the limits implied by the use of the word in this way. A form of communication among those who know the code, manners are a language encompassing both verbal and non-verbal components. Gary Lindberg, in his book on the novel of manners, emphasizes the formal aspect of this language: '[Manners] are the real or implied actions – in gesture, speech, decoration, dress – that provide forms for individual expression, and *within* the social order these forms quicken public feelings by summoning up unspoken meanings and beliefs' (3). In this sense, manners are rather a dialect than a language, having 'their origins and their significance within a specific social order' (3), and not necessarily transparent to those outside the particular group. Lionel Trilling's definition emphasizes the force of unstated communication implicit in a code of manners:

> What I understand by manners, then, is a culture's hum and buzz of implication. I mean the whole evanescent context in which its explicit statements are made. It is that part of a culture which is made up of half-uttered or unuttered or unutterable expressions of value. They are hinted at by small actions, sometimes by the arts of dress or decoration, sometimes by tone, gesture, emphasis or rhythm, sometimes by the words that are used with a special frequency or a special meaning. They are the things that for good or bad draw the people of a culture together and that separate them from the people of another culture ... In this part of culture assumption rules, which is often stronger than reason. (200–1)

Manners are particularly identified with food, in large part because of the heavy cultural associations of mealtime customs. For Norbert Elias, writing in the 1930s, 'the civilising process' has been characterized by an increasing repression of the physical, evidenced by a 'gradual transformation of behavior and the emotions,' and an 'expanding threshold of aversion' (83). Thus, most human activities which respond to biological needs – including sexual activities, bathing, sleeping, and elimination – have become progressively more private in Western culture. Eating, however, has not; on the contrary, as noted in chapter 1, the meal has nearly always been considered a social occasion, one of its main functions to establish, affirm, and mediate not only interpersonal relationships, but larger social ties as well. While remaining social and public, then, the act of eating is ritualized and surrounded by taboos. Nevertheless, attitudes toward food in the West have become increasingly divorced from the fundamental realities of eating both as a bodily function and as the fulfilment of desire. That is, reminders of the physical have become less and less acceptable at the table: there are strict regulations on eating with the fingers, wiping the hands and mouth, and so on. As well, while remaining a public activity, eating has become more personal and individualized: for instance, it has evolved that people do not eat out of the same dishes. By the very fact of their importance, such customs indicate that the physical, although suppressed, is still lurking unpleasantly under the table.

Elias argues that these changes, which he defines as part of the evolving system of manners, while certainly influenced by social, political, and economic factors, have in turn profoundly affected both the society at large and the construction of individual personalities. Both levels of change have occurred gradually and concurrently. Elias links the process of privatization and the expanding boundaries of what is defined as intimate behaviour with an increase in social control and the centralization of power in the state. Further, as the middle class gains prominence, 'Elias suggests ... [a] displacement of merely exterior, superficial aristocratic *civility* into a psychologized *cultivation*' (Litvak 29) – a major shift in both the notion of manners and the definition of the self.

Class differences, then, are crucial in the evolution of manners, with the ascendant class usually setting the tone for change. Novel forms of behaviour at table and specific innovations such as the use of the fork began in the court circle and spread gradually to other sectors of society before finally becoming the norm. As is evident in Edith Wharton's work or in Virginia Woolf's *Mrs. Dalloway*, elite groups set the standard in the early twentieth century as well. In everyday parlance, good manners are frequently linked with good taste, the latter expression –

obviously based on the palate – indicating not only the ability to choose the appropriate food and other consumable items and possessions, but to act with a certain self-restraint. Both qualities are often defined by the behaviour of a certain class. Joseph Litvak, in his discussion of *Pride and Prejudice*, uses the terms 'manners' and 'taste' almost synonymously, arguing that the reader is forced to submit 'consciously or not, to a rigorous aesthetic *discipline*, undergoing subtle but incessant schooling in the ever-finer classifications, discriminations, and aversions that maintain Austen's exacting (because never quite explicit) norms of good manners and good taste' (22). Good manners, by their very definition, then, imply a way of eating. Litvak demonstrates how the value judgments made about individuals and individual behaviour in *Pride and Prejudice* – both by the characters and by the text itself – are often based on explicitly or implicitly stated eating preferences or manners of eating. One example of both the judge and the judged is 'the "indolent" Mr. Hurst, whose vice is confirmed and whose character is irreversibly discredited in the summary observation that, "when he found [Elizabeth to] prefer a plain dish to a ragout, [he] had nothing to say to her"' (Litvak 23; brackets in original). However, beyond such explicit connections, as Litvak points out, the term 'disgusting,' from the Latin word for 'taste,' is commonly applied not only to food items but also to both manners and non-gustatory preferences, not to mention sexual behaviour. In *The Age of Innocence*, this metaphoric root of the phrase 'good taste' is called to our attention in the opening scene, when Newland is shocked that Ellen would dare to appear in the Wellands' Opera box, especially wearing a dress that is rather too décolleté for New York. The narrative voice tells us that 'few things seemed more awful to Newland Archer than an offence against "Taste," that far-off divinity' (14). In a very interesting juxtaposition, immediately before noticing Ellen, Archer was ruminating about Mrs Manson Mingott's chronically bad food.

Despite popular usage, then, a code of manners has a more profound and far-reaching effect than that suggested by the relatively simple and apparently even arbitrary etiquette of the dinner table; manners are represented by, but not synonymous with, social protocol. As well as merely smoothing or facilitating social intercourse, manners may determine the content of both speech and action, and thus of interpersonal relationships and even of thought itself. In this sense, manners are implicit in a given society; often unconsciously followed, they cannot be learned easily by an outsider and are a buttress to the kind of class exclusivity seen in Edith Wharton's work. Richard Godden notes that manners cannot be separated from social economy; in so far as they strengthen 'the stability of the social order' (3), they affirm the economic underpinnings of that order. The economic security of the leisure class both demands and provides the opportunity to develop the highly mannered life which is in the interest of that class. Thus, although the term 'novel of manners' is often used disparagingly, suggesting a superficiality in the concerns of the novel, the portrayal or examination of manners in a novel is potentially more than a mere exercise in structural and social formality. Viewed in the light of Elias, for whom the notion of manners comprises both ritual and the evolving social and psychological history of a people, and Godden, for whom manners are based on social relations grounded in economic realities, the implications of manners are profound.

Edith Wharton's work presents one of the most thorough depictions both of the period before 1914, which Eric Hobsbawm – in the context of Europe and England – calls a golden age for the haute bourgeoisie (166), and of the changes undergone by this society as it was supplanted. As portrayed in Wharton's novels, the late nineteenth and early twentieth centuries present an apparent anomaly of heavily and strictly codified social behaviour existing concurrently with changes in family structure, a redefinition of classes and an increase in geographic and social mobility. The former was in part a response to the latter: that is, the perception and the experience of instability led to a system of tighter controls, which were imposed not by law but by the social group and, as demonstrated by Newland Archer, ultimately accepted and internalized by the individual. But rituals were not created just to maintain exclusivity. Because rituals seem permanent, seem to create a link with both the past and the future, they can reinforce a belief in the rightness of a particular social order. The resulting sense of security, of solidity in the face of geographical and class mobility, might have been reassuring even for those with the most secure and acceptable backgrounds.

Wharton's novels present various incarnations of the American upper class, with *The Age of Innocence* giving the most complete picture of the old New York elite, and thus forming a background to some of her other novels. Although written in the twentieth century, most of *The Age of Innocence* is set some years previously, at a period when the crisis of society was starting to be felt. Even at that time, the old society was not necessarily the most wealthy. Many people were beginning to have money – Ralph Marvell in *The Custom of the Country* calls them 'the

Invaders' (74) – but, although 'a multitude of the newly enriched gravitated to New York as a field for both larger financial operations and social advancement' (Lindberg 5), their wealth was not an immediate guarantee of entry into upper-class society. Wharton captures the difference between the two groups in her description of the 'shabby red and gold boxes of the sociable old Academy [of Music]. Conservatives cherished it for being small and inconvenient, and thus keeping out the "new people" whom New York was beginning to dread and yet be drawn to' (*The Age of Innocence* 3). The new wealthy clamoured for a new opera house: bigger, newer, more convenient, although without historical associations. 'Drawn to' in the above passage suggests not only that, for unstated – perhaps financial – reasons, these new people are becoming unavoidable, but also that the old elite are, almost against their will, somehow attracted to them. This dynamic is illustrated in Howells's *The Rise of Silas Lapham*, published thirty-five years earlier than *The Age of Innocence*, but set at approximately the same time. In that novel, the Coreys certainly have less money than the Laphams have at their height. But they do have history, pedigree, family heirlooms, a tastefully decorated home, education, leisure, manners, and style – none of which the Laphams can ever hope to acquire. Nevertheless, the young Tom Corey not only marries one of the Lapham daughters, but goes to work for her father. In Wharton's *The House of Mirth*, set a few decades later, Gus Trenor realizes, before most of his social set does, that the Jewish businessman Simon Rosedale is an important man to know because of his emerging financial position and influence. At the end of the novel, Rosedale is well on his way to inclusion in Trenor's circle; the self-made Elmer Moffatt in *The Custom of the Country* is also eventually accepted by polite society, despite his small-town origins and lack of social grace.

Richard Godden points out that 'the foundation of manners is economic; and as economic structures change, so manners change' (12). Although money eventually did break down the barriers of society, it did not do so at first. Indeed, against the perceived onslaught, the upper class made a perhaps unconscious, yet desperate and therefore more prescriptive attempt to define its distinguishing characteristics, as well as the appropriate behaviour for its members. Since there were no formal barriers, 'circles of informal but definite exclusiveness ... had to be established' (Hobsbawm 178).[1] As Leonore Davidoff notes about England in this period, 'The domesticating of public life via the dictates of Society was combined with control of individual behaviour and face-to-face interaction through a rigidly applied code of personal behaviour' (33).[2] Thus, in *Mrs. Dalloway*, Peter Walsh remembers an incident from his youth when Clarissa made fun of a housemaid turned squire's wife who did not know the social conventions of dress or conversation.

Wharton's novels demonstrate the degree to which the upper classes in New York defined themselves and clung to the most minute technicalities of this self-definition. Measured against this entrenched conservatism are the fringes of society; the novels also explore the permissible degree of deviation from the norm, and the consequences of nonconformity within the class. Interestingly, *The Age of Innocence* suggests that Americans, despite their democratic traditions, were far more concerned about behavioural distinctions than were their cousins on the European continent, where class distinctions were more definite and perhaps, therefore, not threatened to the same degree by individual aberrations. Newland Archer's first name reflects the resulting ambiguity: is he on the verge of doing something really innovative, original, and modern, or does his name merely refer to an America which is, ironically, far more interested in the old than the new?

If one of the conflicts in Wharton is between the old wealthy and the upwardly mobile, a second is inherent in the notion of manners itself. In Newland's responses to the dominant code of his world in *The Age of Innocence*, he is torn between the security of his society and its repressiveness. Newland's dilemma may be more complex and profound than it first appears. A code of manners, as Joanne Finkelstein points out, potentially has a double function. The use of 'good manners' is frequently seen as a way of putting the common good of society above the interests of an individual; manners, in this sense, constitute 'a language and abstract code of behaviour which promise to enhance the life of the group rather than advancing the singular survival of any individual' (127). This view is based on a kind of fear, wariness or

> ... the underlying assumption that people may not be virtuous by nature; indeed, they may be malevolent and destructive, and in anticipation of this possibility, a general obedience to manners is necessary. Consequently, manners need to be acquired by members of society in order to give the appearance that they will not be socially antagonistic; manners impose a veneer of virtue on everyone's behaviour which will conceal any signs of base or destructive emotions and desire. (131)

This definition, however, becomes a self-fulfilling one: a person who acts like a gentleman must be a gentleman and vice versa. Manners are admitted to be merely veneer, but the surface attributes become the essential reality. Thus, people who do not know the code are considered suspect and, as such, are automatically excluded.

With a slight shift in perspective, then, manners become a conservative force. If one does not look beneath the veneer, then hypocrisies, injustices, defects in society are not revealed or confronted:

> [A]n individual's faithful observance of manners can produce a patterned form of sociality which has the effect of annulling doubts and questions that may arise from anomalies or improprieties encountered in our sociality. From this viewpoint, manners express the mute violence of routine; they ... become a form of social control which effectively maintains the life of the group but, at the same time ... can stifle the private intellectual struggles of the individual. (Finkelstein 131–2)

The exercise of manners disciplines 'both the mind and body,' and the consequent triumph of routine becomes 'an impetus toward the unexamined life' (Finkelstein 131–2). Under an apparent moralism, amorality may be accepted, even encouraged. From this perspective, it begins to seem absurd that, in *The House of Mirth*, Lily Bart clings to 'one of those abstract notions of honour that might be called the conventionalities of the moral life' after having been destroyed in part by hypocritical social codes: 'What debt did she owe to a social order which had condemned and banished her without trial?' (405). Newland's dilemma, while not fatal, is nevertheless a difficult one. Because he has an entrenched interest in the social order, he ultimately understands that he has a good deal to lose if he disturbs it.

Rituals of Dinner in *The Age of Innocence*

The society of old New York described in *The Age of Innocence* is marked by many customs, rituals, and taboos; those surrounding dining and entertaining are the most potent and meaningful ones. Dining practices are central to social identity. Dinners convey multiple levels of meaning both to those around the table and to outsiders: affirming the stability of the social group, defining its boundaries, and confirming membership in that group. Thus it is frequently around the numerous dinners and other social events that the most important issues in *The Age of Innocence* coalesce. As the author, Wharton plays the roles of both hostess and critical guest.

In the upper-class world of Wharton's novels, women are the upholders of mealtime ritual and custom rather than the actual providers of food. In giving a dinner party, the hostess actively participates in endorsing and maintaining the stability of her society. In *The Age of Innocence*, dinners are very rigidly structured and the rituals surrounding them strictly adhered to; indeed, dinners play a large part in structuring this particular segment of New York society and the lives of its members. Dinners are given habitually by the same people at the same time of the year, or to mark a recurring event in the calendar: not only holidays like Thanksgiving, but events such as the opening of the opera season. The form of each dinner is apparently unvarying, with the several courses followed by the segregation of men and women for a period of after-dinner conversation. The novel does not show us too many ordinary family dinners, for the really important meals are those eaten with invited guests – even though, on one level, the social group seems like one big incestuous family. The invitations, the details of the menu, the dishes and silverware used, the seating arrangements – all signify the particular meaning and the importance of the event. Within this prescribed structure, a subtle variation may indicate an important message being conveyed to one or more of the diners or to the society at large.

The organization of meals in *The Age of Innocence* is also almost unvarying. The dinner hour structures the day and does so in the same way for everyone. For instance, we are told that '[o]ld-fashioned New York dined at seven' (100), and, indeed, at the start of the novel, Newland Archer has 'dined at seven, alone with his mother and sister'(4). It is also emphasized that this schedule is strictly adhered to at one of the van der Luydens' dinners: 'Nothing was done without ceremony under the van der Luyden roof, and though there were but four guests the repast had begun at seven punctually, so that the proper sequence of courses might be served without haste before the gentlemen settled down to their cigars' (317). After the dinner hour, 'the habit of after-dinner calls, though derided in Archer's set, still generally prevailed' (100). Thus, walking up Fifth Avenue, Newland can see an almost choreographed parade of callers leaving one house and arriving at another, and, in this very small world, he knows who is visiting whom.[3] This last passage also suggests how difficult it is to change habits. 'Archer's set,' presumably the more self-consciously modern members of the younger generation, is powerless in the face of custom; although they may criticize, eventually they too will most likely follow. Indeed, at the moment of his observation, Newland himself is on his way to make an after-dinner call. This after-dinner circulation is a form of public knowledge accounting for everyone's whereabouts for the evening, and producing a complete picture of both personal and social relations in the group as a whole.

If one knows more or less what everyone else is doing at the dinner and after-dinner hours, one also knows who they are. As the elderly and unconventional Mrs Manson Mingott says, 'Everybody in New York has always known everybody' (29). The same people keep seeing each other at different dinners, and the demographics of New York society are generally familiar to all its members, as are details about each other's histories, genealogies, and even personal quirks. This shared knowledge enforces social conformity and is repeated like a mantra at social occasions. In this sense, society is recreated at every dinner party. In the event of questions, Mr Sillerton Jackson, the unofficial keeper of all this information, can be applied to. With Mr Jackson as a dinner guest, the meal seems to have been sanctioned by the forefathers. It is worth quoting at length the description of his role, in order to capture the flavour of the petty yet powerful forces at work to maintain the network of static social relationships. Jackson

> knew all the ramifications of New York's cousinships; and could not only elucidate such complicated questions as that of the connection between the Mingotts (through the Thorleys) with the Dallases of South Carolina, and that of the relationship of the elder branch of Philadelphia Thorleys to the Albany Chiverses (on no account to be confused with the Manson Chiverses of University Place), but could also enumerate the leading characteristics of each family: as, for instance, the fabulous stinginess of the younger lines of Leffertses (the Long Island ones); or the fatal tendency of the Rushworths to make foolish marriages; or the insanity recurring in every second generation of the Albany Chiverses, with whom their New York cousins had always refused to intermarry – with the disastrous exception of poor Medora Manson, who, as everybody knew ... but then her mother was a Rushworth. (9–10; ellipsis in original)

To people like Mr Jackson, a peculiar form of genetics masks the real socio-economic factors as the nearly absolute determinant of individual characteristics. Thus everyone is not only known but explainable. With some exceptions, outsiders are only minimally tolerated. One anomaly, 'Catherine Spicer of Staten Island, with a father mysteriously discredited, and neither money nor position enough to make people forget it'

(12), was not only accepted into the fold through marriage, but eventually, as the widow of Manson Mingott, becomes one of the doyennes of New York society. The situations for men and for women are a bit different: Julius Beaufort is marginally acceptable because of his money and his ability to live in the appropriate way, but Mrs Lemuel Struthers, the widow of a man who made his money in shoe-polish, is, in the early part of the novel, extremely suspect. Within the inner circles, however, individual eccentricities and failings are generally well known and accepted. For instance, it is considered almost amusing that Mrs Mingott and Mrs Archer have a reputation for serving dreadful food. There is a kind of stability in the knowledge that a meal at one of their houses will be scarcely edible, and, like the quaint habits of a favourite aunt, these dinners are not only tolerated, but play an integral part in the ritual and custom supporting society. Indeed, this culinary deficiency, like others, is seen as so historic as to be almost genetically determined. 'Society,'[4] in its narrative mode, observes:

> But then New York, as far back as the mind of man could travel, had been divided into the two great fundamental groups of the Mingotts and Mansons and all their clan, who cared about eating and clothes and money, and the Archer-Newland-van-der-Luyden tribe, who were devoted to travel, horticulture and the best fiction, and looked down on the grosser forms of pleasure.
> You couldn't have everything, after all. (32–3)

If a socially ambitious person of Undine Spragg's class would not be able to get away with an incompetent chef, the bad food at Mrs Manson Mingott's and Mrs Archer's houses is a fixed constellation in the New York galaxy. The quality of the food itself is not necessarily critical; in this world, dinners have other, more important functions than the enjoyment of food.

In many cultures, mealtimes serve as an opportunity for indoctrinating the young into the mysteries of society; therefore, it is particularly important to uphold social institutions and mores on such occasions. Talk at the dinner table in *The Age of Innocence* follows this rule. The conversation is basically gossip, and Mrs Archer is sometimes worried about what her unmarried daughter Janey may hear; still, the prevailing responses to other people's problems and activities are certainly instructive, and she allows her to hear enough to know the pitfalls to avoid, as well as to participate with her elders in relishing the difficulties of others. Mr Sillerton Jackson is invited to the Archers' specifically for his knowledge of his neighbours' intimate affairs, be they sexual or financial, for these seem to be the two main ingredients of gossip. He is the keeper of scandals, some of them decades old: 'these mysteries ... were loosely locked in Mr. Jackson's breast; for not only did his keen sense of honour forbid his repeating anything privately imparted, but he was fully aware that his reputation for discretion increased his opportunities of finding out what he wanted to know' (10). Jackson is a master at dropping hints, making suggestions, never fully imparting what he knows, and thus keeping himself always at the top of everybody's guest list.

At Jackson's dinner with the Archers early in the novel, the people discussed are those on the fringes, either through birth, like Julius Beaufort or Mrs Lemuel Struthers, or through prolonged absence and questionable behaviour, like Ellen Olenska. Bringing 'fringe' behaviour and 'marginal' people to the forefront helps to better define the standards of the centre. In a comical sequence, Mr Jackson's impressions of the meal are interspersed with his remarks; in fact, the dishes seem to be presented as an accompaniment to the gossip. The bad quality of the food is particularly appropriate. Thus, 'cautiously inspecting the broiled shad, and wondering for the thousandth time why Mrs. Archer's cook always burnt the roe to a cinder' (35), he begins to discuss Beaufort; he wonders 'why no one had ever told the butler never to slice cucumbers with a steel knife' (36) as he begins to talk about Mrs Struthers; and 'Mr. Jackson's "sniff" at the mushroom sauce is "scarcely perceptible" but is enough to suggest that he "would probably finish his meal on Ellen Olenska"' (Knights 25). What he does to his subjects – without losing his acceptably genteel manner – is akin to the chef's treatment of the roe and the cucumbers. Indeed, gossip is food and drink to Mr Jackson: about to produce what to him is a very juicy morsel – that Ellen was seen walking on Fifth Avenue with Julius Beaufort – he 'gave a faint sip, as if he had been tasting invisible Madeira' (39). The infractions committed by Mrs Archer's chef fuel Jackson's comments on the more important sins of Beaufort, Struthers, and Olenska, whose scandalous behaviour is as expected as are the shortcomings of the meal.

The constancy of habits is made clear at this dinner: as Pamela Knights points out, both Newland's grandfathers are mentioned during the meal. Indeed, they almost seem to be present, as Jackson infers one ancestor's probable attitudes toward both the dinner and the subject matter of the dinner conversation: '"Ah, how your grandfather

Archer loved a good dinner, my dear Newland!" he said, his eyes on the portrait of a plump full-chested young man in a stock and a blue coat, with a view of a white-columned country-house behind him. "Well – well – well ... I wonder what he would have said to all these foreign marriages!'" (38; ellipsis in original). The portrait of this gentleman – looking rather like a specimen of stuffed poultry himself – overlooks the dinner table. More important, his views would, if possible, still be solicited by the diners as a relevant part of the dinner-table conversation, and Jackson assumes that the opinions of the deceased would be similar to his own. In fact, the grandfather's era seems still to define the limits to the conversation. Some subjects cannot be discussed, some words not uttered: 'the word [divorce] had fallen like a bombshell in the pure and tranquil atmosphere of the Archer diningroom. Mrs. Archer raised her delicate eye-brows in the particular curve that signified: "The butler –" and [Newland], himself mindful of the bad taste of discussing such intimate matters in public, hastily branched off into an account of his visit to old Mrs. Mingott' (41). The use of the word 'bombshell' – certainly a disruptive image at a dinner party – as a metaphor for 'divorce' implies that the latter word is capable of destroying both the table and the society it represents. It is an understatement to note that such items of discussion are not 'tasteful' in the context of the meal; hints of a woman questioning sexual and marital convention can provoke more disgust, in Litvak's terms, than burnt roe. A second *faux pas*, in the passage quoted above, is breaching the walls between public and private. In this context, the two spheres obviously refer to class rather than to the dinner's location. This is a private meal in a private home; 'public' is a euphemism for 'in front of the servants,' who suddenly seem not merely part of the accoutrements of the meal, but people as capable of gossiping as the diners are. In such a situation it is more 'tasteful' to talk about Mrs Mingott, who, despite her oddly arranged house with its beckoning ground-floor bedroom, is safely beyond the stage of sexual adventures.

Topics that have been launched but dropped and innuendos that have been merely glanced over may be picked up again after dinner. The customary after-dinner rites are gender-specific. In the drawingroom, Mrs Archer and Janey firmly take control of the future domestic arrangements of their son and brother, sewing 'a tapestry band of fieldflowers destined to adorn an "occasional" chair in the drawing-room of young Mrs. Newland Archer' (41), and thereby, in their choice of wildflowers as a motif, civilizing nature into an endless future of after-dinner sociability. Meanwhile Mr Jackson is telling Newland about the rumour of somewhat less conventional living arrangements once entered into by Ellen Olenska. For a young man, indoctrination into the ways of the tribe may occur over cigars and brandy. Thus, for Newland Archer, 'the best fiction, combined with the after-dinner talk of his elders, had long since initiated him into every detail of [the] code [of affairs with married women]' (305). This gender-restricted interlude, after the confirming ritual of dinner and a snifter or two of brandy, also provides the opportunity to speak more freely than usual – although the discussion always ultimately returns within the boundaries of the social code. Newland's disagreement with Sillerton Jackson on the subject of women after this particular meal indicates his attempt to position himself as a rebel in his society. Newland himself, however, seems unaware of 'the terrific consequences' (42) of his own words: 'I'm sick of the hypocrisy that would bury alive a woman of [Ellen's] age if her husband prefers to live with harlots ... Women ought to be free – as free as we are' (41). This remark prepares the reader, of course, for Newland's attraction to Ellen, but it also paves the way for the irony that he ultimately does not find himself to be particularly free.

At Wharton's dinners, then, the mouth is not only used to ingest food: speaking is, arguably, a more important part of dinner than eating. Dinner conversations classify, categorize, and judge people, and in so doing uphold the way of life and affirm for the diners the current attitudes to morality. In this way, they are a means by which society responds to crisis, clarifies its attitudes, and makes its presence and its weight felt. Sometimes, in *The Age of Innocence*, this latter function is the reason for the dinner to be given at all. It is, for instance, the reason why the van der Luydens hold a dinner for Ellen early in the novel. Invitations to the Lovell Mingotts' dinner in her honour have been refused by everyone except the Beauforts and Sillerton Jackson and his sister, people who, for their own different reasons, are interested in the margins of society. The van der Luydens cannot countenance this snub to a New York family, in this case the Mingotts, which has made clear its position of support for an errant member. If the invitation to dine is usually a confirmation of one's place within the group, and acceptance of an invitation an affirmation of conformity with the group's values, here the invitation is not to celebrate a joint conformity – as at a wedding dinner, for instance – but to reinforce the hierarchy within the group, reiterate the rules which govern society, define the boundaries of acceptance, and, in so doing, both contain unconventionality and demand conformity of those on the edge. The higher echelons of the bourgeoisie have more freedom to press the limits of conformity; the irreproachable pedigree of the van der Luydens allows them, then, to resolve for the community the more difficult issues of convention.

The strength of the van der Luydens' defence of Ellen, or more accurately, of the principle of Ellen, is shown first of all by their holding the dinner at all. Any dinner at the van der Luydens' is by definition an important occasion, given their role as the arbiters of New York society. And, as Ellen sees, their dinners have been accorded this weight in part precisely because they entertain so rarely. In this case, even the table-setting raises their dinner to a particular level of significance: 'The van der Luydens had done their best to emphasize the importance of the occasion. The du Lac Sèvres and the Trevenna George II plate were out; so was the van der Luyden "Lowestoft" (East India Company) and the Dagonet Crown Derby' (61). The use of ancestral china and silverware reminds the guests of the historical roots of New York society and of the van der Luydens' place within it.

Moreover, they pair their recognition of Ellen with a second special occasion, the visit of their English cousin, the Duke of St Austrey, thereby at the same time honouring her and calling attention to her foreignness. The conventional Newland feels that Ellen does not adequately appreciate this honour or realize that she has just made a narrow escape from social ostracism. The Duke, like Ellen a semi-stranger to New York society, dresses shabbily and makes little attempt at brilliant conversation. Moreover, neither he nor Ellen obeys the protocol of who should speak to whom after dinner. Ellen does not seem to realize that a woman is supposed to be passive, like a dish waiting to be chosen and eaten: 'It was not the custom in New York drawing-rooms for a lady to get up and walk away from one gentleman in order to seek the company of another. Etiquette required that she should wait, immovable as an idol, while the men who wished to converse with her succeeded each other at her side. But the Countess was apparently unaware of having broken any rule' (63). This behaviour is overlooked because, as outsiders – or more accurately, perhaps, *distanced* relations – both Ellen and the Duke are permitted to seem ignorant of and even uninterested in the petty subtleties of the New York dinner party. It is perhaps not so acceptable to be unimpressed by the honour of being present in so august a company and in such surroundings. After dinner, Ellen shocks Newland by calling the Duke 'the dullest man I ever met' (63), and later by criticizing the gloominess of the van der Luydens' house. Until nearly the end of the novel, however, the van der Luydens, unlike others, continue to excuse Ellen's behaviour because she is 'foreign.' Their eventual rescinding of this indulgence is signalled when, again at dinner, Mrs van der Luyden deplores Ellen's visiting the disgraced Mrs Beaufort, especially in her grandmother's carriage. A more important social protocol has now been breached, this one involving money.

This incident marks a second time in the novel that the van der Luydens hold a dinner to reassure and solidify society. Having returned hurriedly from their country house after hearing of Julius Beaufort's ruin, they give a small dinner solely to demonstrate that Beaufort's bankruptcy is not going to destroy the world of New York. Mr Sillerton Jackson is again the expert on Ellen at this dinner. The chapter opens with his remark, and the table is thus set by him: '"At the court of the Tuileries," said Mr Sillerton Jackson with his reminiscent smile, "such things were pretty openly tolerated"' (316). Ellen's 'imprudence' (318) in visiting Mrs Beaufort is associated by analogy with the sexual and financial standards of the French court: '"At the Tuileries," he repeated, seeing the eyes of the company expectantly turned on him, "the standard was excessively lax in some respects; and if you'd asked where Morny's money came from – ! Or who paid the debts of some of the Court beauties"' (318–19). Neither question is answered or even really asked. Again, much of the dinner-table conversation is made up of tidbits: unfinished questions and answers, suggestions and innuendo. The fact that the talk is interrupted by mouthfuls of food and sips of wine perhaps excuses, but does not completely account for, such interruptions.

The final dinner of the novel, given for Ellen's departure, is the complement of Ellen's welcoming party at the van der Luydens'. It is a ritual in two senses. On the one hand, it is the Newland Archers' first formal dinner party, and, as such, it represents the consummation of their marriage. Certainly, in many cultures, the marriage vow is pledged with ceremonial food: the wedding feast where the newly married couple feed each other wedding cake is a contemporary example. For Newland and May, whose society places such importance on social categories and definitions, this dinner party marks not their marriage, but their full entry into society as a married couple. Since the union of two New York families is an important aspect of the marriage, the mothers-in-law are involved with the dinner preparations, and agree that it is to be 'a great event' (326). The dinner also cements the marriage by affirming its monogamous character, for it marks the departure of Ellen Olenska, the woman Newland believes he loves. It is appropriate that Newland learns of his wife's pregnancy after the party: the text of the dinner party is so strong, it is as if the meal itself impregnated her.[5] For Newland, the marriage vows are then completely sealed.

Second, the party is the ritual of Ellen's banishment: 'There were certain things that had to be done, and if done at all, done handsomely and thoroughly; and one of these, in the old New York code, was the tribal rally around a kinswoman, about to be eliminated from the tribe' (334). The seating arrangements are unusual, thus significant. Ellen's foreignness is emphasized by the apparent tribute of being seated on Newland's right. This designation of status makes the fact of her exile less complicated for the circle of her family and acquaintances. Because so much is unstated at this dinner, there is a sense of unreality about it. Thus, although he takes the customary position of host, Newland does not feel in control; in fact it is a different dinner from what it pretends to be, and he plays a different role from the obvious one. No longer clear about his relationship to social categories, he 'begins to come apart, losing his sense of himself, his language, position, bodily space' (Knights 36). He 'seemed to be assisting at the scene in a state of odd imponderability, as if he floated somewhere between chandelier and ceiling' (334). Newland's sensation is that he is not at the table at all, not actually part of the circle of diners. And, indeed, in a certain sense he is not, for, as he realizes, he has himself become the subject of gossip: everybody believes him and Ellen to be

> lovers in the extreme sense peculiar to 'foreign' vocabularies. He guessed himself to have been, for months, the centre of countless silently observing eyes and patiently listening ears, he understood that, by means as yet unknown to him, the separation between himself and the partner of his guilt had been achieved, and that now the whole tribe had rallied about his wife on the tacit assumption that nobody knew anything, or had ever imagined anything, and that the occasion of the entertainment was simply May Archer's natural desire to take an affectionate leave of her friend and cousin. (335)

It is the dinner that finally conveys to him the reality of his own situation.

Indeed, the power of society is clear in the coming together of this final dinner party, 'a big dinner, with a hired *chef* and two borrowed footmen' (327). The choice of menu, an impressive guest list, and a certain dress code are inseparable components which automatically entail each other, and which, taken together, constitute an important communication about the status of the young Archers: 'the Roman punch ... signified either canvas-backs or terrapin, two soups, a hot and a cold sweet, full *décolletage* with short sleeves, and guests of a proportionate importance' (327). The meal is a coherent, predictable whole; Newland and Ellen must not only be prevented from destroying the structure that it represents, but also be incorporated back into that structure even if, in Ellen's case, by a ritualized banishment. The consumption of the food is presented as almost sacramental: integral to the ritual of banishment and the expression of social disapproval. Despite his feeling of detachment, Newland knows what is happening: 'As his glance travelled from one placid well-fed face to another he saw all the harmless-looking people engaged upon May's canvas-backs as a band of dumb conspirators, and himself and the pale woman on his right as the centre of their conspiracy' (334–5). May's ownership of the ducks – indeed of the dinner – puts her in charge, and the guests rally around their hostess. 'Spatially, ritually, and thus physically and psychologically, so complete is the women's control over their world' (Fryer 139) in *The Age of Innocence* that they automatically come to May's aid to force Newland to give up Ellen. It is perhaps not stretching a point to imagine the dinner guests cutting up and eating the couple at the head of the table – or at least consuming their aberration – along with the ducks. Without anything being said, the meal itself both reinstates the social order and celebrates its return. In this sense, the meal itself speaks.

The social code of dinner in *The Age of Innocence* reinforces the parallel code of sexual behaviour. Despite the fact that 'a certain measure of contempt was attached to men who continued their philandering after marriage' (305), society is not altogether shocked when extramarital affairs do occur; as a bachelor, Newland himself had an affair with a married woman. But any notion that he and Ellen might go away and live together threatens the social cohesion:

Archer felt like a prisoner in the centre of an armed camp. He looked about the table, and guessed at the inexorableness of his captors from the tone in which, over the asparagus from Florida, they were dealing with Beaufort and his wife. 'It's to show me,' he thought, 'what would happen to *me* – '

and a deathly sense of the superiority of implication and analogy over direct action, and of silence over rash words, closed in on him like the doors of the family vault. (335)

The ordinary act of eating vegetables (perhaps imported especially for the occasion) becomes threatening. Are these Newland's own guilty responses or are his dining companions really trying to make a point? As with so much in this novel, the reader does not know for sure. It is noteworthy that nothing is spoken here, that Newland *guesses* that he is the subject of gossip and that others assume that he and Ellen are lovers. Although there is much talk in this novel, there are also significantly profound silences; manners and ritual as a form of language almost always communicate more than words do. Indeed, much is assumed throughout the novel. We do not know exactly what Count Olenski did to his wife; we are not sure whether she and M. Rivière were lovers; we do not really know about Mrs Struthers's background. We think we know about the sexual exploits of Julius Beaufort and Larry Lefferts, but only because, as readers, we have become a part of the grapevine, and ourselves participate in the gossip and speculation. At dinner, then, Newland's assumption is a reasonable one, given the hints, innuendo, and rumour which have been evident throughout the novel, and particularly at earlier dinners. But in the end it makes little difference. Newland himself, as long as he stays in his social role, is in fact one of his own 'captors.'

If dinner parties constantly re-create and reaffirm the characteristics and boundaries of the social group, intimate meals are less important, and, indeed, are scarcely portrayed in the novel. When we do see the Newland Archers dining privately, it is during the crisis following Ellen's return from Washington, and we are told only that 'during dinner their talk moved in its usual limited circle' (294). Bound by conventions and in itself a convention, dinner is not the place to talk about family problems or even to admit that any exist. It is after dinner in Newland's library that more important discussions occur between Newland and May, in a sense reminiscent of the conversations among men over brandy and cigars after the more formal dinners of the novel. From the private space that Newland foresees before his marriage, a room that May 'would probably let him arrange ... as he pleased' (71), the library becomes the site of the most significant events of his married life, or, as he later defines them, 'most of the real things of his life' (344). Looking back at the end of the novel, Archer seems to be oddly satisfied with the invasions of his private sanctuary, a hint, perhaps, that he made the correct choice after all.

However, at various points in the novel there are meetings between Ellen and Newland, sometimes with a small meal or tea, which stand apart from all the usual social rituals. Newland's first visit to Ellen's little house with its unacceptable address is an example. He feels himself to be on foreign soil here; tea is served in 'handleless Japanese cups' (75), and the entire ambiance of Ellen's house takes him away from his normal world, although he is quick to regain his conventional aspect when the Duke of St Austrey enters with Mrs Lemuel Struthers. Knights points out the complexity of Newland and Ellen's later meeting at the Patroon's cottage. There is a feeling of intimacy, of two people together by choice and desire, not just by social arrangement. Although they do not share a meal, the accoutrements of eating are described: 'A big bed of embers still gleamed in the kitchen chimney, under an iron pot hung from an ancient crane. Rush-bottomed arm-chairs faced each other across the tiled hearth, and rows of Delft plates stood on shelves against the walls' (133). There is a sense of history here, of that very old New York upon which their complicated social world is based, a life where fundamental values were more homely, more sound. But there is also a feeling of playing house, as if they are in 'a fairy-tale gingerbread cottage for two lost children' (Knights 37), outside of society, 'transcending time and history' (37). This feeling is recreated to some extent when Ellen and Newland meet in Boston, take a boat out to an island in the harbour, and have tea in an intimate little room at an inn, apart from, although in perhaps an unusual proximity to, the vacationing schoolteachers who fill the main dining-room. The meal or tea *à deux* may sometimes allow an escape from social constraints, and signal the possibility of authentic intimacy. But such meetings, taking place in an unusual setting and sometimes outside of the usual class structures, are also very much associated with the realm of fantasy, that other place which Newland imagines where 'categories like [mistress] won't exist' (290), but which Ellen says is not 'at all different from the old world ... but only rather smaller and dingier and more promiscuous' (290). In fact, despite their sometimes novel physical surroundings, Ellen and Newland remain firmly within the context of society and its roles. For instance, by the time of the meeting in Boston, Newland is married: 'there they were, close together and safe and shut in; yet so chained to their separate destinies that they might as well have been half the world apart' (244).

The manners and rituals of dinner, performed in the usual way, help people get through difficult situations, like the unpleasantness that might result from Newland's infatuation with Ellen and the potential ugliness of Ellen's banishment. Reflections of cultural assumptions and often unspoken rules, they theoretically protect society from deviance and nonconformity, and friends and family members from the consequences of scandal and misbehaviour. Rituals and ritualized behaviour provide a sense of security, a sense of belonging; and acceptance of this way of being is as natural as breathing for most of Wharton's characters. But personal conduct is certainly constrained, and the range of permissible attitudes and activities extremely circumscribed. Confronted by the prejudices of his young wife when he wants to invite to dinner a man who is merely a tutor, Newland thinks: 'After all, her point of view had always been the same. It was that of all the people he had grown up among, and he had always regarded it as necessary but negligible. Until a few months ago he had never known a "nice" woman who looked at life differently' (203).

To return to one of Finkelstein's points, although they may superficially smooth social intercourse, mealtime customs, particularly in the changing economic world of the late nineteenth century, keep people apart, in fact sometimes in competition. To the degree that ostentation, ritual, and the confirmation of social values are uppermost at the dinner party, few new ideas are raised, nothing original or surprising can emerge, and festivity is minimal; moreover very little genuine, in the sense of non-ritualized, personal contact occurs. A notable example, of course, is the final dinner of *The Age of Innocence*, where Ellen and Newland, seated side by side, forced to celebrate their loss, speak in the perfectly acceptable banalities appropriate to two people who are bored with the dinner and the conversation, and perhaps with each other. The sense in which these many layers of ritual seem eternal belies their function of suppressing or at least managing social change and actively reinforcing the cohesion of the whole society. At every Thanksgiving dinner, Mrs Archer laments that New York is changing. These complaints – as much a part of the yearly ritual as Mrs Peniston's fall house-cleaning in *The House of Mirth*, the opening of the season and the holiday dinner itself – have ceased to have any meaning beyond a confirmation of the status quo. Immersed in the ritual of her dinner and her usual ideas, Mrs Archer does not in fact see some of the real changes that have occurred.

Unlike the women in charge of the dinner table in *The Age of Innocence*, Wharton, who has played the role of hostess at the reader's dinner, is off to France with Ellen Olenska. The novelist does not, however, share her knowledge of this other world. The novel ends in Paris with a 'sociable hour' (361) at Ellen's apartment, but we are excluded, left with Newland's view of 'the awninged balcony' (361) from the square below. Within our framework of New York dinner-table sociability, a Parisian social hour is not something that we can know.

4

The Art of Being an Honoured Guest: *The House of Mirth* and *The Custom of the Country*

If Newland Archer thinks of escaping from his social group, with its oppressively formalized dinners and enforced conventions, he ultimately elects to remain a part of that exclusive circle, despite his awareness of its limitations. But what of those on the outside? Even though the upper classes may sometimes have been unconscious of their social assumptions and, until they were broken, of the prescriptive nature of their often unstated rules, those wishing to find acceptance in higher circles were very much aware of the codes of behaviour of that class. The Undine Spraggs of New York certainly see membership in Newland's world as highly desirable, and, despite its apparent solidity, as time went by there were more and more possibilities for entry. Conversely, even for those born into high society, continued membership in the elite circle was not at all a given. It is extremely tenuous for Lily Bart, who does not, for all her reservations about New York society, discover any other way to live. As Pamela Knights points out, 'Some readers would agree with Archer that to be locked in the family is to be buried alive, but the text also suggests, conversely, that *loss* of social being is a form of death' (36; emphasis in original). For Lily, exclusion literally does mean death. Although she is a member of a more modern version of Newland Archer's society, Lily is on her way out, just as Undine Spragg is on her way in.

The Age of Innocence takes place at the acme of New York high society, but, as noted in the previous chapter, this society was already experiencing the threat of change. In *The House of Mirth* and *The Custom of the Country*, Wharton explores two particular manifestations of people on the margins of society: those on the fringes trying to stay in position, and those trying to attain or create a new position for themselves. Both situations are explored in relationship to dinners, and with a particular focus on women. This focus makes sense, for, as Arthur Schlesinger notes, women were 'the principal guardians of decorum in the middle and upper ranks of [American] society' (viii), and in Wharton's novels, it is women who are really in charge of the social world. In *The Age of Innocence*, for instance, it may well be the women who take the lead in banishing Ellen Olenska, and when a conspiracy of women ostracizes Lily in *The House of Mirth*, the men, in general, either merely observe or acquiesce. Following Veblen, Richard Godden argues that women's power derives from their functions as consumers, commodities, and items of display: 'in her double role as display case and womb, the bourgeois woman ... [is] at the centre of the drawing-room' (16), and therefore in charge of the sphere of dinner parties, houses, marriages, and dress – all in one way or another aspects of consumption or the exchange and distribution of accumulated wealth.

It is this world of women that is explored in these two novels. In Lily Bart in *The House of Mirth* and Undine Spragg in *The Custom of the Country*, Wharton shows us the downwardly and the upwardly mobile woman. Lily has birth and knows all the conventions of her class, but does not have money; Undine has money, but is an outsider by birth and by upbringing. Both suffer from a lack of family protection and various kinds of domestic failure: deficiencies which require each to make her own way in the world. The fact that both women are usually guests rather than hostesses at the dinners and other social occasions described in the novels is the key indication of their position on the margins.

From a general anthropological perspective, dinners not only provide nourishment, but create structure, facilitate sociability, and define membership in a group. All of these aspects of meals are at issue in *The House of Mirth*. In this novel, which takes place at least a generation later than *The Age of Innocence*, the rituals which we saw associated with meals in the latter novel barely conceal the jockeying for position that is the real dynamic at dinner. And if the structure of meals is perhaps less rigid, nonconformity is still punished. The focus in *The House of Mirth* is on Lily, who finally fails in the competition, but it is clear that other characters in the novel are involved in similar struggles. Thus the social situation in the novel is characterized by, at the very least, a certain lack of empathy and sometimes even cutthroat rivalry and opportunism.

In Lily Bart, we nearly always have a sense of someone undernourished – emotionally, sexually, and, at the end, aesthetically, and finally even physically. This sense of starvation is connected to a general impression of rootlessness and estrangement which is the legacy of her family: a frivolous mother, an overworked father – both deceased at the time of the novel – an aunt who has taken her in only grudgingly, and cousins who are also *nouveau* poor and, like her, jockeying for position in society. This pervading sense of hunger is fittingly underlined by the fact that the specific act of eating is rarely described in detail in this novel. Yet dinners and other gatherings are extremely significant to the New York social group, and, moreover, mark key moments in the downward curve of Lily's life. The very importance of meals in the structure of the novel and in the society it depicts calls attention to the lack of detail about the food itself: dinners figure as events, but not as meals.

In *The House of Mirth*, the first 'meals' in which Lily participates are not meals at all, but rather performances:[1] the ritual of the table has become almost a parody of itself. In many cultures, the drinking of tea and other beverages has been, traditionally, one of the most ceremonial of food rituals. Susan Williams points out the importance of ritualized tea-drinking in late nineteenth-century America as an affirmation of social values and an expression of women's decorative role (14).[2] It is fitting, then, that two tea ceremonies open the novel. When, in the first chapter, Lily meets Lawrence Selden at the train station, he invites her to his apartment for tea because she acts helpless and asks to be looked after, behaving in a frankly flirtatious way that surprises him, as he cannot believe that she really considers him to be marriage material: 'The provocation in her eyes increased his amusement – he had not supposed she would waste her powder on such small game; but perhaps she was only keeping her hand in; or perhaps a girl of her type had no conversation but of the personal kind' (10). Indeed, it is as if she is incapable of turning off the charm. She exhibits for Selden her elegant manner of pouring tea, as if she is a commodity to be acquired and displayed like a tea service: 'he knelt by the table to light the lamp under the kettle, while she measured out the tea into a little tea-pot of green glaze ... he watched her hand, polished as a bit of old ivory, with its slender pink nails, and the sapphire bracelet slipping over her wrist' (8–9).

Lily's studied charm reflects a hunger and thirst, not for the tea and cakes which Selden provides, but for a certain kind of life in which she would permanently play the tea-pouring hostess, a woman who is a notch above actually having to prepare and serve food, but rather presides decoratively over the household. Yet, even as she plays the conventional role, the rebellious side of Lily's character is suggested. She is breaking the norms of acceptable behaviour by having tea in Selden's rooms; it is unclear whether this is a flippant scoffing at convention or a serious expression of alienation from society and social standards. Although Selden himself seems oddly immune from the hunger for social success, the other characters in this chapter are not. Lily is observed and confronted leaving the apartment building by others who are hungry for higher status and who pay close attention to people like her, waiting for a sign of vulnerability, looking for an advantage. It is the first of a series of compromising situations which will hasten her downfall. The charwoman who refuses to move aside for Lily as she descends the stairs seems to be commenting on their relative worth: a lady leaving a bachelor's apartment is, presumably, no lady. This woman will later try to blackmail Lily with what she believes are her love-letters to Selden. Simon Rosedale, appearing out of nowhere at the entrance to the building – which, as it turns out, he owns – files away his encounter with Lily for future use as a bargaining chip.

Later that afternoon, on the train with Percy Gryce, Lily again makes tea, and her performance is even more marked: she does not actually want any tea, but she wishes to create a certain effect, to be observed in a certain light, and to use this opportunity to buy herself future economic security. Thinking she understands the kind of wife that Gryce wants, 'she resolved to impart a gently domestic air to the scene' (24). By making tea in a jouncing train carriage – and in so doing creating the illusion of a drawing room – she succeeds in impressing Gryce:

> When the tea came he watched her in silent fascination while her hands flitted above the tray, looking miraculously fine and slender in contrast to the coarse china and lumpy bread. It seemed wonderful to him that any one should perform with such careless ease the difficult task of making tea in public in a lurching train ... [S]ecure in the shelter of her conspicuousness, he sipped the inky draught with a delicious sense of exhilaration.
>
> Lily, with the flavour of Selden's caravan tea on her lips, had no great fancy to drown it in the railway brew which seemed such nectar to her companion; but, rightly judging that one of the charms of tea is the fact of drinking it together, she proceeded to give the last touch to Mr. Gryce's enjoyment by smiling at him across her lifted cup. (23–4)

In this scene, the adjective 'inky,' a rather surprising choice of words to describe tea, underlines the communicative role of the beverage. Standing in metonymical relation to the customary social ritual surrounding it, the tea itself functions as the *écriture* of social performance.[3]

The ability to create an elegant and intimate tea party *à deux* even on a train would appear to suggest the ability to create a gracious home under any circumstances. Actually, however, the experiences of Lily's whole life are the opposite: she has had no real home and little knowledge of domesticity. In her childhood, dining meant either dining out, entertaining, or lunching on leftovers from a party the night before: 'it was one of Mrs. Bart's few economies to consume in private the expensive remnants of her hospitality' (40). Born into an old New York family which can no longer afford the level of expenditures demanded by her mother, Lily comes from a 'turbulent element' rather than a home, marked by a 'chaos' of constant visitors and social engagements, a frequently changing contingent of servants, 'precipitate trips to Europe, and returns with gorged trunks and days of interminable unpacking ... grey interludes of economy and brilliant reactions of expense' (37). Later, after her father's death, Lily is literally homeless, as she and her mother 'wandered from place to place, now paying long visits to relations whose house-keeping Mrs. Bart criticized, and who deplored the fact that she let Lily breakfast in bed when the girl had no prospects before her, and now vegetating in cheap continental refuges, where Mrs. Bart held herself fiercely aloof from the frugal tea-tables of her companions in misfortune' (43–4). To Mrs Bart, this degrading life is expressed in terms of meals; for her, meals are a defining symptom of her much-feared 'dinginess,' and her two-year widowhood is described as a period of 'hungry roaming' (46). No matter how little money she has, she refuses to accept the structure of meals that her poverty should decree.

Meals have the same significance for Lily. Gerty Farish, Selden's cousin, offers her shelter on the night she escapes from Gus Trenor's advances and, when Lily is later disinherited by her aunt and ostracized by society, would be willing to accept her as a flat-mate. But although, throughout the novel, Gerty's life is presented as a possible alternative for Lily, living like Gerty is not a choice that Lily can make. When Selden, during their first tea together, mentions that it is possible for a woman to live alone, she says of his cousin's life: 'she has a horrid little place, and no maid, and such queer things to eat. Her cook does the washing and the food tastes of soap' (8). Later, at the Van Osburgh wedding, Lily views with condescension Gerty's excitement at the food that is served:

> 'Did you ever taste anything more delicious than that *mousse* of lobster
> with champagne sauce? I made up my mind weeks ago that I wouldn't
> miss this wedding, and just fancy how delightfully it all came about.
> When Lawrence Selden heard I was coming, he insisted on fetching me
> himself and driving me to the station, and when we go back this evening I
> am to dine with him at Sherry's. I really feel as excited as if I were getting
> married myself!' (118)

Not only enjoying herself, but experiencing the wedding vicariously,
Gerty is ebullient about the whole day. The wedding banquet and the
dinner at Sherry's, like the gifts and the wedding itself, are a fantasy
come true for Gerty, a change from everyday reality. But to Lily, her
friend's enthusiasm demonstrates her lack of hope, her acceptance of
the status of outsider in this social world. Lily herself means to experience marriage first-hand, and to take expensive food and restaurants
for granted.

In the structure of the novel, dinners and parties are particularly
important in defining Lily's social world, setting out the backdrop of
men who are interested in her, and, ultimately, marking her fall. Where
the men are not present – at luncheon at the Trenors,' for instance – the
meal is an opportunity for the catty machinations of the women. These
social gatherings increasingly emphasize Lily's position as an outsider:
underneath the party atmosphere, she is always on a different level
from the other guests. Thus, early in the novel, during a weekend at the
Trenors' country house, she is the only guest who worries about the
money her stay requires, and the only guest whom Judy Trenor asks to
help with secretarial functions, as if to earn her keep. This position is
only exacerbated as the novel continues, and Lily is asked to 'help out'
in more unsavoury ways, finally becoming a paid employee. The tea-
table rituals over which Lily presides at the start of the novel are
gradually supplanted by increasingly anguished and tenuous performances. Lily never attains the position that her role at the tea ritual ought
to represent; she never actually takes her place at the head of a dinner
table or as the lady of the house.

The fact that the food itself is not particularly emphasized at any
of these social events – except, in the example noted above, as a commodity to be consumed by the wealthy, and the object of Gerty's admiration – suggests that the coming together of the social set is for other

purposes than communality, and that, although such events have enormous social, even economic importance, they are not necessarily pleasurable and scarcely even nourishing, either literally or metaphorically. At the Wellington Brys' party, Gus Trenor, sounding rather like one of the more old-fashioned characters from *The Age of Innocence*, and feeling somewhat grouchy because Lily is ignoring him, calls attention to what some of these dinners are like: 'Stay for supper? Not if I know it! When people crowd their rooms so that you can't get near any one you want to speak to, I'd as soon sup in the elevated at the rush hour' (184).

One of the longer dinner scenes is near the beginning of the novel at the Trenors' house party, a weekend event which is even more crucial to her future than Lily realizes. This is the turning point in her life. She begins the weekend with the idea of getting herself engaged to Percy Gryce, but sabotages her own plan. What surprises her later is that she cannot recover from this failure of will and recuperate her advantage with him. Moreover, with her failure to 'land' Gryce, her social status begins its descent. Lily's perceptions at the dinner table – the longest and most crucial of the several meals mentioned during this weekend at the Trenors' – crystallize her change of heart, a fatal one, given that she has no alternative strategy. Although we are parenthetically given an idea of what people are eating at this dinner, details of the menu are not emphasized. In fact, references to eating tend to be rather negative; thus, Gus Trenor is described as 'carnivorous' (72), and George Dorset as unable to eat the rich food because of his jealousy-induced dyspepsia, as he watches his wife flirt with Selden. The meal is not characterized by pleasure or festivity; rather, in forming a backdrop for the various dynamics played out in the group, it reveals a false conviviality. We are introduced here to most of the major and minor characters of Lily's set, and, influenced by Selden, Lily looks critically at them seated around the table: 'How different they had seemed to her a few hours ago! Then they had symbolized what she was gaining, now they stood for what she was giving up. That very afternoon they had seemed full of brilliant qualities; now she saw that they were merely dull in a loud way. Under the glitter of their opportunities she saw the poverty of their achievement' (72). The next day, although she means to follow through with her plan, her dinnertime perception of the Trenors' world as a 'great gilt cage' (71) has stolen her will. Consciously, she does not mean to change her decision to marry Gryce, but the following day she seems unable to pursue her project. Thus, Lily fails to attend church with Gryce, as planned, and also alienates Bertha Dorset, who takes revenge by turning Gryce against her.

Other social gatherings in book 1 of the novel have a similar flavour: dinners remain important as events, but not as meals. And they are peopled by the same group of players, doing and saying the same sorts of things. Beginning with the Trenors' dinner, these social occasions trace Lily's slide. The Van Osburgh wedding, mentioned earlier, 'was the kind of scene in which Lily had often pictured herself as taking the principal part, and on this occasion the fact that she was once more merely a casual spectator, instead of the mystically veiled figure occupying the centre of attention, strengthened her resolve to assume the latter part before the year was over' (115). Ironically, considering her 'resolve,' it is at the wedding that Lily finds out that she has lost Percy Gryce for good. Instead, the novel pairs her with Gerty. The two seem to be somewhat outside the main group of diners at the wedding banquet: '"Do let us go and take a peep at the presents before every one else leaves the dining-room!" suggested Miss Farish, linking her arm in her friend's' (117). The narrative jumps directly from the church to the after-dinner display of wedding gifts; dinner itself is skipped by the novel. Lily is not depicted eating at this wedding, then, but rather working: trying to discover the truth about Gryce's engagement, walking a thin line with Gus Trenor, working her charms on Sim Rosedale in order to defuse his potential danger to her. Similarly, at the Wellington-Brys' entertainment, where she reaches the apex of her beauty in the *tableaux vivants*, Lily speaks with Selden instead of eating: 'they moved away, not toward the supper-room, but against the tide which was setting thither' (181–2). If, earlier, Lily gave up her 'meal-ticket' in Percy Gryce for Selden, here she gives up her meal, and, once again under Selden's influence, distances herself from the rest of the group heading for the table. The encounter seems to promise the start of a love affair, but Selden is more tied to the social values of his world than he admits, and, therefore, nothing ever comes of their mutual admiration.[4] It is more possible for a man than for a woman to maintain an ironic distance from this social world and still belong to it.

Dinner invitations also play a pivotal role in the novel, even without the actual dinner; invitations can constitute a social minefield rather than a welcome opportunity to enjoy food in pleasant company. Thus, the day after the Wellington-Brys' party, Lily's tentative relationship with Selden is thwarted because she is trapped between two dinner invitations. An adept at social juggling, she tries to enjoy Carrie Fisher's 'indefatigable hospitality' (186) and, on the same evening, to 'reëstablish [her] former relations' (186) with Judy Trenor. Although she already plans to dine with Mrs Fisher, 'who had gathered at an informal feast a few of the performers of the previous evening' (186), when the jealous Gus Trenor decides to cash in on his investment by sending Lily a dinner invitation supposedly from his wife, she tries to attend both dinners. For once, Mrs Fisher's party is a gathering that seems genuinely enjoyable: 'Lily was reluctant to leave, for the dinner was amusing, and she would have liked to lounge over a cigarette and hear a few songs; but she could not break her engagement with Judy' (186). Thus, she arrives late at the Trenors,' to discover that Judy is not really there. In a parallel to her leaving Selden's apartment at the start of the novel, she is seen by Selden himself as she leaves the house, having narrowly escaped the amorous Gus, and Selden, who the novel implies is the potential 'true mate,' is thus dissuaded from pursuing her.[5]

An invitation to one of Mrs Peniston's apparently rare dinners is also particularly important, even though, again, the dinner is never described. The issue in this case turns on the difference between the stodgy dinners of the old-fashioned and the 'smart' (163) entertainments of the younger set:

> Mrs. Peniston disliked giving dinners, but she had a high sense of family obligation, and on the Jack Stepneys' return from their honeymoon she felt it incumbent upon her to light the drawing-room lamps and extract her best silver from the Safe Deposit vaults. Mrs Peniston's rare entertainments were preceded by days of heart-rending vacillation as to every detail of the feast, from the seating of the guests to the pattern of the table-cloth ... (162)

In order to have a more interesting circle at the dinner table, Lily advises her aunt, 'who leaned helplessly on her niece in social matters' (163), not to invite Grace Stepney. In retaliation, the latter informs Lily's aunt of her extravagances, and therefore ultimately takes Lily's place as the beneficiary of Mrs Peniston's will. The fact that 'Mrs. Peniston ... had been prevailed upon to pronounce Grace's exile' (163) leads to Lily's own eventual exile.

In the second section of the book, meals are one of the few constants in the highly irregular situation of the Dorsets' marriage. Life on the Riviera with the Dorsets and other members of the New York set – which seems to be life in New York merely transplanted – is defined by a continuous succession of breakfasts, lunches, and dinners. These culminate in the restaurant dinner where Bertha Dorset publicly banishes Lily. In Selden's eyes, this dinner, an extreme version, perhaps, of earlier meals in the novel, is marked by

> the stupid costliness of the food and the showy dulness of the talk ... the freedom of speech which never arrived at wit and the freedom of act which never made for romance. The strident setting of the restaurant, in which their table seemed set apart in a special glare of publicity, and the presence at it of little Dabham of the 'Riviera Notes,' emphasized the ideals of a world where conspicuousness passed for distinction, and the society column had become the roll of fame. (289)

The 'labyrinth of courses' (288) at that dinner corresponds to the Byzantine relationships, conspiracies, and deceptions engaged in by Bertha Dorset and her set. It is a 'triumphant' (290) occasion for Mrs Wellington Bry, the hostess of the party, one of the 'new people' (184) who has long been aspiring to become a full member of the social set. But if this dinner marks her ascent, it punctuates Lily's fall.

Still, the acceptance of new people into society creates a temporary niche for Lily. If her invitation to France is not essentially a social one, but rather a mandate to keep George Dorset busy while his wife has an affair, Lily finds more regular employment, upon her return, as social consultant to Mrs Hatch, a newcomer trying to establish herself in the social world of New York. In the United States, as in England, newcomers to the social scene acknowledged and assented to 'a hierarchy of exclusiveness, without closing the possibility of climbing the steps of [the] social stairway' (Hobsbawm 174); they wanted to know what they had to do to achieve social status and they wanted 'barriers to entry' (Davidoff 41), so that their own success would be worth something. Thus, Lily is to teach Mrs Hatch what she needs to know and how she needs to act in order to find acceptance; ironically, however, this position contributes to society's final rejection of Lily herself. Mrs Hatch, like Mrs Bry, will ultimately become acceptable to New York society, but, even though this is more honest work than that on the Dorsets' yacht, Lily's association with Mrs Hatch before the latter gains acceptance is one more step in her downfall.

Mrs Hatch is considered to have a disorderly and hence disreputable life. This quality is described in terms of her mealtime habits: the manicurist might be invited for luncheon and Mrs Hatch might be 'in the hands of her masseuse' (373) rather than available to visitors during the 'tea-hour.' Even Lily does not question social norms to this extent. She herself is uncomfortable that, at Mrs Hatch's house, 'no definite hours were kept; no fixed obligations existed: night and day flowed into one another in a blur of confused and retarded engagements, so that one had the impression of lunching at the tea-hour, while dinner was often merged in the noisy after-theatre supper which prolonged Mrs. Hatch's vigil till daylight' (370). The recognized conventions that structure the day represent conformity to a larger set of social values; Mrs Hatch's failure to keep normal mealtime hours suggests a threatening chaos. Moreover, the confusion about meals and mealtime exacerbates Lily's own confusion about her identity and her place in the world. With little definite structure in her life, and incapable of generating her own, Lily needs an imposed sense of order to keep her from fully realizing the terror of time passing.

Lily misses 'the smiling endurance of tedious dinners' (352) when she is no longer invited. Although she seems to become progressively more conscious of her situation and critical of the social world and the efforts and compromises it requires, she is never able to extricate herself from it fully or to construct her life differently. Nevertheless, she shows a good deal of perceptiveness in telling Gerty:

> You think we live *on* the rich, rather than with them: and so we do, in a sense – but it's a privilege we have to pay for! We eat their dinners, and drink their wine, and smoke their cigarettes, and use their carriages and their opera-boxes and their private cars – yes, but there's a tax to pay on every one of those luxuries ... the girl pays it by tips and cards ... and by going to the best dressmakers, and having just the right dress for every occasion, and always keeping herself fresh and exquisite and amusing! (358)

As noted in the discussion of *The Age of Innocence*, for the hostess, details about the invitations, the china, the menu, and the clothing are all automatically prescribed as part of the trappings of a formal dinner. Similarly, the guests must present themselves in a certain way. Dresses – like manners and social conventions, part of the accoutrements of dinner – are not an issue in *The Age of Innocence* because being well dressed is assumed. But such is not the case in *The House of Mirth*; rather, Lily struggles with dressmakers' bills throughout the novel. Thus, the evening before her death, when Lily looks at her dresses one last time and packs them away, each dress evokes the social occasion upon which it was worn. Entry tickets to dinners and parties, they are now useless, yet '[a]n association lurked in every fold: each fall of lace and gleam of embroidery was like a letter in the record of her past' (428). The dresses are also the equivalent of a diary, a text of her social performances and of her attempts to fit into 'the life she had been made for' (428).

If, for Lily, dinners and other social events are, in the beginning, the occasion for showing herself to prospective husbands, and for keeping herself a part of the social world, food becomes more real as she descends the social scale. Throughout most of the novel, dinners are the stage for an obligatory performance, a stage upon which one manoeuvres for position, makes connections, watches others for potential weaknesses, and, with luck, is oneself seen to advantage. The purpose of dinners has not been to enjoy a good meal. For Lily and her set, food itself is assumed, a given that one need not think or worry about. This may be another reason why the actual dishes are hardly mentioned in the descriptions of dinners. If Lily does not think about the biological necessity of eating, however, she is aware that invitations to and attendance at various entertainments are in fact essential for life in this world. In the end, for Lily, social 'life' does, in fact, literally mean living. She is incapable of any other kind of survival. Thus, ostracism from the social world puts her physical survival in question as well. In the last part of the novel, she suffers aesthetically, as her mother would have, from the dinginess of the basement dining-room in the boarding house. As well, the novel mentions for the first time that she is hungry. The fact that the ritual of tea has changed by the end of the novel is an indicator of Lily's decline. In contrast to her having gracefully and elegantly poured and sipped tea in the early chapters, she drinks tea hungrily, almost desperately at the end. If tea was at first important for its social value, and as a backdrop to flirtation, it is finally important as a stimulant and as a substitute for the meals she can no longer afford.

Thus, the vague feeling of exile which always attaches to Lily Bart becomes a real exile from the only world she knows. At the somewhat melodramatic end, which Norris calls 'pure Dickens' (436), she momentarily feels at home in Nettie Struthers's kitchen, where she watches Nettie feed her baby. She is for the last time a guest, this time in the kitchen of a working-class woman who was once the recipient of her charity, rather than in a salon or a dining-room. Offered coffee, she does not take any. Instead she watches while the baby is fed: another little girl taking nourishment and beginning life. Later that night she imagines the baby in her arms as she falls into her deadly sleep. There is a sense here not only of a change in generations, but of the waxing and waning of two classes. Although poor, Nettie has displayed an energy and a recuperative ability that the decadent Lily lacks; as a result, the former has, at least, a family and a warm kitchen, where she can offer food and drink to others. Incapable both of compromising as required to create a home in her world, and of searching for an alternative, Lily is unable to nourish herself either spiritually, emotionally, or, in the end, physically. She ingests the final overdose of chloral in lieu of dinner.

The novel proposes that Lily is right to question certain aspects of the old society; indeed, although she does not appear to have any impact on the process, society has been changing. In *The Age of Innocence*, a greater degree of openness is represented by Ellen Olenska, and later by the young Dallas Archer. Members of old families, both are also people who have, because of their experiences or their generation, become more progressive, more modern. Already the form and the purpose of dinners in *The House of Mirth* have evolved from those of *The Age of Innocence*. The acceptance of 'new people' into the social elite also certainly represents change. On the other hand, some of these people, in embracing the apparent values of the old society, fail to grasp what lies beneath the surface of the social ritual, and create a new world that is merely a parody of the old one. Godden explains the fall of the traditional elite society thus: 'What capital increasingly needs after 1900 is a highly mobile, highly reproducible and highly controllable system of manners. That is to say, fashion must supplant manners: where taste once stood, style must stand ... Fashion penetrates the mannered self and opens it for the market' (20). And, in Gilles Lipovetsky's terms: 'In order for fashion to come into being, the "modern" had to be accepted and desired; the present had to be deemed more prestigious than the past; in an unprecedented move, what was novel had to be invested with dignity' (47–8).

In *The Custom of the Country*, traditional New York dinners and the values they represent are presented in a somewhat more positive light. Wharton suggests that the new superficiality, represented by Undine Spragg, is worse than the old repressive sociability epitomized by the dinners of *The Age of Innocence*. Undine is one of the people changing New York society, although, of course, she does not set out to do so, but rather to join it. In a very different way from Lily Bart, Undine also conveys a feeling of being undernourished: she is constantly hungry for wealth, admiration, status, and an indefinable sense of security and acceptance which is perhaps unattainable for those born outside the world she covets. Such a hunger cannot, in fact, be assuaged by the novel's dinner parties. Her hunger to be in the spotlight is literally insatiable because she wants an unspecific 'everything.'

Undine is the daughter of one of those wealthy men who, having recently made their money in trade, manufacturing, or investment, sought, particularly for their children, the social imprimatur that could only be conferred by association with the old families of inherited wealth. The fiction of the early part of the twentieth century – Dreiser's is an excellent example – is full of people who are trying to 'make it,' not only financially, but socially as well. The fact that *some* people changed classes encouraged a belief that social mobility was at least possible; that it was not common or likely made it all the more desirable. Thus, in *The Custom of the Country*, the Spraggs move to New York to improve their daughter's chance of success. But it is she who knows that more than money is necessary, and, like others aspiring to a higher class, she engages in what Stephen Mennell calls 'anticipatory socialisation': that is, 'consciously or unconsciously adopting the ways, tastes and manners of a social group to membership of which one aspires' (Mennell 75). Thus, Undine is in charge of telling her parents how to live, even if she changes her mind with experience: a hotel is not, she realizes, after having demanded the move to the Stentorian in the first place, the most fashionable place to live; and, by the time she has divorced Ralph, she sees that stalls, not boxes, are more desirable at the Opera.

For a woman like Undine, the right invitations are the surest sign of acceptance into the higher echelons. Once she is told about the social status of the Marvells, Undine Spragg knows that her invitation to dinner at the home of Ralph Marvell's sister means that she is on her way. In *The Rise of Silas Lapham*, when Silas and his family are invited to the Coreys for dinner, they study etiquette books in preparation. Silas knows nothing about behaviour at dinner: the use of various forks and glasses, conventions such as the ladies' leaving the table first, and so forth. To deal with the gaps left by the etiquette books, Silas tries to act the way he has seen other people act. Undine is a far more astute observer, but much of her knowledge of society and of etiquette has been formed by faithfully reading the society pages of newspapers, rather than the etiquette manuals that the Laphams study. However, there is a difference between the popular journalistic image of the

wealthy and the way New Yorkers of long-standing social status behave. Undine is very disappointed by her dinner at Mrs Fairford's.
Accustomed to the view of society described in the newspapers,

> ... she had expected to view the company through a bower of orchids and
> eat pretty-coloured entrées in ruffled papers. Instead, there was only a low
> centre-dish of ferns, and plain roasted and broiled meat that one could
> recognize – as if they'd been dyspeptics on a diet! With all the hints in the
> Sunday papers, she thought it dull of Mrs. Fairford not to have picked up
> something newer; and as the evening progressed she began to suspect that
> it wasn't a real 'dinner party,' and that they had just asked her in to share
> what they had when they were alone. (44)

For Undine, a 'dinner party' does not mean the honour of being invited
to share dinner, to enter the intimate family circle, but rather a photo-
genic society event to celebrate the social standing of the guests, an
event which is less important in itself than as a subject for a society-
page reporter. Moreover, in this view of the world it is the originality of
the menu and the appearance of the dishes rather than the taste of the
meal that is important. Mennell notes that, whenever food supplies
have been dependable and plentiful, the rich have distinguished themselves not so much by eating large quantities, as they did in periods of
relative scarcity, but by the innovativeness of their menus, the talents of
their cooks (34). However, in an old and socially secure family like the
Marvell/Dagonet clan, subtlety is appreciated; there is no need to
impress with fancy dishes or display. Thus, later in the novel, Clare Van
Degen will give Paul Marvell a 'battered old Dagonet bowl' (160) for his
birthday. Undine is insulted by this gift; if Elmer Moffatt understands
that solid history is both classier and more valuable than showiness,
Undine never really learns this lesson. Less concerned about social
niceties, Elmer Moffatt, to his wife's chagrin, never achieves a really
polished manner, but, as an American businessman, he certainly becomes more aware than Undine is of the distinction between what has
real value and what is merely faddish.

Inviting a guest to dinner is an offer to share not just one's table, but
also one's home. It is not, therefore, the place of the guest to criticize the
furnishings, arrangement, or decoration of the hostess's house. But, at
this first dinner party, just as Mrs Fairford's dinner offends her, Undine
is also shocked by Mrs Fairford's house:

The house, to begin with, was small and rather shabby. There was no gilding, no lavish diffusion of light: the room they sat in after dinner, with its green-shaded lamps making faint pools of brightness, and its rows of books from floor to ceiling, reminded Undine of the old circulating library at Apex, before the new marble building was put up. Then, instead of a gas-log, or a polished grate with electric bulbs behind ruby glass, there was an old-fashioned wood-fire, like pictures of 'Back to the farm for Christmas'; and when the logs fell forward Mrs. Fairford or her brother had to jump up to push them in place, and the ashes scattered over the hearth untidily. (44)

In *The Decoration of Houses*, Wharton and Codman emphasize simplicity and respect for architectural structure rather than ornamentation and veneer. Undine's 'preference for display and artifice' (Waid 135) might be termed simply an expression of bad taste. However, in fact, she has no personal taste – in food or anything else – but for that which she believes, based on her reading or other sources, to be modern. She prefers a style which, in its showiness, might allay the insecurity of one of the newly wealthy and reassure her, in its lack of subtlety, that she has truly 'arrived.' The role of advertising in creating taste is also important in this context. As noted in an earlier chapter, at the turn of the twentieth century, not only had advertisements for consumer products already begun to emphasize the desirability of the new and modern – a trend which continued throughout the century – but mass-market periodicals also displayed that ambiguity between advertisements and editorial text that is still evident today in women's magazines like *Vogue* and *Better Homes and Gardens*. In Undine's reading of the society pages, she is susceptible to the presentation of consumer goods which form part of – indeed, to her, seem to create – the larger context for what might be called today a certain 'lifestyle.'

To return to Mrs Fairford's meal, it is not only the physical setting that Undine fails to understand; it is the way the dinner party is constructed. Indeed, some conventions are not easily learned. Silas Lapham, having somehow weathered the manipulation of dinner utensils, experiences terrible moments as a dinner guest when everyone looks at him, expecting him to speak. Although he has observed others, he does not understand what dinner-table conversation might comprise and, having drunk an unaccustomed number of glasses of wine, proceeds to make a fool of himself. Neither does Undine comprehend what is below the surface of the simpler rules of etiquette: 'All was blurred and puzzling to the girl in this world of half-lights, half-tones, eliminations and abbreviations; and she felt a violent longing to brush away the cobwebs and assert herself as the dominant figure of the scene' (47). Thus, she does not understand the conversation at Mrs Fairford's dinner, neither the subject matter, nor the conventions of who speaks to whom, nor indeed the hostess's role of drawing out her various guests: 'with Mrs. Fairford conversation seemed to be a concert and not a solo. She kept drawing in the others, giving each a turn, beating time for them with her smile, and somehow harmonizing and linking together what they said' (45). Undine assumes that the hostess reigns over the dinner party, as indeed she does, but in a rather more complex and subtle way than Undine understands. Still, Undine is an apt learner. Although she never understands the difference between manners and mere etiquette, by the time of her dinner with Ralph's mother and grandfather, 'Her quickness in noting external differences had already taught her to modulate and lower her voice, and to replace "The i'dea!" and "I wouldn't wonder" by more polished locutions' (82), even though her own conversation still consists largely of meaningless responses. Judith Fryer finds that 'Undine is quite literally unable to speak' (113); however, when she does in fact speak, she does so inappropriately. She shocks the table with her outspoken and rather flippant views on divorce, certainly tactless at an engagement dinner.

For Undine, then, dinners are important social occasions, but not to meet and converse with people or even to pay homage to the hostess: the point is to be invited in the first place and then to be admired. From her perspective, dinner parties are quantitative: the number of dinners per week is an index to one's popularity and to the status of one's circle. In this attitude she reflects that of the unsophisticated Mrs Heeny: 'They certainly do things with style over here [in France] – but it's kinder one-horse after New York, ain't it? Is this what they call their season? Why, you dined home two nights last week. They ought to come over to New York and see!' (332). For Undine, the ideal is to live in 'a house in which no one ever dined at home unless there was "company"' (H of M 37), like the house where Lily Bart grew up. Indeed, although she may seem crass compared to the refined Fairfords and Marvells, Undine is not so different from many of the people in Lily Bart's social circle; just, at first, unpolished and a bit too obviously eager.

Undine is correct in believing that guests are expected, even required, to shine, and she gradually learns the acceptable boundaries of dining behaviour. As a guest, being observed is never the problem for Undine that it is for Silas Lapham; she expects people to comment on her appearance, she herself constantly observes her reflection in mirrors, and, indeed, she even sees herself in other objects: the Boucher tapestries, for example, become 'mirrors reflecting her own image' (360). But eventually her hosts want more.[6] Thus, during her period as the Marquise de Chelles, when the dinner invitations stop arriving, her American friend Madame de Trézac divulges that this perceived neglect is because, although people still find her beautiful and are 'delighted to bring [her] out at their big dinners, with the Sèvres and the plate' (368), they also find her boring: thus, 'those who regard conversation as a necessary part of ritual finally stop inviting her to small dinners because she has nothing to say, because she does not understand' (Fryer 113).

What is more difficult for Undine than being a guest, however, is playing the part of hostess.[7] To some extent, this difficulty reflects her insensitivity as a guest, her unease in making conversation and her inability to defer to others. The skills of being a guest and of being a hostess are, to some extent, linked, and the hunger – indeed the vacuum – at Undine's centre makes it difficult to play either role. The striking fact that Undine is never actually portrayed as a hostess – striking because her whole world revolves around socializing – reflects her desire to be out rather than at home, her measuring her social progress by the number of invitations she receives. Not until she is married to Raymond de Chelles is there even any reference to the possibility of guests. When Mrs Heeny arrives in Paris with Paul, she says, 'I suppose you'll begin to give parties as soon as ever you get into a house of your own. You're not going to have one? Oh, well, then you'll give a lot of big week-ends at your place down in the Shatter-country; that's where the swells all go to in the summer time, ain't it?' (332–3). But these 'week-ends' do not happen; other than the mention of family parties, which are torture for Undine, the only other references are to parties that do not occur because of the mourning period for her father-in-law or a lack of money.

Whatever the novel's explanation for these particular parties not being given, Undine's playing the guest rather than the hostess is typical of her chosen social persona: although she is an active, not to say aggressive, participant in getting where and what she wants, she fights first to be noticed, then to be observed and admired, but not to play a dynamic role. Just as Undine wants to be desired, but never loves, a certain passivity is also apparent in her avoidance or refusal of the role of hostess. In fact, she does not understand the function of the hostess: that the hostess must be ready to receive homage, but also to supply socialization; she does not *need* society because she *is* society. Undine would not be capable of playing such a part. The only life she really knows is that of aspirant. Upon marriage into the upper classes, her driving ambition remains, but its goal becomes confused; hence her several marriages. She keeps achieving what she wants, but because her initial desire was for the outward appearance of something undefined, what she gets is always empty for her and just generates more desire. Because she continues to view the world with yearning, Undine never feels settled or established, and thus she never has a solid base as a hostess. The hostess should feel at home when she welcomes her guests, and, in one way or another, Undine is ashamed of or ill at ease in most of her houses: the West End Avenue apartment is badly located, the Paris apartment too small, the château too much part of the de Chelles family history.

Finally, Undine cannot play the role of hostess because, although she masters the basic conventions of etiquette and style, she never learns that there is a deeper level to the appropriate codes of both social behaviour and language. It is not that Undine is unable to speak, but that she does not speak the same language as the Marvells and the de Chelles – representatives of the traditional American and French social milieus she thinks she wants to join. As Waid points out, when Raymond tells her that she does not speak his language, he is not just referring to French. The courtly, kindly aspect of the manners of the old wealthy class is missing for her; and only the naked competition under the 'veneer of virtue' (Finkelstein 131) is evident.

Undine is portrayed planning to host a dinner party only in the last chapter of the novel, after her remarriage to Moffat. Perhaps this finally occurs, as she suggests to Mrs Heeny, because she only now really feels as though she has a house of her own. Also, even though Undine again shows hints of dissatisfaction in this marriage, the novel implies that she has found her appropriate match. The preparations for the dinner party are poignantly juxtaposed with Paul Marvell's lonely wandering through the unfamiliar house. His alienation in this house and in his new family is emphasized by his discovery that his mother has lied about his 'French father' and that both she and Elmer Moffatt are pleased about having tricked and defeated his beloved de Chelles in acquiring the Boucher tapestries. When he finally seeks out Mrs Heeny for some help in trying to make sense of his life, she pulls out her bag of newspaper clippings about Undine: this is the only explanation ever given to Paul of his mother's divorce and remarriage. Just as the dinner parties reported in the newspapers are more interesting than the actual events, it is the interpretation of Undine's life by the society pages – in a sense, standing in competition to Wharton's book – which gives it validity and even reality for Mrs Heeny, Undine herself, and that society which they represent. On the last pages of the novel, Paul wants to tell his mother about a composition prize he has won, but she brushes him away to dress and place the dinner cards. Uninterested in his writing, as she was in his father's (unless he were to have made a lot of money at it), her only use for language, other than reading the society pages, is to place the guests at her table: applications of reading and writing that appropriately complement each other. If her son is confused and distressed, and she is not capable of or interested in giving him direction, her guests, at least, will be guided to their appropriate seats at the table.

If we were given many details about May Archer's first dinner party, we have none about Undine's. Although it is going to happen, it remains unrealized; in the last sentence of the novel, Undine only 'advance[s] to welcome her first guests.' There is no reference to the meal that is being prepared; as in *The House of Mirth*, the food itself is less important than the social scene to which it gives an occasion. Still, the Moffatts' dinner party is a signal of social change. The society that Undine wanted to enter is definitely finished, both in New York and in Europe; she sees that herself during her marriages to Marvell and de Chelles, even if she is not able to articulate her realization. She has proved that she can be accepted by this society, but people like her, coming into ascendancy, are inevitably changing its values. Although the novel is critical of the Undines and the Elmers, still, as Cynthia Wolff reminds us, it does not idealize the old society of New York. Clare Van Degen, although kind and sensitive, has bartered herself for 'the Van Degen diamonds and the Van Degen motor [which] bore her broken heart from opera to ball' (Wolff, *Feast of Words* 73). Ralph, although perhaps tragic, is a dilettante, the final product of a dying society and incapable of making the transition into the new one.

In this contrast between the new and the old lies the difference between Undine in *The Custom of the Country* and Lily Bart in *The House of Mirth*. Both women are guests, but while Undine desperately wants social invitations, Lily desperately needs them. Lily, like Ralph from a decaying class, similarly finds herself incapable of constructive action. Through the course of the novel, dinner and other social invitations come to her less and less frequently and, ultimately, Lily finds herself truly hungry, alone, homeless, and with no solutions, crippled by her very restricted set of values, which have been defined by a particularly conservative reading of the conventions of the dinner party. She has a decorative manner of pouring tea, and can present herself as a rare work of art to be collected, but she does not have the drive to succeed of Undine's class: men like Moffatt who are capable of cutthroat business deals, women like Undine who barter themselves aggressively to the highest bidder. Undine's ultimate success occurs, however, because the new values and manners of her class are in the process of defeating the old, and because she finally links up with a man like herself. It is Undine and, in *The House of Mirth*, the Gormers and Mrs Hatch, who, once they have achieved a veneer of social manners, will demonstrate that, in a profound sense, the social rituals of dining and the deeper code of manners dear to the society of *The Age of Innocence* have indeed changed, and, from Wharton's narrative perspective, not necessarily for the better.

It is significant that neither Lily nor Undine is depicted eating or serving dinner throughout these two novels. Neither woman is capable of enjoying a good meal because, for related but somewhat different reasons, each is completely concerned with the social ramifications of dinner parties. And the notion of service, as well, is laden with social and economic implications. Lily, because she has neither a husband nor a home, both requirements for a hostess, does not have the opportunity to serve guests. Undine has both husbands and homes, but only understands the most superficial formal aspects of a dinner; thus we do not see her dinner party itself, but only the placing of the name cards. This important and suggestive link between eating and serving dinner will be explored further in the next chapter.

5

'Hungry Roaming': Dinners and Non-Dinners in the Stories of Katherine Mansfield

Homelessness and Hunger

In her depiction of old New York, Edith Wharton points the way to changes in consciousness that are typical of the modernist period and that affect women and are expressed in the writing of women in very particular ways. The social change traced by her work is well established in the fiction of Katherine Mansfield. If, in Wharton, society is defined in large part by customs of dining and sociability, in Mansfield's short stories, dining and attitudes to food in general are linked to the modern predicaments and modernist themes of homelessness, rootlessness, alienation, and isolation. In sum, Mansfield's meals elucidate the contradictions surrounding changing roles for women in the context of the larger social changes which marked the first part of the century.

Because meals are so central to notions of the home, their literary treatment is a key index to modern experiences of homelessness or a sense of homelessness, and, in Mansfield, reflects a profound ambivalence about that state of being or state of mind. From childhood, as noted in chapter 1, food plays a crucial role in people's lives, not only in forming our habits and tastes, but in defining our feelings of warmth and security. Food figures strongly in our memories of home, usually evoking positive associations: a nostalgia for 'mom's home cooking' is expected, a cliché. In adult life, meals are a crucial element in creating a home – usually the job of a woman. For various reasons, homes are problematic in both *The House of Mirth* and *The Custom of the Country*; however, they are particularly so in Mansfield's work. If circumstances in some of her stories seem to make it impossible for characters to create a home, it may also be a character's choice not to do so, an attempt, perhaps, to liberate herself from the constraints a home might impose. Mostly, the lines are blurred between longing for and rebellion against home, and the two apparently contradictory positions of desire for liberation and anxiety about isolation may fade into each other.

Mansfield's people can be viewed as caught between the limitations of two eras. Consciously rebelling against lingering and tenacious Victorian ideals about the proper role of women, her female characters may be trapped by another constraint: that sense of estrangement – itself, in part, a consequence of the reaction against Victorianism – which is intrinsic to modernity. In other words, the very forms of rebellion contain this sense of alienation; what looks like freedom may, in fact, be oppressive in another way. This peculiarly twentieth-century dilemma is reflected in the structure of a number of stories, which seems to trap the characters, at the same time as the content of the stories explores or at least hints at new ways of living. For instance, although Mansfield's characters present an impression of being in motion, actual mobility is minimal; many of the stories are very contained in both time and space. Indeed, even though the characters may have broken away from the traditional home and family setting, some of the stories seem scarcely to give them breathing room.

Rita Felski writes that '[t]he so-called private sphere, often portrayed as a domain where natural and timeless emotions hold sway, is shown to be radically implicated in patterns of modernization and processes of social change' (*Gender of Modernity* 3).[1] Modernist expressions of alienation and homelessness are indeed congruent with actual historical changes in gender roles and family structure. Although the food reformers succeeded in establishing food science in school and university curricula, they did not, in so doing, cure social ills or solidify the family unit as they had originally hoped to do. The First World War pushed women into new situations which forced them to see themselves differently. In addition, the cultural disillusionment arising from its battlefield horrors had a huge impact on social structures. But even before the cataclysm of the war, there had been changes in the family. Despite the focus of early advertising on the family, referred to in a previous chapter, one can trace a breakdown in family structure beginning in the nineteenth century. Ernest Groves and William Fielding Ogburn's *American Marriage and Family Relationships*, published in 1928, cites the statistic that in the United States, 'Divorce between 1870 and the mid-1920s had risen 35 percent for each ten year period' (Ewen 120).

Certainly, the most cursory look at early twentieth-century fiction reveals a concern with fragmented families. If Ellen Olenska's possible divorce in *The Age of Innocence* is a matter for some discussion among members of the New York aristocracy, divorce is relatively common in *The House of Mirth* and nearly unremarkable in *The Custom of the Country*. As well, many early twentieth-century novels portray orphaned children and parents who do not fulfil a traditional role. As already noted, etiquette manuals were so popular partly because parental guidance was no longer sufficient for the upwardly mobile; thus children of newly wealthy but old-fashioned families like the Spraggs might take charge of the family themselves.[2]

Some early twentieth-century works of fiction portray families in the process of disintegrating completely. One or both parents may be entirely absent, and guardians – like Mrs Peniston in *The House of Mirth* – not completely committed to their responsibilities. Given the destruction of black family structure by slavery, it is perhaps not surprising that in Zora Neale Hurston's *Their Eyes Were Watching God*, Janie is raised by her grandmother. In Nella Larsen's *Quicksand* and *Passing*, the parents of Helga Crane and Clare Kendry are dead, and in both cases, the biracial family situation made the parent-child relationship a complicated and painful one in the first place. However, white families are also portrayed as fragmented. In Kate Chopin's *The Awakening*, Edna's mother has died young, and her father is not a reliable source of paternal guidance; moreover, she leaves her own two young sons motherless. By the end of *The Custom of the Country*, Paul Marvell, having had two fathers rather violently taken away from him, is a lonely and neglected little boy.

The differences in meaning, referred to earlier, between nineteenth- and twentieth-century fictional portrayals of dinner signal a change in the portrayal of families as well. The history of the novel is full of orphans like Pip or Jane Eyre, making their way in the world. In this tradition, however, the family itself is not questioned. What we see in the early twentieth century, on the other hand, is not the unfortunate and unpredictable loss of the family, but the rejection of the family. In the literature of the early modernist era, when characters leave home and set out on their own, it may be because they have to, but, more likely, also because they consider the beliefs and values of their parents and their home to be hopelessly old-fashioned. Thus F. Scott Fitzgerald's Jay Gatsby not only leaves the Midwest but tries to eradicate his origins completely. Carrie in Theodore Dreiser's *Sister Carrie* and Ellen in John

Dos Passos's *Manhattan Transfer* are women making their own way in the world more out of desire than because of dire financial necessity.

Geographical mobility, then, also contributes significantly to the sense of homelessness in this period: indeed, it is well known that many of the writers discussed in this study themselves lived in a self-imposed exile, an exile which they found necessary for intellectual, artistic, or psychological survival, even though they may have written longingly and frequently or – as Joyce did – even exclusively about their home country.[3] Edith Wharton's experience is presumably mirrored in that of Ellen Olenska, who, despite her short-lived attempt to integrate back into New York, ultimately does better alone in Paris. It is groundbreaking for a woman to be on her own, creating, by herself, her own home and, thereby, her own stance in relation to society. The conventional marriage plot with the conventional role for women is upended in *The Age of Innocence*.

As Marshall Berman argues, there may be economic reasons for the modernist emphasis on the solitary individual struggling with both loneliness and – apparently inconsistently – the desire for distance from home or roots: the notion of striving and the feeling of mobility are, Berman says, inherent in modern capitalism. Because expansion is necessary, change is necessary as well.[4] On the one hand, in both Marxist and standard capitalist terms, this philosophy is profoundly optimistic; in another sense, it is both frightening and profoundly isolating, as notions of family, community, and even selfhood become fluid. Thus we see a desperate need for intimacy at the same time as traditional group relationships can no longer be assumed, and as it becomes increasingly difficult to be certain of one's own identity (Berman 110).[5] As indicated by the rising interest in psychoanalysis during the early twentieth century, the notion of the self becomes more important at the same time as its very existence becomes questionable. Djuna Barnes's dreamlike *Nightwood* is a striking example of a piece of modernist fiction in which the characters – and indeed the entire narrative – evince a sense of distance and dissociation from self and from what is generally constituted as reality. In Mansfield's fiction, the shifting quality of personal and social identity is frequently associated with a change in the relationship to the home. In particular, the treatment of dining and of food itself expresses both this loss of tradition and the search for a new way of being, especially for women. Loss or rejection of food habits, customs, and rituals may signal various other losses as well.[6]

Much recent criticism of Mansfield includes a strong biographical element. While such criticism may be valuable – interesting and insightful – I am wary of interpreting works of fiction in the light of excerpts from journals and letters.[7] Nevertheless, even as a historical example of women's relationship with food, it is worth noting a 'preoccupation with eating' (Moran, 'Unholy Meanings' 108) in Mansfield's personal writing as well as in her fiction. Like Virginia Woolf, who could not eat during her several breakdowns (Poole ch. 8), Mansfield may have suffered from food-related anxiety and health problems. As a child, she was sensitive about being plump, and her weight remained a source of some tension, especially in her relationship with her mother, until tuberculosis finally cured that problem with a more serious one.

It has been suggested that eating disorders are more common in times of social change, that the disruption, dislocation, and instability inherent in such periods may be indicators for anorexia, and specifically, that the condition 'afflicts many women during periods of change in female roles' (Perlick and Silverstein 81). Thus anorexia has been seen by some as a disease peculiar to the twentieth century. Indeed, there is an anorexic quality to the experience of many of Mansfield's women characters, a rejection of meals which is not based in the popular understanding of anorexia as an obsession with weight dictated by cultural norms of beauty, but which nevertheless involves self-rejection. The potentially liberating movement away from the roles that usually tie women to the provision of meals and the creation of a home seems, in much of Mansfield's fiction, to entail an alienation from the physical self and a lack of interest in the nourishment – both literal and metaphorical – required to sustain that self. In other words, the roles of server and consumer of meals may be conflated: the rejection of the former may involve the rejection of the latter as well. Male modernist characters may generally have been able to assume that, in the end, dinner would somehow be cooked. And, with notable exceptions such as Joyce's Bloom cooking breakfast, they did not need to pay too much attention to how. But Mansfield's women who divorce themselves from such details of mundane existence may sometimes seem to be at risk of starvation. At the very least, they seem to have no pleasure in eating; moreover, the magical, transformatory quality of meals may be lost, forgotten or even deliberately avoided.

In Mansfield's work, then, women who view themselves or are viewed by the author as resisting the mould of Victorianism have a particularly complex and difficult relationship with dinner. Mansfield writes about women alone, in couples, and within the family; in each of these circumstances, characters may evince an attempt to find meaning in food and the rituals of dining, and yet, at the same time, an alienation from eating that reflects a larger sense of social and personal alienation, even despair: what Thomas Hardy, in a very different context, calls 'the ache of modernism' (180). Moreover, as chapter 1 pointed out, food is inextricably tied up with language, and Mansfield's sense of the relationship of food with the forms of discourse that structure people's lives is quite acute. If the dinner table fails in these stories, this failure is frequently linked with a failure of communication as well.

'Ghosts of Saucepans & Primus Stoveses'

Yes, I hate hate HATE doing these things that you accept just as all men accept of their women. I can only play the servant with very bad grace indeed. Its all very well for females who have nothing else to do ... & then you say I am a tyrant & wonder because I get tired at night! The trouble with women like me is – they cant keep their nerves out of the job in hand – & ... I walk about with a mind full of ghosts of saucepans & primus stoveses & 'will there be enough to go round' ... & you calling ... isn't there going to be tea. Its five o'clock.[8]

Katherine Mansfield to John Middleton Murray

If Lily Bart is on the cusp of modernity, most of Katherine Mansfield's women lead a definitely 'modern' life. Many of her stories are about independent, mobile people, often young, and looking to reject the past. On the surface, at least, class may be unimportant to them. Sometimes they are intellectuals or artists, people who could be classified as bohemian; often they are single and may have had many lovers, or, if married, have a consciously different view of marriage from their parents. They are the mould for the kind of characters found in the popular short stories of writers like Dorothy Parker, Jean Rhys, and Kay Boyle in the 1920s and 1930s. Unlike Lily, who only begins to recognize the degree of her alienation from society and to discover the depth of her loneliness late in The House of Mirth, many of Mansfield's characters do not need to discover their own solitude and anomie: it is rather the milieu in which they move, the air that they breathe. In some of the stories, alienation is so much an accepted state of being that people would be as hard pressed to live otherwise as Lily is to survive outside the Trenors' circle.

In Mansfield, this alienation is frequently expressed in terms of food.

The emphasis on eating is a striking characteristic of Mansfield's work: most of her short stories include at least a reference to some kind of meal, tea, or snack. Lily Bart's failure to nourish herself, although in a very different context, has become the norm in many of the stories, where the serving and consuming of dinner and other meals represent major sites of conflict and conceal a tangle of anxiety and unease. Some stories present an arguably neurotic obsession with eating; in many, a meal or a lack of meals is foregrounded as an integral part of the dissociated, solitary, or fragmented lives that the story follows. A character's state of spiritual or psychological well-being, on the one hand, or malaise, on the other, is reflected and made concrete in her relationship with the dinner table. The strong emphasis on food suggests a pervasive hunger that cannot be assuaged, a constant question about survival – physical, emotional, and financial – and the means of survival.[9] However, the importance of the issues raised by meals goes beyond the problems of individual characters; as descriptors of a particular view of the modern and modernist world, issues of food are an integral part of the narrative consciousness and, as such, are woven into the context of the story as a whole.

Overall, two major emphases emerge in Mansfield's treatment of food. First, in many stories, the social event of the meal is reduced to the merely biological level. Thus the presence of food in the story has an almost ironic effect, if not intent: meals underline the absence of that very communality, commensality, intimacy, and warmth which the rituals of sharing food are supposed to create or enhance within families, among friends, and between lovers. Even when such positive associations with food seem about to appear, they are either shown to be false or undercut in some way. In some stories, love, friendship, or family is directly parodied. Although Mansfield usually focuses on the loss of mealtime ritual from a woman's perspective, its effect on men is also demonstrated in a number of stories. Second, the treatment of meals, as part of the larger framework of domesticity in general, particularly reflects and reveals the tensions in women's lives; that is, for women, the modern sense of alienation expresses itself in the context of their traditional roles – especially that of organizing meals – and through each individual woman's position within or against these roles.

In much of Mansfield's work, then, if eating is at all associated with pleasure, sociability, and intimacy, it is solely as an expression of a lack of pleasure, of the absence of sociability or intimacy, of a general sense of unfulfilled desire. The meals in Mansfield's stories often occur within

an atmosphere of loneliness, repression, even moral corruption – as in
'Je ne parle pas français' – and suggest the failure of intimacy, the
dashing of hopes. Many of the meals in Mansfield's stories are eaten
alone, largely because 'her people are ceaselessly on the move, traveling,
wandering, often in foreign or threatening situations ... Mansfield wrote
almost compulsively of outcasts, exiles, minorities, and fringe dwellers'
(Robinson 4). In some of Mansfield's stories, then, eating is done on the
fly; meals are consumed in nameless restaurants or are replaced by
snacks. When eating in restaurants because they are away on holiday,
vacationers may seem more like exiles. Sometimes people simply do
not get to eat: in 'Poison,' for instance, the table is set for lunch, but
lunch is not eaten; in 'Marriage à la Mode,' the fruit that the husband
brings home for the children somehow just disappears into the chaos of
fashionable guests, sardines eaten out of the box for supper, and van-
ished leftover salmon. In these last two examples, it is largely the man's
alienation within the couple that is explored. In both cases, the men
seem to be looking for the traditional marriage that their partners reject.
Although spurning the traditional couple, the women in these two
stories are still in control of meals, and exercise their power by leaving
the men hungry, if not physically, then emotionally.

Such an unstructured, if possibly frustrating, manner of eating does,
of course, suggest a possible release – for both men and women – not
only from the entrenched rituals of the Victorian dinner table, but from
the social structures implied and reinforced by such rituals: those, for
instance, described in Wharton's *The Age of Innocence*. Most important,
perhaps, is the potential liberation from gender roles, even if such does
not always actually materialize. However, modern changes to meal
structures can also imply a loosening of class distinctions. Eating in
restaurants is one expression of the partially illusory democracy inherent in the anonymity of the modern crowd, the twentieth-century street
scene which figures prominently in the work of many modernists.[10]
Like these street scenes, the fictional restaurant setting conveys the
impression of equality. As Joanne Finkelstein says, '[b]y following the
formulated modes of sociality accepted in the restaurant one can appear as one desires without the risks of actually crossing social barriers
or attempting to realize these imagined postures' (15). In Nella Larsen's
Passing, Irene Redfield and Clare Kendry drink tea in the roof-top
restaurant of a whites-only hotel; with the appropriate clothes and class
demeanour, a light-skinned woman can 'pass' in such a situation. When
Miss Kilman has tea with Elizabeth Dalloway in the restaurant of a

department store – itself a leveller of classes – the anonymity of the tea-room momentarily erases class. However, when Elizabeth has to leave to get ready for her mother's party, the differences of class – and the material and social advantages of class – reappear between her and Miss Kilman. The older woman is left wallowing in self-pity: "'I never go to parties," said Miss Kilman, just to keep Elizabeth from going. "People don't ask me to parties ... Why should they ask me? ... I'm plain, I'm unhappy'" (200).

Public dining, then, creates only a superficial equality – defined strictly by one's ability to pay the bill. Moreover, Finkelstein argues that, although it is public, the restaurant meal may not be truly social, even when it is shared. Highly 'stylized' (Finkelstein 13), such meals may in fact preclude rather than encourage interaction. Certainly, the restaurant setting does not inspire the profound resonance of meaning associated with the historic rituals of a culture. Despite its liberating aspects, then, this new world of dining out is not without its price; it may in fact entail a loss of ritual and sociability, which creates or reinforces a sense of loneliness or rootlessness. The above example from *Mrs. Dalloway* suggests not only that Doris Kilman's craving for sweets emerges from her feeling of deprivation, but, moreover, that the tea-room brings out this feeling:

> Elizabeth rather wondered whether Miss Kilman could be hungry. It was her way of eating, eating with intensity, then looking, again and again, at a plate of sugared cakes on the table next them: then, when a lady and a child sat down and the child took the cake, could Miss Kilman really mind it? Yes, Miss Kilman did mind it. She had wanted that cake – the pink one. The pleasure of eating was almost the only pure pleasure left her, and then to be baffled even in that! (197)

Miss Kilman's desperate loneliness, envy, and unhappiness are espe-cially evident in this tea-room setting, which seems to suggest just the opposite: camaraderie, intimacy, festivity, pleasure.

For women in general, the restaurant meal certainly represents free-dom from domestic fetters and liberation from such potentially oner-ous tasks as organizing, cooking, and serving meals. Yet Mansfield's stories emphasize that dining on the run, especially alone, is both rooted in and symbolic of other things that are missing in a character's life. Obviously, many of the people in the stories eat alone because they are literally alone in the world; others may feel alone or experience themselves as profoundly divided from society or within themselves. Mansfield's heroines may demonstrate at any age a profound aliena- tion from both meals and the world around them. Their sometimes very minimal diet is in keeping with their minimal pleasure and mini- mal expectations. Moreover, the fact that very small details about food or changes in diet are so terribly important in their lives and carry such subtle nuances of meaning for them shows the tenuousness of their accommodation with life, the fine line between joy and despair.

If left with only the physical necessity of eating, the person feels spiritually bereft. Yet, at the same time, food habits can create meaning even for those who are alone or alienated from social life. 'Miss Brill,' reminiscent of some of Joyce's stories, describes the simple rituals of the lonely and suggests the importance of these rituals for survival. An English teacher living in France, Miss Brill makes a habit of a weekly Sunday afternoon outing to a park where a band plays. The stop on the way home to buy herself a Sunday piece of honey-cake is a high point of the week, and central to her life: 'Sometimes there was an almond in her slice, sometimes not. It made a great difference. If there was an almond it was like carrying home a tiny present – a surprise – some- thing that might very well not have been there. She hurried on the almond Sundays and struck the match for the kettle in quite a dashing way' (335). Miss Brill's weekly treat of cake, like Miss Kilman's desper- ate consumption of pink cakes and éclairs, seems laughable, pathetic. But buying the cake reflects more than greed, self-pity, or sublimated desire; it is a ritual, and as such, not only fills a need for Miss Brill, but creates meaning in her life. The secret possibility of a nut hidden in the cake represents a chance prize or gift, a hoped-for yet unexpected bonus or reward, and thus the possibility of optimism. No meal is portrayed in this story; still, even on this very limited scale, food can transform reality. For Miss Brill, finding an almond in her slice of cake creates feelings of gaiety, frivolity, excitement and transforms her after- noon, so that she even lights the gas 'in quite a dashing way.'

The almond in the cake is also related to her sense of a hidden part of herself: sexual, perhaps, or in any case unknown and unappreciated by anyone else. Like buying the cake, wearing her rather moth-eaten old fur piece, a special possession that she treats almost as a pet, is part of the weekly ritual; it represents that weekend self which is hidden from others, a part of her which would surely surprise her pupils and 'the old invalid gentleman to whom she read the newspaper four after- noons a week while he slept in the garden' (334). Although her words are surely wasted on the sleeping man and perhaps on her students as well, Miss Brill is a person who deals in language. She has created for herself a highly significant personal script to describe her Sundays. Wearing her Sunday fur, she is part of the crowd in the park, someone with a place in the world and a knowledge of character and of life, an accomplished actress with a role in a play, a woman who is curious, interested, almost beautiful. Thus, she is devastated when two young lovers sharing her park bench make fun of her fur. The fact that she does not buy her slice of cake that day, depriving herself of that little pleasure and the meaning inherent even in the possibility of finding an almond, indicates the degree of her humiliation. She returns directly home to 'her room like a cupboard' (335) after hearing the couple laugh at her: 'The box that the fur came out of was on the bed. She unclasped the necklet quickly; quickly, without looking, laid it inside. But when she put the lid on she thought she heard something crying' (336). Denying herself her ritual of cake expresses her despair; indeed, it is a kind of suicide of the spirit.

In Mansfield's early story 'The Tiredness of Rosabel,' the main character is young, and not only lonely, but poor; the fact that she has had little to eat for tea opens the story and sets its context. For a young woman on a limited budget, a shop-girl who understands the world of exchange, dinner must be weighed against other needs. Thus flowers replace the meal.[11] Rosabel has bought 'a bunch of violets, and that was practically the reason why she had so little tea – for a scone and a boiled egg and a cup of cocoa at Lyons are not ample sufficiency after a hard day's work in a millinery establishment ... [S]he would have sacrificed her soul for a good dinner – roast duck and green peas, chestnut stuffing, pudding with brandy sauce – something very hot and strong' (513). Although written in the third person, this passage represents Rosabel's own text of her life. In fact, despite the cliché of the last sentence, it is obvious that Rosabel would *not* sacrifice her soul: the flowers she buys are 'soul food,' and are at least part of the reason for her eating a minimal dinner.

But Rosabel has also written a second, more romantic script for herself. Fantasizing about the wealthy young couple who came into the shop that day, she imagines the life she would lead if she were in the other woman's place: the food and drink, the invitations to social events, the house, the clothes, and especially the man. She sees herself sharing an elaborate dinner with him – 'the soup, and oysters, and pigeons, and creamed potatoes, and champagne, of course, and afterwards coffee and cigarettes' – and later tea: '"Sugar? Milk? Cream?" The little homely questions seemed to suggest a joyous intimacy' (517). Eating together is part of Rosabel's fantasy of sexual desire and fulfilment. As in many of Mansfield's stories, however, food is minimal and desire repressed. For the independent, solitary woman, both social conventions and economic pressures make the expression of sexuality problematic except in fantasy. In fact, Rosabel's fantasy reflects economic realities: delicious meals are linked with both financial security and emotional intimacy. For the self-supporting woman who lives outside the traditional family structure, both may be lacking. Rosabel is not alone in this situation: as she daydreams on the bus, the woman next to her reads a romance novel, the text of which quite probably parallels Rosabel's own rewriting of her life. If nineteenth-century bourgeois dining rituals are disappearing in the early twentieth century, a version of them may still exist in fantasy for the working class.

Even when parts of Rosabel's dream come true for other women – women, that is, who have some money and are not alone – intimacy itself often stays at the level of fantasy. A number of Mansfield's stories depict meals shared by a man and a woman, meals which might automatically suggest intimacy, as the waiting lunch table does for the male narrator in 'Poison': 'As always, the sight of the table laid for two – for two people only – and yet so finished, so perfect, there was no possible room for a third, gave me a queer, quick thrill as though I'd been struck by that silver lightning that quivered over the white cloth, the brilliant glasses, the shadow bowl of freesias' (674). Although such meals *à deux* occur in various situations in Mansfield, any sense of intimacy they suggest always remains potential, if not false. 'Sexually, one devours or is devoured,' Fullbrook (88) says of Mansfield's stories. However, the recurring link between food and sex is more varied and usually more subtle than Fullbrook suggests, and is always part of the all-encompassing context of alienation. To one extent or another, frustration permeates many of the stories, and superficial trappings of intimacy may make the situation all the more painful. If a meal brings the potential for closeness, the failure of this potential is demonstrated sometimes in the inadequate menu, sometimes in the lack of joy or pleasure in eating, and usually in the halting, stunted conversation. As talk sputters and falters, the dinner table fails as the setting for intimacy or even conviviality, as well as for any profound degree of communication.

'The Honeymoon,' for instance, is about a newly married couple, but as they drink tea and eat éclairs in the south of France, the story delves beneath the surface of love and the novelty of marriage. The sexual attraction between them is apparent, but the reader is aware of their differences, the woman's attempts to overlook flaws, the beginnings of questions which remain suppressed – perhaps the seeds of the failure of their marriage, as they negotiate the gaps between everyday life and their idealized notions of love. George, practical, insensitive, somewhat boorish, is incapable of understanding his wife's desire for intimacy, a desire that she can scarcely express, even awkwardly: 'So often people, even when they love each other, don't seem to – to – it's so hard to say – know each other perfectly. They don't seem to want to. And I think that's awful. They misunderstand each other about the most important things of all' (396). Even as the couple hold hands across the table, the distance between them cannot really be breached. In the few minutes described in the story, their relationship appears insubstantial, superficial, although sweet and delicious, like the pastries they are eating. Their marriage is, so far, a sweet snack, their vacation a month of honey; whether it will ever really become nourishing remains open to question, but, the story suggests, is unlikely.

A different version of this faltering tea-table discourse appears in 'Psychology,' where another meal of cake and tea reflects a different kind of limited relationship. A man and a woman – each a writer and an intellectual – are having tea at the woman's home, and seem to be on the verge of becoming lovers. In this story there is a lot of talk, much of it about books and writing, but it is almost compulsive, ultimately boring even for the talkers, covering their fear of being together in silence and of considering another level to their conversation and their relationship. Each is afraid of broaching the subject of the attraction between them. However, the woman tempts the man with her cake: '"Do realise how good it is," she implored. "Eat it imaginatively. Roll your eyes if you can and taste it on the breath. It's not a sandwich from the hatter's bag – it's the kind of cake that might have been mentioned in the Book of Genesis ..."' (113; ellipsis in original). The man observes that their eating together is significant, but can only speak about it in a halting way: 'It's a queer thing but I always do notice what I eat here and never anywhere else. I suppose it comes of living alone so long and always reading while I feed ... my habit of looking upon food as just food ... something that's there, at certain times ... to be devoured ... to be ... not there' (113; ellipses in original). Although the man associates the enjoyment of food with the presence of his companion, and sees that, in her company, food is transformed from a mere physical necessity, to be ignored in so far as possible, into something pleasurable, he seems unable to go any further with this thought, and his resistance to intimacy remains. Both are quick to break a silence or to change the subject to intellectual banalities. In this story, it is not a lack of facility with language that precludes closeness, but the limitations and barriers reinforced by their language itself.

A dinner table or tea table, then, can set the framework of both a relationship and a story. In the humorously titled 'A Dill Pickle,' a restaurant is the setting for a chance meeting of ex-lovers for the first time in six years. Even though the story is about a man and a woman in a restaurant, it does not describe a meal, a relationship, or even a date, but is almost a parody of all of the above: food is not shared, and the two characters remain separate. A very limited description – 'He was seated at one of those little bamboo tables decorated with a Japanese vase of paper daffodils' (167) – suggests a stylish but anonymous décor. Other diners do not seem to exist; the interior reality of memory, imagination, and emotion dominates the external surroundings. Yet years of personal history are evoked at the restaurant table, and food plays a part in their shared but different memories – his, perhaps, romanticized; hers more negative – and defines both their closeness and their distance from each other. Past intimacy is suggested in the fact that the man's eating habits are still recognizable to Vera: 'There was a tall plate of fruit in front of him, and very carefully, in a way she recognised immediately as his "special" way, he was peeling an orange' (167). She, however, declines fruit and takes only coffee, her refusal to eat emphasizing their separateness. There is also a sense of austerity about this choice: Vera takes her coffee black, a detail noted only because, after her departure, the man insists that he not be charged for the unused cream. Both seem to be worried about money. Yet the man presents himself as well off and vaguely successful; Vera, on the other hand, has presumably had to choose food over art and pleasure, for she mentions 'with a little grimace' (170) that she has sold her piano.

The man's story of eating a dill pickle during his trip to Russia, a trip that they once spoke of taking together, sparks Vera's imagination, and she feels that she is 'sitting on the grass beside the mysteriously Black Sea' (171). She even seems able to taste the pickle: 'She sucked in her cheeks; the dill pickle was terribly sour ...' (171; ellipsis in original). The pickle is more real than what is actually on the table, and the past seems more tangible than the present. The congruence between the pickle and

the soured love affair is too comically obvious, yet, indeed, the relationship returns almost as palpably as the taste of the pickle. Across the
table, their old dynamic is picked up again: a fleeting illusion of intimacy, as well as competition, ambivalence, pain both felt and inflicted.
The vividness with which Vera imagines the pickle also suggests the
hunger that characterizes her life – and perhaps her ex-lover's as well.
Indeed, both are still alone.

   Playing with an even harsher vision of physical vulnerability implicit
in sharing a meal, Mansfield takes to the limit her pessimism about the
possibility of communion at a shared table. As Margaret Visser observes, during dinner, people have always had to relax their guard and
put their weapons aside, even though they are surrounded at the table
by tearing teeth and sharp instruments. Moreover, unless we have
cooked the meal ourselves, we are ingesting unknown substances. The
fear of poisoning is a terrible one, suggesting an absolute failure of
trust; if sharing food is a bond, poisoning is the most insidious betrayal,
occurring, as it does, from inside the site of communal intimacy. Some
of Mansfield's stories draw an analogy between this kind of culinary
betrayal and that occurring in love: for example, a husband's poisoning
his wife figures in the unfinished 'A Married Man's Story.' In 'Poison,'
the physical danger of meals is linked with the emotional danger of
relationships. Like 'The Honeymoon,' this story takes place in the south
of France, but the couple are sophisticated, even world-weary, and the
story is far more cynical, although rather flippant and glossy. The man
is trying to convince himself that he is finally sure of his aptly named
lover Beatrice: this, despite the fact that her impatience for the postman
to appear strongly suggests to the reader that she expects a letter from
another man. As noted earlier, the sight of the table set for two people
implies a happy intimacy to the man, but not to Beatrice: 'She took my
arm. "Let's go on to the terrace –" and I felt her shiver. "Ça sent," she
said faintly, "de la cuisine ..."' (675; ellipsis in original). Her aversion to
the smell of cooking suggests a disgust with the physical, the sexual,
and her avoidance of the table a rejection of love and intimacy. No
lunch is eaten during the story; instead the man is served up an intense
and rather dramatic discourse on poisoning. Beatrice becomes 'pale
with excitement' at the subject: '"It's the exception to find married
people who don't poison each other – married people and lovers"'
(679). The 'gleam of the pearl' on her ring begins to look ominous: a
poison ring, perhaps? Finally, Beatrice's words transform the taste of
his drink into something unpleasant and frightening: 'Good God! Was

it fancy? No, it wasn't fancy. [His apéritif] tasted chill, bitter, *queer*' (680; emphasis in original).

If loneliness, unhappiness, a failure to communicate, and even cruelty seem to be endemic and even inevitable at the tables described in these stories, the option of traditional family life, which some characters have either missed or rejected and others still hope for, is not without its drawbacks in Mansfield's fiction. While the treatment of meals in 'The Daughters of the Late Colonel' is, on one level, quite funny, it also points to the oppression and repression of the family. The very title of the story indicates the family relationship which has destroyed its main characters: Constantia and Josephine ('Jug') have, indeed, been defined as daughters for their entire lives; that they do not know how to be adult women is demonstrated in their relationship to both cooking and eating.

A preoccupation with food runs throughout the story. Tea, meals, and discussions about food occur during the actual time frame of the story, a week after their father's death, and also form a significant part of the sisters' recent memories. Their own role as consumers of food has apparently always been secondary to their father's; now, having lived within the oppressive limits of their father's house for so long, the two women do not know what they want to eat, if they want to eat, or even what it is possible to eat, a state of indecision which causes friction with their servant, Kate:

> 'I think it might be nice to have it fried,' said Constantia. 'On the other hand, of course, boiled fish is very nice. I think I prefer both equally well ... Unless you ... In that case –'
> 'I shall fry it,' said Kate, and she bounced back, leaving the door open and slamming the door of her kitchen. (279; ellipses in original)

If they fire the servant, of whom they are terrified, they are not sure what they can manage to cook, or indeed what kind of food there is to buy; nevertheless, the prospect seems childishly exciting:

> 'What it comes to is, if we did' – and this [Jug] barely breathed, glancing at the door – 'give Kate notice' – she raised her voice again – 'we could manage our own food.'
> 'Why not?' cried Constantia. She couldn't help smiling. The idea was so exciting. She clasped her hands. 'What should we live on, Jug?'
> 'Oh, eggs in various forms!' said Jug, lofty again. 'And, besides, there are all the cooked foods.' (280)

The lack of regular meals seems to them to be liberating, and they are annoyed that when they rather naïvely invite the voracious Nurse Andrews to stay an extra week, it means having to hold 'regular sit-down meals at the proper times, whereas if they'd been alone they could just have asked Kate if she wouldn't have minded bringing them a tray wherever they were' (265). However, the anticipated informality of their mealtimes is double-edged: if it is liberating, it is also symptomatic of their repression and self-denial. Meals are for other people, perhaps mostly for men; with their father dead, they may not need the cook.

The daughters can, however, organize a tea and serve others. They invite their nephew Cyril from time to time: 'one of their rare treats' (275), if not one of his. Although the form of the family meal is here, there is no content to it. The sisters look to the tea party to transform their everyday reality, to draw their nephew into their world and to create the family they do not have. But Cyril is a disappointing guest; he merely tolerates the tea table, remains detached and leaves as quickly as possible for the real world of friends and business connections. At the last awkward tea before the colonel's death, Cyril – mindful, perhaps, of Persephone's fate – does not want to eat the extravagant cake and meringues which they press upon him: 'Josephine cut recklessly into the rich dark cake that stood for her winter gloves or the soling and heeling of Constantia's only respectable shoes. But Cyril was most unmanlike in appetite' (275). Since there is really nothing to say, food becomes the only subject of conversation at tea, and a banal and meaningless one at that. The discussion of whether or not Cyril's father likes meringues continues from the table into the absurd and finally pathetic scene in the colonel's sickroom where the young man, at his aunts' insistence, tries to tell his grandfather about his father's taste for meringues. The old man has difficulty hearing the young man's words, and then comprehending why they are being spoken; it is a ridiculous exchange across the generations that neither Cyril nor the old man wants.

The sisters, however, do not see the absurdity; for them, speaking is as divorced from meaning as eating is. Both are also potentially terrifying: either making a choice about what to eat or stating something in real words could, perhaps, lead to the frightening prospect of admitting desire, articulating hopes, maybe even seeking fulfilment. At the end of the story, both Constantia and Josephine want to speak about their fragile and tentative desires for the future, but each backs away, claiming to forget what she intended to say. If food is, literally, the text of

Cyril's trivial communication about his father, the text of their lives has comprised domestic duties of the most trivial and meaningless sort. Since they have only been servers in their father's home, they have found in domesticity neither content, nor meaning, nor nourishment – only a marking of time.

A preoccupation with the physical and symbolic value of food itself is most evident in Mansfield's first published collection, *In a German Pension*.[12] The stories, most of which are set at a German spa, are both a parody and a critique of bourgeois family life: the ersatz family of guests viewed through the eyes of a young Englishwoman. Diet is presumably one component of the cure, but, more than this, food is the constant obsession of the '*Kurgäste*,' who, under the narrator's ironic gaze, appear comical, pathetic, neurotic, even revolting. The opening story, somewhat crudely called 'Germans at Meat,' begins with the following passage, a dinner-table discussion about food:

> Bread soup was placed upon the table. 'Ah,' said the Herr Rat, leaning upon the table as he peered into the tureen, 'that is what I need. My "magen" has not been in order for several days. Bread soup, and just the right consistency. I am a good cook myself ... Now at nine o'clock I make myself an English breakfast, but not much. Four slices of bread, two eggs, two slices of cold ham, one plate of soup, two cups of tea – that is nothing to you.'
>
> He asserted the fact so vehemently that I had not the courage to refute it.
>
> All eyes were suddenly turned upon me. I felt I was bearing the burden of the nation's preposterous breakfast – I who drank a cup of coffee while buttoning my blouse in the morning. (683)

This is more an accusation than an interchange, and is typical of much of the dialogue in the stories. Food is discussed aggressively and eaten aggressively at the large, family-style meals. The '*Kurgäste*' talk about the benefits of a good diet throughout 'Germans at Meat,' at the same time enjoying a multi-course dinner, and finally applying themselves without restraint to cherry cake with whipped cream. Characters in other stories may demonstrate a more dogmatic approach to their choice of food. For instance, a woman in 'The Luft Bad' attests to 'living entirely on raw vegetables and nuts, and each day I feel my spirit is stronger and purer. After, all, what can you expect? The majority of us are walking about with pig corpuscles and oxen fragments in our brain.

The wonder is the world is as good as it is' (731). In either case, food is at the centre of their universe: an explanation and a cure for the ills of individuals and of the world, the subject of talk and testimonials.

In contrast to the other guests, the narrator, like the heroine of 'A Dill Pickle,' is unmistakably the sort to eat and run. While she dines with the other guests and participates in some other group activities, 'she sets herself in squeamish, often derisory opposition to what is depicted as the gross physicality of those around her – particularly the men – in relation to food, sex and health' (Parkin-Gounelas, 'KM's Piece of Pink Wool' 501). Thus, as a critical observer of the self-righteous, somehow perverse gluttony of most of the characters – women as well as men, contrary to Parkin-Gounelas's point – the narrator seems ascetic, almost ethereal; she never describes herself eating.[13] The narrator also remains an aloof observer of the spa flirtations, in 'Frau Fischer' concocting a story about a sea-captain husband away on a 'long and perilous voyage' (702). Given the description of the other spa guests, the narrator's detachment seems eminently sensible and may also enhance her powers of observation as a storyteller. But, conversely, her role isolates her, and she herself expresses an ambivalence about being an outsider, admitting to feeling 'a little crushed ... at the tone – placing me outside the pale – branding me as a foreigner' (692). Her lonely position calls to mind Mansfield's statement of her own internal division: '"I am a writer first and a woman second"' (Parkin-Gounelas, *Fictions of the Female Self* 22).

Swirling around the focal point of food, then, is an exploration of what it means to be a woman, and, beneath that, of the tension between the woman and the artist. Moran argues, from the journals, that 'Mansfield connects eating, impregnation, and engulfment; more ominously, she perceives these "female" functions as inhibiting analysis and self-examination' ('Unholy Meanings' 112). Again, in the *Pension* stories, eating is, in itself, not especially gendered; yet, the stories link women's reproductive capacities with their ingestion of – and general connection with – food. In 'Germans at Meat,' a widow who has nine children advises the narrator that she is childless because she is a vegetarian, and goes on to recount, 'A friend of mine had four at the same time. Her husband was so pleased he gave a supper-party and had them placed on the table. Of course she was very proud' (685). Here, both dinner and children seem to have been produced by the woman to enhance her man's status. In 'Frau Fischer,' the English woman is thus advised to produce 'handfuls of babies, that is what you are really in need of ... Then, as the father of a family he cannot leave you' (703). Clearly, the true womanliness of the English narrator is suspect. Frau Fischer refuses to accept seriously her provocative comment, 'I consider child-bearing the most ignominious of all professions' (703), and speculates that the young woman must have suffered greatly to have such views, impossible for a real woman. In 'Germans at Meat,' the whole table reacts with horror that she does not know her husband's favourite meat: 'A pause. They all looked at me, shaking their heads, their mouths full of cherry stones' (687). And in 'Frau Fischer' it is considered highly unusual that she is travelling alone, and admits to enjoying sleeping without her husband at her side. Yet widows generally seem glad that their husbands are gone, although they speak of them in a formalized mournful way: for instance, 'Frau Hartmann, in an ashamed, apologetic voice: "We are such a happy family since my dear man died"' (697). For the speaker, there seems to be no inconsistency in this odd statement.

Although always associated with food, which is certainly attacked with vigour, and, generally, pleasure, by both women and men, sexuality, in some *German Pension* stories – particularly those characterized by an omniscient narrative voice and set outside of the spa – is presented as frightening and harsh, or at best, confusing for women. In 'At Lehmann's' and 'Frau Brechenmacher Attends a Wedding,' images of candy or cake describe fantasies of love, marriage, and motherhood. In the former story, Sabina, a young servant and waitress in a café, 'loved to stand behind the counter, cutting up slices of Anna's marvellous chocolate-spotted confections, or doing up packets of sugar almonds in pink and blue striped bags' (722–3), an image of baby colours underlining the girl's feeling that perhaps 'it would be very sweet to have a little baby to dress and jump up and down' (724). Hitherto apparently ignorant about all matters sexual, and frightened and disgusted by her mistress's pregnancy, she is seduced in the cloakroom by a young man who appears in the café with photographs of naked women. At the end of the story, Sabina, her mistress, and the latter's newborn infant are linked by their intermingling cries of pain, passion, fear, and birth.[14] In 'Frau Brechenmacher Attends a Wedding,' the bride herself is described as a piece of cake: she wears 'a white dress trimmed with stripes and bows of coloured ribbon, giving her the appearance of an iced cake all ready to be cut and served in neat little pieces to the bridegroom beside her' (706). Just as an intimate meal may be a prelude to seduction, the eating, drinking, and other wedding festivities are a prelude to sexual consummation. But married love is portrayed as an unpleasant, even cruel experience that women must endure, a reality contrary to the sugary, pink confectionery image. Most of the older women express a kind of glee that the bride will soon share their burdens. Frau Brechenmacher's drunken husband recalls their own wedding night: 'Such a clout on the ear as you gave me. ... But I soon taught you' (ellipsis in original). And things do not seem to have changed between them since. Back at home after the wedding, Frau Brechenmacher 'lay down on the bed and put her arm across her face like a child who expected to be hurt as Herr Brechenmacher lurched in' (711).

As Moran and other recent critics have pointed out, the literal and symbolic connection of food with women's lives and with sexuality in *In a German Pension* sets the stage for Mansfield's later New Zealand stories. The themes of homelessness, loneliness, and alienation found in her other stories continue here, although in a rather more subtle and complex way. The stories centring around the Burnells are about an apparently stable family, not lonely, single people, a young woman in exile, or uneasy couples wandering around Europe. Yet an underlying sense of dislocation is implied by the fact that in neither 'Prelude' nor 'At the Bay' is the family at home: in the former they are in the process of moving house, as Roger Robinson also points out (4), and in the latter on vacation. In addition to the sense of disruption, there is also a pervasive feeling of isolation experienced by at least some of the family members, and reflected in the context of the stories as a whole. In 'Prelude,' the family has moved away from town; in 'At the Bay,' the reader feels the 'sense of isolation of the little summer colony, the sense of there being no "others" in the background' (Alpers, *The Life of KM* 346).[15] In other words, despite the fact that these two stories are about a family, they take place within an uneasy or temporary space rather than an established family setting. Nevertheless, most of the characters are actively working to create a home: Stanley Burnell's role as wage-earner and provider of the home is emphasized, and much of the women's time – especially that of Mrs Fairfield – is spent on domestic chores. As well, Beryl Fairfield dreams of marrying and establishing her own household.

The fact that meals are somehow askew is a major factor contributing to the sense of uneasiness. The first meal in 'Prelude' introduces, right at the beginning of the story, a sense of being homeless, of bitter satisfactions in exile. The meal is not eaten at the Burnells' home, but at the Josephs,' neighbours with whom Kezia and her sister Lottie have been left behind because there is not enough room in the wagon taking their mother, grandmother, and sister Isabel to their new house: '"We shall simply have to leave them. That is all. We shall simply have to cast them off," said Linda Burnell. A strange little laugh flew from her lips; she leaned back against the buttoned leather cushions and shut her eyes, her lips trembling with laughter' (11). Abandoned, at least temporarily, in favour of what their mother calls 'absolute necessities that I will not let out of my sight for one instant' (11), the girls have tea with a surrogate family, whose dinner-table behaviour is pointedly unfamiliar, as are their customs of discourse. They are outsiders at the family table, excluded from the habits and rituals of a group of initiates. Thus, Kezia does not understand that one of the menu choices is a joke. Offered 'strawberries and cream or bread and dripping' (13) for tea, she naturally chooses the former, much to the delight of the whole table. Everyone laughs at her, and 'beat[s] the table with their teaspoons' (13) because only the latter is in fact available. 'Even Mrs Samuel Josephs, pouring out the milk and water, could not help smiling' (13), an echo of the girls' own mother's laughter at leaving them behind. The fact that the boy who teases her is named Stanley, like her father, sets up another parallel to her own family. In fact, in the first pages of the story, the 'storeman' who drives them to their new house that evening is more friendly than members of either the Burnell or Josephs family.

Fullbrook defines Kezia's licking her tears away at the table rather than allowing the Josephs to see her cry as 'a gesture of emotional self-consumption that ... sends ripples of meaning through the story' (70). Indeed, her tears become food, while Kezia tries to control her feelings by transforming the actual food into another kind of object: 'Kezia bit a big piece out of her bread and dripping, and then stood the piece up on her plate. With the bite out it made a dear little sort of a gate. Pooh! She didn't care!' (13). A gate is a potent symbol of transitions and limits: an entry, an exit, a potential point of access in a barrier. Mansfield tells us that the two girls stand 'just inside the gate' (11) – a place that was within the family circle but now is on the wrong side – as the cart leaves for the new house. The fundamental loneliness of family life is suggested by Kezia's returning, after the meal, to her family's former house, now empty; indeed, the sentence 'After tea Kezia wandered back to their own house' immediately follows her whisking her tears away. She enters the house through the scullery and the kitchen, and, wandering through the dining-room, drawing-room, and the bedrooms of her parents, her grandmother, and the servant girl, looks for treasures in the detritus of family life.

Throughout 'Prelude,' there exists an uncomfortable relationship with food. Left outside the Josephs' inner circle, Kezia finds this first meal confusing and painful; however, her mother seems to have put herself permanently in a similar position, outside the normal pattern of eating and away from the table. Thus, when the children arrive at the new house, Stanley and Linda's sister Beryl are having dinner, but Linda sits apart: 'Linda Burnell, in a long cane chair, with her feet on a hassock and a plaid over her knees, lay before a crackling fire. Burnell and Beryl sat at the table in the middle of the room eating a dish of fried chops and drinking tea out of a brown china teapot' (19). Later in the story Stanley says to Beryl, 'You and I are the only ones in this house with a real feeling for food' (50). Only once is Linda portrayed eating, and the occasion is a snack, not a meal. On the first morning in the new house, she comes into the kitchen and says, 'I'm so hungry ... where can I get something to eat, mother?' (30). Yet she takes only a piece of gingerbread, and offers Beryl half of it.

Patricia Moran sees as particularly significant Linda's refusal to eat meat: 'Like the narrator in the *German Pension* stories, Linda connects eating with reproduction and initially sees men as devourers and consumers; when with her husband, who is always eating, she refuses to eat meat, as if she can thereby reject sexuality and childbearing' ('Unholy Meanings' 118).[16] It is difficult, however, to argue that an appetite for meat is an integral part of gender identification in this story, since other female characters do eat meat: the story pointedly shows Beryl and Isabel eating chops. In fact, Isabel, who has arrived at the new house without her sisters, boasts that she has had meat for supper as if it is symbolic of entry into the adult world. Still, if the consumption of meat is not necessarily linked with men, the technical skills involved in preparing meat are indeed presented as the purview of men in the division of domestic labour:

> Burnell ran his eye along the edge of the carving knife. He prided himself very much upon his carving, upon making a first-class job of it. He hated seeing a woman carve; they were always too slow and they never seemed to care what the meat looked like afterwards. Now he did; he took a real pride in cutting delicate shaves of cold beef, little wads of mutton, just the right thickness, and in dividing a chicken or a duck with nice precision ... (50; ellipsis in original)

The source of meat is also emphasized, and specifically the fact that the animal was killed by a man. The duck eaten at dinner in section XI may taste like 'a kind of very superior jelly' (50), but the children have seen the animal beheaded by Pat, the handyman, whose gender is emphasized in Kezia's surprise at a man wearing earrings: 'She put up her hands and touched his ears. She felt something. Slowly she raised her quivering face and looked. Pat wore little round gold ear-rings. She never knew that men wore ear-rings. She was very much surprised' (47).[17]

In any case, it is not just meat that Linda avoids. She shows little interest in her breakfast gingerbread and she also puts aside the gifts of a pineapple, oysters, and cherries that Stanley brings her, calling them 'silly things,' and giving the excuse – a rather lame one, given her general lack of interest in meals – 'You don't mind if I save them. They'd spoil my appetite for dinner' (37). The couple treat the fruit in a 'silly' way – Stanley has placed some of the cherries in his buttonhole and she hangs them over his ear. 'Don't do that, darling. They are for you' (37), he says. Her playfulness masks both her reluctance to eat and her rejection of his gift.

Linda's attitude toward food seems to be the opposite of that of the Germans in the *Pension* stories; however, her *not* eating indicates an obsession with food as much as their gluttony does. In her very interesting work on the Middle Ages, Caroline Bynum argues that it was in the area of food that medieval women felt they could make some choices and exert some control: 'Women's food behavior – fasting and feeding – was an effective way of manipulating the environment in a world in which food was woman's primary resource' (30).[18] Fasting was one way for women to assert themselves against their parents and the church; it could be, for instance, an effective way to avoid marriage. Bynum's argument may also have relevance in more recent times. Certainly, in the early twentieth century, a period when the number of cases of eating disorders may have increased,[19] food was still largely women's domain. In 'Prelude,' it is too late, of course, for Linda to avoid marriage and, indeed, her husband seems to pay little attention to her eating habits. Still, her avoidance of food makes a statement about her life, at least to herself, and expresses an attitude toward the physical in general: her children, her husband, her body, sexuality – in short, the fecundity, the mortality, and the daily routine of adulthood. In addition, Linda often appears to be somewhat sickly, a reaction, perhaps, to her apparent pregnancy, but also a withdrawal from her identity and responsibilities as a wife and a mother.

While I do not find it helpful to an understanding of 'Prelude' to debate whether or not Linda suffers from clinical anorexia, to some extent, Linda's case does fit the view of anorexia as an expression of confusion about or a rejection of the sufferer's femininity.[20] Certainly, Linda does not take on the usual roles for a married woman, either in cooking and serving meals or in other aspects of domestic management. Moreover, her attitude toward the children seems at best uninterested. Not only do her belongings have priority over Lottie and Kezia at the start of the story, but, when the two girls reach the new house that evening, her response to their arrival is minimal: '"Are those the children?" But Linda did not really care; she did not even open her eyes to see' (19). She refers to her daughters as 'three great lumps of children' (54), as if still experiencing their bulk in her body before birth. However, it is hard to tell whether Linda is fundamentally questioning gender roles or acquiescing in them. Her response to having finally given birth to a boy in 'At the Bay' is a standard one, seeming to resolve some of her predicament by ending the necessity of child-bearing, but also affirming her success as a woman in finally giving her husband a male heir and filling the empty place that Stanley sees at the nursery table (38). Moreover, her own preference for boys becomes clear as, looking at the sleeping infant, Linda for the first time feels drawn to one of her babies.[21] The child also reminds Linda of her own youthful fantasies of *being* a boy, of her father promising that the two of them would sail up a river in China: '[W]e'll escape. Two boys together' (221).

Moran insists on Linda's behaviour as a neurotic response to her own mothering. This approach follows Showalter's sources in proposing another definition of anorexia: 'in the rigid control of her eating, the anorexic both expressed her fear of adult sexual desire and enacted an exaggerated form of the deadening life of the dutiful daughter' (*The Female Malady* 129).[22] But it is too simple to cast Mrs Fairfield as the villain of the piece, as Moran sometimes seems to do. It is likely that Mansfield is indeed critical of – or at least ambivalent about – the characteristic expressions of mothering in the culture at large; however, if Mrs Fairfield's effect on her daughter can be read as destructive, her presence also allows Linda the space to protest against and to refuse certain cultural demands and definitions of womanhood. If Linda will not or cannot take on a woman's role, she is able to take this stand – to some extent, perhaps, remaining a child herself – because her mother is still there to run the Burnell family for her. Given the limited possibilities of her world, by refusing to act as a mother, she necessarily remains emotionally a daughter, both supported and repressed by the continuing presence of her own mother.[23] By the standards of her culture, like the standards of the women in the *Pension* stories, Linda must, of course, be considered neurotic or she would be a better mother. However, especially in the context of Mansfield's corpus, Linda's questioning of femininity – inconsistent, to be sure, and expressed in a passively 'feminine' way – cannot be seen as an individual failure, but rather as an indictment of social roles. 'Prelude' calls into question the culture's standards, even if the existence of any other role for Linda is scarcely imaginable within the story.

Women who more actively seek non-traditional roles in other Mansfield stories also rarely find fulfilment; most of Mansfield's people are split, anguished, searching. In 'Prelude,' and 'At the Bay,' this fragmentation is made real, as women are divided in two: on the one hand Mrs Fairfield, the nurturing, motherly cook; on the other, the imaginative, but detached, hungry, and unhappy Linda. It is a challenge for the fragmented individual to live in the modern world: stereotyped roles are at the very least unsatisfying, and an identity outside of these roles both dangerous and hard to find. Thus, throughout Mansfield's corpus, the options of the dependent spinster, the independent bachelor girl, the traditional wife and mother, the 'liberated' married woman are all oppressive, each in its own way.

In the wake of Victorianism and, with it, the questioning of traditional social values, roles, and conventions described by meals, many of Mansfield's stories depict a void in people's relationship to the table. For women especially, the collapse of mealtime roles and rituals leaves a hungry vacuum. In portraying the failure of the communality of the table, Mansfield's work examines other failures as well, asserting the difficulties not merely of being human in the twentieth century, but particularly of functioning fully as a female human being. New ideologies may be in the process of replacing the old, but, although Mansfield's fictional worlds at first seem far more open and full of possibilities than, for example, Lily Bart's world in *The House of Mirth*, ultimately there may be a similar lack of room to manoeuvre.

The fact that food is constantly present in Mansfield's stories, then, does not necessarily indicate either physical or spiritual nourishment, but rather a pervasive anxiety about home, security, and loneliness. As I have argued, meals are linked to language on a profound level: not only allowing an opportunity for conversation, but also reflecting its success or failure. Failed, insufficient or non-existent meals mean that meaning-ful communication suffers as well. The dinner itself – or the non-dinner – is an expressive vehicle for communicating the loss. In Mansfield's work, it is only in the New Zealand stories that there is the beginning of a resolution to this situation. The following chapters will propose other perspectives on these stories which suggest the potential of a more positive relationship to meals.

6

Through the Dining-Room Window: Perspectives of the Hostess in the Work of Mansfield and Woolf

Behind the Scenes in the Kitchen

Kezia's looking through the dining-room window of her family's abandoned house at the start of 'Prelude' serves as a metaphor for Katherine Mansfield's work: much of her insight into modernity, into gender roles, into marriage and the family, and into art is developed from the perspective of a woman's relationship with meals. Yet the dining-room can also be a desolate place. Many of Mansfield's characters, although they regard food with wary, tempted, or envious eyes, are nevertheless unwilling or unable either to cook or to eat. They avoid occupying the dining-room and seeing the world from this vantage point. Still, despite the anxiety about food and meals which emerges in much of Mansfield's fiction, in her own work and in that of other women writers of the modernist period there are also examples of meals served with pleasure – both to the family circle and to the larger social world.

In most modernist, as in pre-modernist, works of fiction where the dinner table plays a part, the emphasis is on the guests, rather than on the hostess of the party or the server of the meal. In other words, the fictional meal is presented as an outcome only, with no reference to the history, labour, or intention that went into organizing, planning, cooking, and serving it. Some twentieth-century women writers, however, have foregrounded the role of women as cooks, servers, and hostesses – indeed have made it the centre of their work, not only thematically but structurally as well. In such cases, the central role of dinner-maker defines women's spaces within the novel. The dining-room, as the centre of the woman's world, may form the central focus of an architectural model or metaphor that is used as a primary structuring device of the novel: the dining-room is literally and figuratively the hub of the fictional house as the dinner is at the centre of the fictional world. Daphne Spain writes, '[D]omestic architecture mediates social relations, specifically those between women and men. Houses are the spatial context within which the social order is reproduced' (140). Looking at the ways in which 'spatial and social relations mutually reinforce one another,' Spain quotes architectural historian Gwendolyn Wright, who 'proposes that homes serve as metaphors, "suggesting and justifying social categories, values, and relations"' (111). As Robert Harbison says, the architecture of a home may sometimes be read 'as the expression of an individual life' (22), yet to a great extent, the architecture of most European or North American homes in the early twentieth century reflected a similar role for women.

If women's domestic role – varying, of course, with class differences – was largely assumed in the nineteenth century, it was seldom the subject of fiction. Although nineteenth-century novels are redolent with meals described in detail, rarely is there any sense of their having been cooked or even planned. Similarly, in the twentieth century, Gatsby's celebrated parties in Fitzgerald's novel seem almost to happen of their own accord. Although Gatsby's role as party-giver is a crucial part of his character and of the novel, the party guests hardly see their host and often do not even know who he is. Moreover, there is no sense of who actually organized the parties and did the work. Still, a different perspective begins to emerge in some twentieth-century fiction by men. Joyce's 'The Dead,' a story which centres around the Misses Morkans' traditional Christmas party, gives at least some details about the providers and the providing of the feast. The Morkan sisters and their niece are structurally, thematically, and symbolically central, and their role as hostesses is emphasized. Thus the two older women worry about when Gabriel will arrive, whether Freddie Malins will be drunk again, and who will do the carving. The reader is given such homely details as the fact that there has been a dispute over whether the goose should be accompanied by applesauce and that it is Mary Jane Morkan who chose the way to serve the potatoes. This story does suggest the work involved in serving dinner, albeit in a comic vein and from a male viewpoint. For instance, rather than sitting down with their guests, the hostesses fuss about the dinner table:

Aunt Kate and Aunt Julia were still toddling round the table, walking on each other's heels, getting in each other's way and giving each other

unheeded orders. Mr. Browne begged of them to sit down and eat their
suppers and so did Gabriel but they said there was time enough so that, at
last, Freddy Malins stood up and, capturing Aunt Kate, plumped her
down on her chair amid general laughter. (197–8)

But the story is called 'The Dead,' not 'The Christmas Dinner.' The
thoughts and motivations of the hostesses are not presented; the three
women are seen largely from the perspective of their nephew and
cousin Gabriel – like Joyce, a writer. The fact that Gabriel's is the central
consciousness of the story suggests two levels of narrative control:
Joyce has created a second writer, a character like himself, to interpret
and define both the story and the dinner. Ultimately, the women's role
as cooks, hostesses, servers, organizers is only marginally important to
the story; although crucial to its framework, secondary to larger philosophical and political issues and to the relationship between Gabriel
and Gretta. It is Gabriel, as the chosen speaker, who plays the central
role at the table. The wordsmith is ranked higher than the cooks.

To clarify this point, I will turn briefly for contrast to a later story, Isak
Dinesen's 'Babette's Feast.' Published in 1952, although set in the late
nineteenth century, this is one example of a piece of fiction in which the
meal is seen from the perspectives of both the guests and the cook.
Although, after making the dinner, Babette does not sit at the table or eat
the food, and is largely forgotten during the meal by most of the diners,
she reappears after dinner and ends the story. Thus both the dinner and
the story are framed by the cook: it is her idea to prepare the feast, her
unexpected money that pays for it, her history as a great chef in Paris
that it celebrates; and, although the extent of her talent remains unac-
knowledged by most of the guests, her work has a major – almost
magical – impact on their lives. The meal is in every way the centre of
the narrative, and Babette, despite her subservient role in the social
hierarchy of the small Norwegian town, is completely in control.

It could be argued, of course, that in the world of nineteenth-century
fiction, there is little emphasis on the actual preparation and serving of
the meal because these activities would have been performed by servants. Thus, nineteenth-century novelists, both male and female – Austen,
the Brontës, or Hardy, for example – might have ignored the details of
cooking and serving meals because neither they nor, in some cases,
their characters would have known anything about these activities.
(Dickens's A Christmas Carol, on the other hand, does include details
about the servantless Mrs Cratchit's cooking Christmas dinner.) And,

although a governess could be a main character in the nineteenth century, a cook could not; if a servant in a nineteenth-century novel happened to have a background like Babette's, her employers would generally not have known it, nor would writers and readers have been interested in such a character. But a lack of servants is not the only explanation for the increased attention to the organizing of dinner in some modernist work. True, as the nineteenth century moved toward its close, reliance on servants, originally relatively common even fairly far down the social scale, evolved into the 'servant problem' of the century's end, and, by the 1920s, servants had become rare in middle-class homes on both sides of the Atlantic. Still, the early twentieth-century women writers who portray the serving of meals, as well as other domestic tasks, depict a variety of social milieus, including up-per-class households with servants. And, whether or not a servant or cook is present, a woman of the house – wife, mother, grandmother, daughter – is usually described as being in charge of the meal.

Rather, the modernist focus on meals occurs partly because women writers were becoming more willing to admit the importance of this aspect of their lives, and partly because, during the late nineteenth and early twentieth centuries, the ideology of women's role as homemaker was being shaken. No longer taken for granted, the role was increasingly perceived as problematic, and embraced – or acceded to – far more consciously, if at all. I noted earlier that the proliferation of books, periodicals, and advertising which set out to define models of domes-ticity and to give advice on cooking and other domestic chores is, in itself, evidence of change. The set of ideas about housework that was in the process of evolving, in varying manifestations according to class, was a response not only to technological, economic, and social change, but also to the accompanying anxiety about women's role. Given that the novel reflects the crises and preoccupations of a culture, this uneasi-ness surely influenced the presentation of female roles in fiction.

If the roles of cook and hostess are relatively recent sites of emphasis and loci of uneasiness in fiction, the questions about these roles tend to be expressed by younger characters in the novel or story; the women portrayed cooking and serving meals are frequently, although not al-ways, of an older generation and are seen by younger characters – and sometimes by the text itself – as old-fashioned. The most notable exam-ple discussed here is Mrs Fairfield in 'Prelude'; however, Woolf's Mrs Dalloway and Mrs Ramsay are also middle-aged, and, at certain points in their novels, each is regarded critically both by younger women and by men. In Joyce's 'The Dead,' of the three single women giving the Christmas dinner, two are elderly, and the attitude of the younger guests toward this annual event is ambiguous, if not exactly critical. It is questionable whether any of the other women will take over the tradition when the elder Misses Morkan are dead. Gabriel, although he attends faithfully each year, enjoying and taking seriously the role of master of ceremonies conferred on him, does so with a somewhat condescending, if nervous, air. In some cases, then, the presentation of cooks and hostesses is double-edged: these women may be a nostalgic element in the piece of fiction as a whole, viewed critically or even disdainfully by other characters and by the writer.

In their work overall, both Mansfield and Woolf see the security and stability generated by these older characters as anachronistic, lost, based on a set of traditional roles which are disappearing. As the narrative focus of her Burnell stories moves among several women characters at different ages and stages of life – now alighting here, now there among the widowed grandmother, wife and mother, young single woman, and little girl – Mansfield explores the real losses as well as the potential gains involved in the modern reaction against these roles. Some of her other stories demonstrate the difficulties in creating a new model of traditional domesticity in the twentieth century: if girls and young women continue to be trained as homemakers and hostesses, their work may seem to have lost its meaning and the meal to have become a mere formality or an empty shell. Woolf, on the other hand, in both *Mrs. Dalloway* and *To the Lighthouse*, explores the traditional role from the inside, situating one of the central consciousnesses of each novel in the traditional woman herself – the giver of parties, the provider of food, and the focal point of the novel.

Women's Domestic Space in Mansfield's Stories

There are different terrains for men's and women's activities and, as Spain says, the differences are associated with power.[1] In Mansfield's stories, men are more often portrayed leaving the house and women more frequently staying at home. Yet even though it may generally be assumed that separate spaces imply domination, exclusion, or inferiority, the notion of women's space is not necessarily a negative one. Mansfield's 'At the Bay,' for instance, valorizes the household of women, delighted to be alone when Stanley leaves for work each day. The early-morning activities in the Burnell household are arranged around

Stanley's needs. Although the older, more sanguine Mrs Fairfield is 'unruffled' (210) by her son-in-law's series of orders for such things as his polished shoes and a slice of bread, Beryl's frustration at Stanley's petty but tyrannical demands to be served at the breakfast table – 'You might go and see if the porridge is ready, Beryl?' and 'Hallo! ... you've forgotten the sugar' (210) – is turned upon Kezia, who feels unfairly and unaccountably criticized for digging 'a river down the middle of her porridge' (211). But after Stanley's departure, Beryl gives 'a little skip' (212), and Linda, Mrs Fairfield, 'even Alice, the servant girl' share in the feeling of 'reckless' (213) gaiety. Not only the kitchen and the dining-room, but the whole house is theirs:

> Oh, the relief, the difference it made to have the man out of the house. Their very voices changed as they called to one another; they sounded warm and loving and as if they shared a secret. Beryl went over to the table. 'Have another cup of tea, mother. It's still hot.' She wanted, somehow, to celebrate the fact that they could do what they liked now. There was no man to disturb them; the whole perfect day was theirs. (213)

In Mansfield, satisfaction or serenity may be found in these moments, these 'glimpses' (Sandley),[2] even if such interludes always give way to other moments of unfulfilled, even undefined, desire.

Although anxiety about food is particularly acute in Mansfield, her work also demonstrates the profound importance of the meal in the structure of women's lives and at various stages in their lives, even if some women resist its centrality. As chapter 5 pointed out, Mansfield's Linda Burnell has little or no association with meals either as a consumer or a server, except in so far as she rejects these roles. Her refusal of even the social structure of meals is expressed in her physical position within the house: in a passage quoted earlier, she sits apart from the diners eating at the table, and, in the following passage, enters the kitchen only as a visitor:

> Someone tapped on the window: Linda was there, nodding and smiling ...
> 'I'm so hungry,' said Linda: 'where can I get something to eat, mother? This is the first time I've been in the kitchen. It says "mother" all over ...' (30)

On the other hand, her mother, Mrs Fairfield, is strongly identified with food preparation and with the kitchen. Even though the family is just settling in, the kitchen of their new house is already described as hers by the narrator as well as by Linda:

> It was hard to believe that she had not been in that kitchen for years; she was so much a part of it. She put the crocks away with a sure, precise touch, moving leisurely and ample from the stove to the dresser, looking into the pantry and the larder as though there were not an unfamiliar corner. When she had finished, everything in the kitchen had become part of a series of patterns. She stood in the middle of the room ... (29)

Mrs Fairfield not only makes the space her own immediately upon moving in, but creates 'patterns': that is, organizes to create meaning. The room seems to emanate out from her in orderly symmetry; every corner has become hers and her. It is her domain.

We see Mrs Fairfield serving others more than eating; her association with food preparation and the kitchen is explicitly coupled with her maternal quality. Mrs Fairfield does not share her daughter's fear of nurturing: perhaps she never felt Linda's fear, because she is of an earlier generation which accepted this role without question; or, equally likely, since her child-bearing years are over, she no longer perceives the danger in the role that her daughter does. Thus, walking together in the garden at night, Linda wonders why she should bother staying alive, and thinks how surprised Stanley would be if he knew that hatred was among her feelings for him; her mother, on the other hand, thinks of canning for the winter: 'I wondered as we passed the orchard what the fruit trees were like and whether we should be able to make much jam this autumn. There are splendid healthy current bushes in the vegetable garden. I noticed them to-day. I should like to see those pantry shelves thoroughly well stocked with our own jam ...' (55; ellipsis in original). Mrs Fairfield takes charge of both the kitchen and Linda's children. Indeed, she has a far closer bond with the little girls than Linda does.

The grandmother never really leaves her role as the keeper of the house; indeed, the fact that we do not know her first name suggests that she has no other identity. Thus she is the last one to sleep, having waited until the household is safely shut down, and she climbs into the bed she will share with Kezia for the night accompanied by cries of owls which seem to refer to the chops eaten at the evening meal: '"More pork; more pork." And far away in the bush there sounded a harsh rapid chatter: "Ha-ha-ha ... Ha-ha-ha"' (23). As Patricia Moran points out, owls also appear on Mrs Fairfield's brooch: as 'the symbol of female wisdom' (*Word of Mouth* 109), an appropriate motif for an older woman. Yet the odd laughing in the woods – outside of and encircling the house – suggests an undercutting, a mocking, a negation. And Moran sees a sinister cast in the imagery as well: 'owls are predators as well as the emblems of Athena, the goddess who affirmed father right' (*Word of Mouth* 109). She finds that Mrs Fairfield's apparently unquestioning acceptance of mother-identity implies an absolute acceptance of the traditional male role as well, and therefore of the patriarchy. But, as noted earlier, Moran's real concern is with Mrs Fairfield's motherliness itself: she argues that Mansfield portrays her as smothering. However, in the story itself there is never any specific negativity associated with Mrs Fairfield, never any actual sense of the oppressively engulfing mother about whom Moran writes; she seems, rather, particularly in her relationship with her granddaughters, to be associated with meals, nurturing, and women's wisdom in a positive way.

In 'Prelude,' it is largely because of Mrs Fairfield's strong presence in the story that women's spaces are central. The identification of the grandmother with the kitchen is obvious, and the dining-room, where the meals she prepares are served, is the centre of family life. In fact, in seven of the twelve sections of 'Prelude,' there is a scene either in the dining-room of the new house, in the dining-room of the old house, at a nursery dining table, or in a make-believe dining-room. One other section is set in the kitchen and another is about killing the duck which is to be dinner that night. In other words, only three of the sections have nothing directly to do with meals; and in one of these (V), Stanley is called to breakfast from his bedroom, in another (XII), Beryl called to lunch. The dining-room is the first room described when the children arrive at the house, and is portrayed as especially important for Beryl and Stanley. In what is presumably the story's commentary on the role of men, the latter is only depicted either leaving for work, coming home from work, in the bedroom, or eating.

The fact that it is Linda's sister Beryl, rather than Linda herself, who helps Mrs Fairfield clean and set up the kitchen may suggest either that she is more fit for the life of a housewife than Linda is or that the fantasy and the reality of marriage are two different things. For Beryl, the dining-room seems to hold significance even between meals. In one scene, Beryl plays her guitar in the dining-room; it is as if the music she plays might have the transformatory power to give her access to her own dining-room and her place in the world as a married woman, presiding over her own table. Beryl is annoyed when the maid asks her to leave so that she can set the table. However, as the maid well knows, while the kitchen is completely women's territory, the dining-room is a place of service where the woman waits on her man and meets the needs and demands of others. It is not meant as a setting for a young woman to please herself by dreaming alone.

In 'Prelude' and 'At the Bay,' Stanley has an access to town that the women do not have; his sister-in-law Beryl, especially, bemoans her isolation. Still, there is a certain power in women's space, too. In 'At the Bay,' Stanley's freedom to leave the house seems to him like banishment. He feels cast out when he leaves for work, and is hurt that his wife and the other women in the family so obviously want him to leave, that they are happy to be alone in the house. Since these stories are written from the perspective of the women and of the house, we do not see Stanley at work. For Linda's brother-in-law, Jonathan Trout, in 'At the Bay,' however, the office is a closed space, a trap, claustrophobic, and the apparent freedom of men an illusion: 'On Monday the cage door opens and clangs to upon the victim for another eleven months and a week' (236), he says, and 'I'm like an insect that's flown into a room of its own accord. I dash against the walls, dash against the windows, flop against the ceiling, do everything on God's earth, in fact, except fly out again' (237). In the architecture of the home there is at least more space – and perhaps more control – than this.

Mansfield's story 'The Doll's House' reinforces the notion of the power of women's space, especially in terms of competition among women. The miniature house of the title is at the centre of the story, sitting in the Burnells' courtyard like a parody of its larger neighbour. The possession of this 'perfect, perfect little house' (383), an imitation of their mother's, gives the Burnell children status with the other girls at school, much as a married woman with her own home has more status than a single woman. Moreover, by choosing which girls to invite to see the doll's house, and in what order, the children use it as a social demarcator, separating those who are more privileged from those who are less so. Class is reinforced as well as individual favouritism: just as their parents would never invite Mrs Kelvey, the washerwoman and a single mother, to their home, so the girls are forbidden to invite the Kelvey children to see the house. Beryl chases Lil and 'our Else' away when Kezia breaks the rule.

The story also suggests in concrete terms how little girls learn to become adult women, the various rooms of the doll's house denoting their various roles: hostesses in the dining-room, cooks in the kitchen, mothers in the nursery, and housekeepers overall. The realism of the doll's house makes it special: every room is perfectly furnished. However, the toy house also mimics the less than perfect reality of family life. Somehow the people seem not to fit, even though they are placed in the appropriate rooms: 'The father and mother dolls, who sprawled very stiff as though they had fainted in the drawing-room, and their two little children asleep upstairs, were really too big for the doll's house. They didn't look as though they belonged' (384). The constraints of the home are inflexible: it is up to the inhabitants to live within its norms.[3]

Thus do little girls learn how to invite guests, play hostess, and make family members conform. The Burnell children also learn how to feed a family. In section VIII of 'Prelude,' the children's activities centre around food, as the girls play house and invent meals. The section begins with the game already in progress:

> 'Good morning, Mrs. Jones.'
> 'Oh, good morning, Mrs. Smith. I'm so glad to see you. Have you brought your children?'
> 'Yes, I've brought both my twins. I have had another baby since I saw you last, but she came so suddenly that I haven't had time to make her any clothes yet. So I left her ... How is your husband?' (40; ellipsis in original)

This scene is presented with no introduction, and, up until the misinformed reference to childbirth, the reader may not realize that these are children playing, so acute is their imitation of the adult female world. In a lovingly detailed sequence, the table is laid with 'two geranium leaf plates, a pine needle fork and a twig knife. There were three daisy heads on a laurel leaf for poached eggs, some slices of fuchsia petal cold beef, some lovely little rissoles made of earth and water and dandelion seeds, and the chocolate custard which she [presumably Kezia] had decided to serve in the pawa shell she had cooked it in' (41).

Gender roles are further emphasized with the arrival of the Burnells' two male cousins. The boys are the proud furnishers of gingerbread, although their participation in its creation is limited to having licked the spoon, beater, and bowl. The younger brother, Rags, is delighted to be able to play with the girls and thus indulge his 'shameful' (42) secret passion for playing with dolls. Pip, the leader, and more typically male, emphasizes danger and experimentation in his attempts at cooking, which consist largely of concocting various supposedly explosive mixtures to feed to the long-suffering dog. And he is proud of having skinned the almonds for the gingerbread, an activity which he presents as a feat of bravery and domination: 'I just stuck my hand into a saucepan of boiling water and grabbed them out and gave them a kind of pinch and the nuts flew out of the skins, some of them as high as the ceiling' (42). In contrast to Pip's adventurous attitude to food preparation, the girls' playing house seems to be straight out of a popular women's magazine. Moreover, their flower-food blooms; the boys' food blows up.

The hostess's tasks are an extension of those of the provider of food, of the mother at the family table; a party makes a public statement about a woman's domestic and culinary abilities. In 'The Garden Party,' the adolescent Laura Sheridan undergoes a further stage of apprenticeship, as she learns to be a hostess at a real party. The job is shared with her sisters, her mother – who claims to be leaving the work up to the children – and the household servants. The whole day is described from the hostess's point of view; if the party itself scarcely appears in this story, there is a good deal of emphasis on the preparation. A party requires a transformation of the domestic space – in this case both the house and yard – as well as of the party-givers themselves, from the private to the public, the ordinary to the marvellous. The chores involved in the transformation imply organizational, aesthetic, and social skills. Mansfield also makes it clear that social values and ideological priorities are reflected in all aspects of party-giving, from the ordering and arranging of the flowers to the inspection of cream puffs sent by the bakery and the labelling of sandwiches. Laura particularly learns about the applicability of 'class distinctions.' Even as she thinks of them as 'absurd ... Well, for her part, she didn't feel them. Not a bit, not an atom' (247–8), she shows that the lesson has already been internalized. Thus, sent to instruct workmen on where in the yard to erect a canopy – an exercise in supervision which is certainly valuable practice for a future hostess – Laura is painfully conscious of what she says and does.

More important, she learns that the death of a workman who lives near her home is not a reason to cancel the party. Proximity of dwelling does not make someone a neighbour: class is more important than propinquity, and Laura's notion of 'nearly neighbours' (255) is very heavily qualified, for there is a solid demarcation between rich and poor districts, no matter how near to each other geographically. The border can be traversed only for certain reasons, under certain conditions, and in certain ways. Moreover, the party sets up new boundaries, creating a temporary but clearly defined psychological and physical space which does not allow intrusion. Thus news of the accident is subsumed to the priorities of the party: ironically, as Nathan points out (43), it is the man delivering cream puffs – some of which are later sent to the workman's survivors – who brings the news. The pretty hat that her mother gives her – black for fashion, not for mourning – distracts Laura from the death. In her bedroom, the domain of the young girl, she catches a glimpse of herself, transformed, in the mirror:

> ... she saw ... this charming girl ... in her black hat trimmed with gold daisies and a long black velvet ribbon. Never had she imagined she could look like that ... Just for a moment she had another glimpse of that poor woman and those little children and the body being carried into the house. But it all seemed blurred, unreal, like a picture in the newspaper. I'll remember it again after the party's over, she decided. And somehow that seemed quite the best plan ... (256; last ellipsis in original)

In the ideology of a garden party and the world of the story, this plan is as it should be: both in terms of her being a young, pretty girl, who is not at all dead, and in terms of her class.[4]

Because the story is focused on the young hostess, the reader sees very little of the actual party: only a half-page summary of Laura's impressions, including compliments on her appearance and on her hat, and her own proud self consciousness as a hostess offering her guests tea and ices, and looking after the band. The guests, conversations, and party activities are not described. What is important is the party euphoria Laura experiences, that sense of heightened sensibility which is evident in other fictional parties as well. And her elation is not just frivolous; the story demonstrates that certain truths are much easier to perceive at such moments. Thus, the mysteries of sex, love, life, and time seem to be fleetingly but profoundly grasped under such festive circumstances.

After the party ends, the underside of the festivities is brought to light. Although it may at first seem an odd juxtaposition, death has had a central, although concealed, place at the party, as it does in *Mrs. Dalloway*,[5] and, as Christopher Ames points out, in 'The Dead.' Laura, stepping into adulthood, is ready both to take on fully her role within the class system – not only as a hostess but also as the wealthy lady on the hill, giving charity to the poor – and to confront death first-hand.

Although she considered it absurd to cancel the party because of the workman's death, Mrs Sheridan deems it appropriate to deliver party leftovers – 'sandwiches, cakes, puffs, all uneaten, all going to be wasted' (258) – to the grieving family: 'it will be the greatest treat for the children. ... And she's sure to have neighbours calling in and so on. What a point to have it all ready prepared' (258). Mrs Sheridan envisions the widow as a hostess, and imagines the problem of serving food to the mourners to be paramount for her. The funeral dinner will thus become a rather skewed reflection of the garden party.

Laura's venturing outside her family's rose-filled yard and the paradise of the party is like a trip into the underworld: 'It was just growing dusky as Laura shut their garden gates. A big dog ran by like a shadow. The road gleamed white, and down below in the hollow the little cottages were in deep shade' (258–9). The unnamed workman's house, with its 'wretched little low kitchen, lighted by a smoky lamp,' is dark and 'gloomy'(260), especially as compared to the Sheridans' sunny, open garden. Although a small house, its arrangement of rooms appears somehow obscure, even labyrinthine, with the word 'passage' repeated several times, as if the house itself is the tunnel to the underworld. To Laura's family, death is 'other' on this particular day, not only secondary to the party but very much associated with the working class. The cream puffs sent to the worker's family are themselves absurd, if not insulting – more a reminder of class than anything nourishing or consoling. Nevertheless, this trip is part of the coming-of-age ritual defined by the garden party itself. If, afterwards, Laura cannot really speak about or define her experience, it has an impact on her, and she finds it wonderful:

> Laurie put his arm round her shoulder. 'Don't cry,' he said in his warm, loving voice. 'Was it awful?'
> 'No,' sobbed Laura. 'It was simply marvellous. But, Laurie–' She stopped, she looked at her brother. 'Isn't life,' she stammered, 'isn't life –' But what life was she couldn't explain. No matter. He quite understood. (261)

The ordeal of visiting the dead man's cottage and seeing his body does not ruin the party for Laura; rather, it enhances the day and underlines the rightness of the world of the garden party. Laura's reservations about both holding the party in the first place, given the workman's death, and sending the extravagant bits of food seem to have been banished at the end, as his death is incorporated into the world of the party: 'While they were laughing and while the band was playing, this marvel had come to the lane. Happy ... happy ... All is well, said that sleeping face. This is just as it should be. I am content' (245; ellipses in original).

Also about the hostess's experience of a party, in this case a dinner party, Mansfield's 'Bliss' describes that further stage in a woman's life for which the young Burnell and Sheridan girls are preparing. As the title of the story suggests, the heightened perceptions and emotions of party euphoria are also depicted in 'Bliss.' The dinner party given by Bertha, a thirty-year-old married woman, is a success: the table is beautiful, the food attractive, the soufflé 'very admirable' (100), the coffee machine new. The atmosphere is pleasant and the conversation brilliant, by the hostess's standards. But, overall, there is an uneasiness, a blurriness of vision in the depiction of the gathering, and, in the end, the story is a devastatingly mocking critique of modern marriage and social life, and the 'artsy' crowd. The dinner party, rather than being a triumph for Bertha, ultimately demonstrates her failures as a woman.

At the start of 'Bliss,' Bertha is outside on the street, returning to her house, which is unquestionably her centre; she does not seem to have the life outside it that her husband does. In a rather detached tone lent by the use of the second-person pronoun, she describes herself as filled with joy at returning home: 'turning the corner of your own street, you are overcome, suddenly, by a feeling of bliss – absolute bliss!' (91). Once at home, Bertha's only apparent contribution to the upcoming meal is to arrange a bowl of fruit: 'There were tangerines and apples stained with strawberry pink. Some yellow pears, smooth as silk, some white grapes covered with a silver bloom and a big cluster of purple ones' (92–3). The fruit is beautiful, even sensual, but it is its appearance that is emphasized. The fact that Bertha has chosen purple grapes to match the carpet suggests that, for her, the fruit is purely aesthetic.

As in other Mansfield stories, the serving of food is linked with maternity. Before receiving her guests, Bertha assists at her baby daughter's dinner. Her interaction with her child recalls her arrangement of the fruit. She is interested in her baby as a delightful possession. Although, despite the nursemaid's reluctance, she insists on feeding the child herself, she is obviously unused to doing so; she is awkward, shy, inept, and there is an air of novelty and of unreality in the scene:

The baby looked up at her again, stared, and then smiled so charmingly that Bertha couldn't help crying:

'Oh, Nanny, do let me finish giving her her supper while you put the bath things away.' ...

She ate delightfully, holding up her lips for the spoon and then waving her hands. Sometimes she wouldn't let the spoon go; and sometimes, just as Bertha had filled it, she waved it away to the four winds.

When the soup was finished Bertha turned round to the fire.

'You're nice – you're very nice!' said she, kissing her warm baby. 'I'm fond of you. I like you.' (93–4)

As if she is just another beautiful object in the house, the baby seems one more small piece of a perfect life. The scene adds to the overall impression that Bertha is playing at being married and running a household.

In 'Bliss,' as in 'The Garden Party,' the values of Bertha and her set are reflected in the party. The superficiality of this world is underlined by the fact that the dinner party is reduced to a contentless form: decorative, but not nourishing, either physically or spiritually. The dinner itself seems two-dimensional, a tableau, and the group of dinner guests around the table an extension of the fruit arrangement, part of the colour scheme of the dining-room. Bertha has given great attention to inviting splendidly modern, interesting people to her party, people she finds 'delightful' because they are 'a decorative group ... they seemed to set one another off and ... they reminded her of a play by Tchekof!' (100). Mansfield very much admired, and indeed imitated Tchekov, but the reference to him here signifies life which is pretending to be art, the dinner table as a stage and the diners as both actors and spectators, watching themselves eat and talk. Bertha finds her dinner guests 'dears – dears – and she loved having them there, at her table, and giving them delicious food and wine' (100). Yet their conversation seems false, their interests and their projects superficial, and their social poses several levels removed from any sense of a genuine self. Although she enjoys her guests as much as she expects to, Bertha's only real sense of communion at the dinner is with the woman who turns out to be her husband's mistress.

The story satirizes both dinner parties and modern literature. Eddie Warren, one of the dinner guests, calls Bertha's attention to a poem called 'Table d'Hôte,' which begins with what he calls the 'incredibly beautiful line: "Why Must it Always be Tomato Soup?"' If Eddie finds this obviously silly poem 'so *deeply* true, don't you feel? Tomato soup is so *dreadfully* eternal' (105; emphasis in original), the poem undercuts and trivializes both Bertha's aesthetic sense and her choice of menu: 'the beautiful red soup in the grey plate' (100) served at dinner, apparently chosen more for its colour than for its taste. In other ways too, the dinner is paralleled and parodied by images of food. Mrs Norman Knight wears a 'banana skin dress' and earrings 'like little dangling nuts.' She recounts that, on her way to the dinner party, 'the train ... rose to a man and simply ate me with its eyes' (97). Mrs Knight, whose abilities as an interior decorator seem somewhat questionable, also mentions her idea of redecorating someone's house with a fish and chips motif: '"You know, my dear ... I am so tempted to do a fried-fish scheme, with the backs of the chairs shaped like frying-pans and lovely chip potatoes embroidered all over the curtains"' (102–3). Such references to food are fun, silly, playful, even stylish, but a veneer on the real importance of the meal in terms of nourishment or desire or pleasure or communality. Food loses its reality in 'Bliss' to become a bad poem, a fashion statement, an object of art rather than a source of sustenance or, for most of the diners, of pleasure.

Bertha's husband, Harry, is the character who seems most to appreciate the meal. Although the reader begins to understand him, Bertha does not know whether his pleasure in eating is genuine or affected: 'Harry was enjoying his dinner. It was part of his – well, not his nature, exactly, and certainly not his pose – his – something or other – to talk about food and to glory in his "shameless passion for the white flesh of the lobster" and "the green of pistachio ices – green and cold like the eyelids of Egyptian dancers"' (100). In a social world of poses and masks, Harry's 'real' character is unknown to his wife. Bertha is also incapable of knowing whether a 'passion' for food could exist because she seems to live largely on a non-physical, 'slightly hysterical' (Moran, *Word of Mouth* 67) level – indeed Bertha, before the start of the party, refers to herself as 'hysterical' (93). Bertha shares her guests' pretension to being terribly modern, a pose which provides her with a justification of her lack of sexual desire for her husband:

Oh, she'd loved him – she'd been in love with him, of course, in every other way, but just not in that way. And equally, of course, she'd understood that he was different. They'd discussed it so often. It had worried her dreadfully at first to find that she was so cold, but after a time it had not seemed to matter. They were so frank with each other – such good pals. That was the best of being modern. (104)

The profundities that Bertha, like the much younger Laura, believes she grasps during the party are not what they at first seem, and she achieves only a somewhat confused understanding. She never fully sees, as the reader does, that in her marriage she, like the Burnell children, has been only playing house. Still, despite its superficiality, Bertha's dinner party does, after all, open her in an unexpected way. Although Bertha has never felt any kind of passion, during the course of her party she begins to desire her husband for the first time. She also, without exactly admitting it, feels strongly attracted to Pearl Fulton. It is both ironic and sad – for, despite her self-delusion, Bertha is, in her innocence and repression, a somewhat sympathetic character – that her awakening is too late. Yet her own glimpse of passion seems to be necessary before she is capable of seeing that her husband is in love with Miss Fulton.

Bertha's most important view of the outside world, which she shares with Miss Fulton during the party, is of the pear tree from the drawing-room window. However, she does not go into the garden herself, with its hints of beauty, eroticism, and other mysteries of life; rather she is bounded by the house and by the framework of her passionless marriage, her social world, and the dinner party which is the expression of that world. It is because Eddie wants to show her the foolish poem about tomato soup that she is at the drawing-room door, able to see her husband embracing Pearl Fulton in the hall. Their positions are significant: while Bertha, at the entrance to the drawing-room, is at the boundary of her domain, Harry and Pearl are near the door to the exterior world that Bertha seems scarcely to know. As other works by both Mansfield and Woolf suggest, once underway, a meal or party creates its own discourse, one affecting the hostess herself as well as the guests. Like Laura Sheridan's garden party, Bertha's dinner party finishes by leading the hostess in a different direction from that she foresaw. But in this story, Bertha cannot absorb her new knowledge or incorporate it into the assumptions and values which she believed to be at the basis of her dinner party, her home, and her life. She can only return to the window and cry out to the 'lovely' but silent pear tree, 'Oh, what is going to happen now?' (105). Although, Bertha has, up until this point, happily accepted her role, the story certainly suggests, first, that she has not understood it, and, second, that, transplanted and translated to a modern urban setting, woman's task as an organizer of dinner can be a very different and far less satisfactory business than in the world of the traditional Mrs Fairfield.

Mrs Dalloway's Party, Mrs Ramsay's Dinner

Although Mansfield's Bertha follows the forms expected of a hostess, as well as of a wife and a mother, these roles are, for her, powerless and ultimately meaningless ones, and what is really happening at her dinner party and in her home is beyond her understanding. Traditionally, however, women's power is based in women's domestic work, in the agglomeration of small daily tasks that ultimately define a life. Virginia Woolf's *Mrs. Dalloway* and *To the Lighthouse* raise the significant question of how women's work, defined and exploited by a patriarchal society, can be channelled creatively by women themselves. For Woolf, this is a major issue for the modern woman trying to emerge from nineteenth-century Victorianism. In both *Mrs. Dalloway* and *To the Lighthouse*, Woolf explores the burden of meaning inherited by twentieth-century hostesses and providers of food: the Victorian ideological model of woman's domestic work as a civilizing force. Woolf's Mrs Ramsay and Mrs Dalloway present two versions of the bourgeois ideal of the wife/mother/hostess. Each in her own way represents a forging of community, a bringing together of disparate elements into at least a temporary whole around a table, at a party – within a house. Thus, Mrs Ramsay creates order for her husband and children, succeeds in bringing about a marriage, and integrates loners and confirmed individualists into the community of her table. In *Mrs. Dalloway*, the pre-party dinner occurs behind the scenes; yet its very privacy communicates a definition of the party, and the role of the hostess emanates from that undescribed meal. Clarissa Dalloway sees her party as almost religious, calling it 'an offering for the sake of offering' (185). As Christopher Ames puts it: 'Acknowledging the separateness at the heart of life, Clarissa proposes her parties as a solution ... [H]er parties are an attempt to bridge the separateness of selves, to create a community ... The party, she thinks, will be magical and unifying' (90). In their own domestic contexts, in their own domestic centres, Mrs Dalloway and Mrs Ramsay are powerful. At the same time, Woolf's ambivalent relationship to the traditional female role is clear,[6] both in *To the Lighthouse*, where the life of Mrs Ramsay is affirmed and, at the same time, undercut by the text, by other characters, and by Mrs Ramsay herself, and in *Mrs. Dalloway*, where the position of hostess is presented both critically and compassionately.

There are a number of obvious similarities between Mansfield's 'Bliss' and Woolf's *Mrs. Dalloway*. In each case, the social gathering is presented from the hostess's point of view and emphasizes the hostess's central role, although in Woolf's novel the reader is also allowed inside the minds of several party guests. Each piece opens with the main character on the street, feeling girlish and excited about her party; yet for both women there is a strong pull back to the home, which is clearly their centre. Each work culminates in an image of the hostess looking through a window and experiencing a sort of personal realization or epiphany, although of a very different nature in each case. There are similarities in the main characters as well.[7] Clarissa Dalloway is older than Bertha, however, more adept and probably more wealthy, as well as less insistent on being 'modern,' and more consciously rooted in a class and a society. As – in part – a post-war and urban version of Woolf's Mrs Ramsay, she retains and endorses many of the strongly established ideological foundations which sustain the latter. She plays a similar domestic role to that of Mrs Ramsay – indeed, the very title of the novel indicates her station in life as a wife – but it is a role changed significantly by the context. Even though most of the characters in the central plot of *Mrs. Dalloway* must have grown to adulthood in the nineteenth century, the novel is about the modern era. And Mrs Dalloway is very much a Londoner.

Still, although she seems much less tied to her house and family than is Mrs Ramsay, and the depiction of her daughter Elizabeth riding the buses around London suggests even more mobility and freedom for the next generation of women, Mrs Dalloway is hardly liberated from domestic concerns. If her party only begins late in the novel, her whole day – and everything in the novel – leads up to it in some way. Her leaving the house on the first page of the novel to buy flowers for her party is directly related to her role as hostess. And she is back at her front door on page 42.[8] Her outing to Bond Street is a prelude to the party in another way as well: for Clarissa, as for Woolf, the crowded London streets provide an inspiration for the evening to come. With a specific purpose and specific errands in mind, Clarissa is hardly the '*flâneuse*' that Rachel Bowlby (214) sees in Woolf's 'Street Haunting,' yet her love of London is evident, or rather, a love of *her* London, the London that her party will affirm and celebrate.[9] Throughout the rest of the novel, a strong sense of the city remains, but the London scenes are described through the eyes and the activities of others: Richard and Elizabeth Dalloway, Peter Walsh, and Septimus and Rezia Warren Smith.

Beginning in this first scene, then, *Mrs. Dalloway* underlines the fact that, in certain classes at least, women's position as wife, mother, keeper of the house, and provider of the meal also encompasses the responsibilities of hostess and, to some extent, consumer. Clarissa is presented less as the mother of Elizabeth and the wife of Richard than as a hostess, although the former roles are certainly integral to the latter. Mrs Dalloway likes giving parties, and, although she is, at times, criticized and indeed criticizes herself for this passion, she is in her element when playing hostess. Peter Walsh remembers that even as a young girl, she had this quality: 'Clarissa came up, with her perfect manners, like a real hostess, and wanted to introduce him to some one – spoke as if they had never met before, which enraged him. Yet even then he admired her for it. He admired her courage; her social instinct; he admired her power of carrying things through. "The perfect hostess," he said to her, whereupon she winced all over' (93). Peter's youthful impression of her as hostess does not seem to have changed. The good hostess is democratic, giving every guest equal attention. That evening, Peter, wanting to be special, and not just another party guest, again reacts negatively to Clarissa's greeting: '"How delightful to see you!" said Clarissa. She said it to every one. How delightful to see you! She was at her worst – effusive, insincere' (254). Clarissa herself still hates to be defined as a 'perfect hostess'; she can feel the connotation of superficiality in that phrase, even though, in fact, giving a perfect party is one of the most important things in the world to her, and even though the novel suggests that the functions of the hostess and of the party are meaningful on several levels.

The party is both the culmination and the centre of the novel: if the novel's structure is viewed as circular rather than linear, the party is the hub around which, for that day, at least, the entire world of Mrs Dalloway revolves. As readers, we are invited guests at the party, if perhaps somewhat out of our element like cousin Ellie Henderson or the inappropriately garbed Mabel Waring in Woolf's preliminary story, 'The New Dress.' Our status outside the inner circle is made clear by our not being invited to the pre-party dinner. The dinner remains so private that even the guest list is not divulged; we do not know which of the party guests were among the select few invited. Although a party supper will also be served later in the evening, neither meal is described in the novel. In terms of what the novel tells us, Clarissa seems to have been less concerned with what dishes to serve than with other details of organizing the evening. The fact that neither Clarissa nor the text pays much attention to the party meals underlines the importance of women's social role in this class, an emphasis on the hostess rather than the provider of the family meal, on the public rather than the private realm.

This lack of attention to the meal is different from that generated by the anxiety about gender roles or the general turn-of-the-century malaise seen in some of Mansfield's work. A psychological interpretation might posit that it reflects Clarissa's general repression, in keeping with the 'fear of embodied existence' that Moran (*Word of Mouth* 78) notes elsewhere in the novel. Such 'fear' is seen most readily in Septimus Warren Smith and Doris Kilman. The former cannot eat and the latter eats desperately: '[F]or both, food functions as a symbolic expression of distress about living within the confines of the body' (Moran, *Word of Mouth* 79). Although in Clarissa's case, no specific dissociation from food or obsession with eating is described, Moran sees evidence of her sharing this 'distress' in her simultaneous retreat from heterosexuality and repression of homoeroticism, except at a safe distance in memories. She cites, as evidence of Clarissa's disembodiment, Jane Marcus's analysis of 'the cloistered imagination' (72) suggested by the monk-like attic room where Clarissa naps. However, there is more going on in this novel. As others have noted, the party is in many ways an expression of a particular nation, class, and set of values and beliefs. The lack of emphasis on the dinner is, most of all, a signifier of class structure: only the servants refer to the meal. Although it is not emphasized, it is certainly an important part of Mrs Dalloway's responsibilities to ensure that the kitchen, like the rest of the household, runs smoothly and without any visible effort on her part; there is always a post-mortem meeting the morning after a dinner party, the cook tells us. In fact, it is *because* her work is not emphasized that we know she and her household staff have succeeded in their efforts to make it seem effortless. We do not need to be shown the dinner table because in this class, the form of meals is unvarying, and their excellence assumed, as is made clear in the description of Lady Bruton's lunch, characterized by a 'grand deception practised by hostesses in Mayfair ... this profound illusion ... about the food – how it is not paid for; and then that the table spreads itself voluntarily' (158).[10] Peter Walsh's solitary restaurant dinner, his table manners and way of eating are described in the novel only because he is observed admiringly by the more common Morris family of Liverpool, on holiday in London (241–4).

Still, the placement of the servants' conversation about the meal indicates its importance, as well as the importance of their work in preparing it. In the structure of the novel, the servants open the party: 'Lucy ... running full tilt downstairs' (250) so as not to be caught in the drawing-room by the arriving guests, followed by the servants' gossip about whether the prime minister is coming, and their reports of the ladies going upstairs, while the gentlemen are served their after-dinner drinks. Here, in the below-stairs attention to cleaning up and worries about matters such as the salmon having been underdone, are presented the bones – the leftovers but also the essential skeleton or framework – of the party.[11] Indeed, it is from the kitchen perspective that the reader learns about the menu, after the meal itself is over:

> Did it matter, did it matter in the least, one Prime Minister more or less? It made no difference at this hour of the night to Mrs Walker among the plates, saucepans, cullenders, frying-pans, chicken in aspic, ice-cream freezers, pared crusts of bread, lemons, soup tureens, and pudding basins which, however hard they washed up in the scullery seemed to be all on top of her, on the kitchen table, on chairs, while the fire blared and roared, the electric lights glared, and still supper had to be laid. (251)

The dinner has been consumed and reconstructed as a pile of organic and inorganic objects in the kitchen. The above passage translates the meal from a series of, presumably, carefully planned and beautifully presented courses into a wonderfully chaotic list – almost reminiscent of Stein's *Tender Buttons* – composed of food, dishes, and the kitchen utensils that were used in cooking. In the after-dinner chaos, the distinctions between preparation, serving, and eating, between kitchen and dining-room have been eliminated.

The dinner takes place before the party, and, in the architecture of the house, one comes to the dining-room first; that it is a floor below the party level is certainly not an unusual arrangement in London houses of the time, but, in the novel, also suggests that, even though the meal is not depicted, the fact of eating dinner together still has some basic and prior importance. The narrative takes the reader smoothly up the social scale as we climb the stairs to the party with the guests arriving after dinner: from the kitchen staff, invisible to the party guests, to 'Mrs. Parkinson (hired for parties)' (253), who greets the guests, and Clarissa's old nurse, Ellen Barnet, who helps the ladies with their garments. From there, we accompany Lady and Miss Lovejoy up the stairs to 'Mr. Wilkins (hired for parties). He had an admirable manner, as he bent and straightened himself, bent and straightened himself and announced [each guest] with perfect impartiality' (254). It is only after passing through the structure of servants that we arrive finally at the hostess, standing at the top of the stairs. Like the dining-room, the below-stairs world of the kitchen and the downstairs world of the cloakroom are the building blocks which support the upstairs party.

Except for Peter Walsh, and, in another context, the Bradshaws, we see the guests only after they have entered the house, having left their everyday selves behind, and, in most cases, after we have followed them upstairs. This upstairs area of the house is scarcely described except as a space for the party; it is as if these rooms have been transformed and cease to be part of the Dalloways' everyday house. Details of the environment are unimportant; there is little description. The family's furniture and possessions are seen only from the point of view of a maid, who imagines that the guests 'must think how clean, how bright, how beautifully cared for, when they saw the beautiful silver, the brass fire-irons, the new chair-covers, and the curtains of yellow chintz' (250). But Lucy is incorrect: precisely because everything is so cared for, so completely as expected, the surroundings go unnoticed both by the party guests and, except for the curtains,[12] by the novel. As in the case of the dinner and the supper that we learn of through the cook's passing reference that it 'still ... had to be laid,' it is only the preparation and the clean-up which we hear about, and only the household staff who need to be concerned.

The lack of emphasis on the meal at the party also suggests a particular definition of the event. In the Dalloways' world, the notion of a party is expanded from an opportunity to share food and conviviality with friends to a more political gathering, partly motivated by pragmatic objectives, if not the specifically utilitarian goals that inspire Lady Bruton's renowned luncheons.[13] Clarissa is somewhat hurt that Lady Bruton invited only Richard to lunch that day. But there is a clear purpose to her guest list; the lunch party is not merely a social function. If Clarissa's party is less clearly focused and can, therefore, to some extent become a festive world unto itself, it is also a creature of the real social, political, and economic world. Thus, the party is about more than celebration, and if, as the hostess, Mrs Dalloway seems to be involved only at arm's length in preparing and presenting the party meal, her political function is a major and an evident one. In contrast to Mansfield's parties, where the guests are presumably friends, relatives, acquaintances, members of a small social world, at Clarissa's party many of the guests are also important in the larger political world. As the wife of a member of Parliament, Clarissa plays hostess not to the philosophers who visit the Ramsays, but to the prime minister; her parties support her husband's political career. Richard Dalloway is not an extremely prominent politician, although influential enough. There are, presumably, legions of such men – some more, some less success-ful – and women like Clarissa playing hostess for them, some more effectively than Clarissa does.[14]

Clarissa's party is political in a larger sense as well: it reflects and endorses the values of the British Empire. It is evident in the novel that women have been delegated the responsibility of upholding these val-ues. The Empire shrinks to the size of a drawing-room and the party conversations resonate with its compressed magnitude. The political meets the private; the most personal of interactions encompass the most public. The prime minister is present, and Lady Bruton, who has 'the thought of Empire always at hand' (275), monopolizes his ear. Clarissa arranges that those with imperial experience abroad should speak together. Miss Parry nostalgically evokes a romantic and glorious time to have been a Briton in Asia:

> For at the mention of India, or even Ceylon, her eyes (only one was glass) slowly deepened, became blue, beheld, not human beings – she had no tender memories, no proud illusions about Viceroys, Generals, Mutinies – it was orchids she saw, and mountain passes and herself carried on the backs of coolies in the 'sixties over solitary peaks; or descending to uproot orchids (startling blossoms, never beheld before) which she painted in water-colour; an indomitable Englishwoman ... (271)

Through the presence of such guests, however, the party also makes it clear that times have changed; other truths – sometimes more human truths – emerge from beneath the veneer of British nationalism. If the morning on Bond Street suggests that history has speeded up and that the old tweed shop where Clarissa's father bought his clothes is already two eras behind,[15] it is also clear that Miss Parry belongs to a past which is becoming more and more remote. Peter Walsh, a modern bureau-crat in India, is seen rather as a failure. Certainly, the response to the prime minister's entrance, although more discreet among this privileged crowd, is similar to the effect generated by the important-looking passing car on the people in the street earlier that day: 'Nobody looked at him. They just went on talking, yet it was perfectly plain that they all knew, felt to the marrow of their bones, this majesty passing; this symbol of what they all stood for, English society' (262). Yet, from the perspective of Ellie Henderson, a cousin invited grudgingly at the last minute, the prime minister is like the emperor in his invisible clothes: 'He looked so ordinary. You might have stood him behind a counter and bought biscuits – poor chap, all rigged up in gold lace. And to be fair, as he went his rounds, first with Clarissa then with Richard escorting him, he did it very well. He tried to look somebody. It was amusing to watch' (261–2). Beneath the trappings of his office, the economic base of the country shows through in the man, as if England is, literally, a nation of shopkeepers.

If Mrs Dalloway's dinner is not at the centre of either the party or the novel, it can be argued that death, in fact, occupies this place. As in 'The Garden Party,' the story of a death parallels the story of the party. In Woolf's novel, however, we follow Septimus Warren Smith's day as closely as we follow Clarissa's, and we are privy to the thoughts and perceptions of both Septimus and his wife, Rezia. Moreover, the death is reported to the hostess *during*, not before, the party, thus becoming an integral part of the festivities, although unforeseen, like Sally Seton's arrival. Christopher Ames, in his very thorough discussion of the importance of death to 'the festive vision,' emphasizes that, ultimately, celebrating life means celebrating, or at least coming to terms with, death. In Bakhtin's words, '[T]hrough all the stages of historic development feasts were linked to moments of crisis, of breaking points in the cycle of nature or in the life of society and man. Moments of death and revival, of change and renewal always led to a festive perception of the world. These moments, expressed in concrete form, created the peculiar character of the feasts' (9). In this sense, Septimus is rather a scapegoat for the new century, and his death underlines the degree to which Clarissa's party occurs in the context of not only a changing but a painful world, in which the cataclysm of the war still reverberates. Septimus's run-in with the twentieth century has been particularly acute. Dr Holmes's admonition to him to act like a man emphasizes the cage of limited roles and possibilities where Septimus, like Clarissa and others, finds himself: 'Are we not all prisoners?' Sally Seton asks (293). At least some of Clarissa's guests have had a hand in the institutions and values that precipitated this personal destruction and international ruin: the Bradshaws, to be sure, but presumably others as well, in their own ways. Still, although the novel stops short of endorsing or celebrating their world, it is, as other critics have noted, forgiving, if not of the Bradshaws, at least of the other party guests. Just as the novel does not hide Clarissa's failings, yet looks at her tenderly, so the social satire of her class, its habits, and its values is muted. Underneath – or alongside – the social criticism, there is compassion. Peter Walsh, to some degree an outsider now to his class, sometimes seems to be the voice of the novel, critical of Clarissa and her world, but at the same time still in love with her.

At least temporarily staying with the hostess's consciousness, the narrative leaves the party with Clarissa, following her to the small room where Lady Bruton and the prime minister talked together about India.[16] Her withdrawal from the party in response to the news of the suicide brings to a climax all the large issues which have reverberated in the party and in the novel which it comprises. Clarissa's complicated personal response to Septimus's suicide is also a response to the public social and political issues personified by the people in the adjacent rooms and inherent in the party itself. If Clarissa's drawing-room pulls into her centre a certain segment of London, its history and its people, it also brings together the major people, places, and events of her own life; it represents a culmination of her own private and public history.

Clarissa has served up a party from a remarkable set of ingredients: not only the party guests themselves – aging, regretful, despairing, nostalgic, hopeful, proud, insecure – but the social and historical crises which they have lived and in which some have had a hand. If Septimus felt both desperately alone and at the same time haunted by ghosts and at the mercy of the social establishment around him, Clarissa's own ghosts and many of the pillars of that establishment surround her on this particular evening. Giving her party allows Clarissa some control over the spectres that destroyed Septimus. The final line of the novel, 'For there she was,' emphasizes not only her own beauty and power – qualities she herself doubts – but also her work, her success in creating and hosting this human banquet, this homage to time, history, and human imperfection.

Woolf's *To the Lighthouse* is perhaps the best modernist literary evocation of women's work, of that domestic life that Mansfield's perpetual wanderers desire and yet reject. In *To the Lighthouse*, this work is focused around the dinner table, both the literal centre of the Ramsays' house and a potent symbol for all of domestic life. Mrs Ramsay is of Clarissa Dalloway's generation, born perhaps a decade or so earlier, although slightly younger than Clarissa during the day depicted in 'The Window,' the first section of the novel. Like Clarissa, Mrs Ramsay is portrayed at home or associated with the affairs of home; however, although her dinner includes several guests, her role as a hostess is more rooted in the immediate family. She is, indeed, the mother of eight, while Clarissa has only one nearly adult child.

Although the Ramsays presumably have another house in London, we only see them in the country. Running a large household of her family and their guests, Mrs Ramsay is only minimally subject to the stimuli of outside events even on the most ordinary level of street life, chance encounters, and so forth. There are references to past and future outings to the beach or to the circus, but within the frame of the novel, she leaves her home only to do the marketing and to visit sick people in the village, a direct continuation of her role at home. Mrs Ramsay could belong to another century. Certainly the modern world is present in *To the Lighthouse*: the availability of household appliances, the existence of mail-order catalogues, the centralized distribution system for agricultural products all reflect the industrialization and the boom in consumerism at the turn of the century. But, although there are also hints of the complexities of a twentieth-century life led by the house guests when they are not in Scotland, Mrs Ramsay scarcely seems affected by modernity. If, for us, as for Woolf, it is hard not to feel the Great War hovering over the first section, the fact that an era is about to end is not apparent to the characters.

In *To the Lighthouse*, the material world seems to be gendered. While for Mrs Ramsay a table is the real – and for the novel, the metaphorical – centre of her day, for her husband its very existence is questionable, its function – indeed its relationship to human life – a matter of perception. Andrew Ramsay – the budding mathematician in the family, whose death in the war will be as appropriate to his gender as is his sister Prue's in childbirth – tells Lily to 'think of a kitchen table, then ... when you're not there' (38) in order to help her understand his father's philosophical work on '[s]ubject and object and the nature of reality' (38).[17] Mrs Ramsay's ways of being, knowing, creating, and communicating are continually contrasted with her philosopher husband's highly abstract way of thinking and of using language. Unlike her husband, Mrs Ramsay is grounded in the everyday, in the domestic objects which surround her. Even her speculations, meditations, and dreams are based there. At times she feels herself merge with the domestic environment: 'Often she found herself sitting and looking, sitting and looking, with her work in her hands until she became the thing she looked at – that light, for example' (97).

Of course, *To the Lighthouse* does not leave us completely mired in these gender distinctions. It bears remembering that the overriding consciousness controlling and interpreting both the everyday and the philosophical in this novel is that of Woolf, a woman, and that an amalgamation, if not a fusing, of the two gendered perspectives occurs at the level of the literary text. Still, the two focuses around which *To the Lighthouse* is built echo and reinforce gender differences and divisions within the world of the novel. The lighthouse is both the central symbol and the central feature of the novel's landscape. It is not where we – either characters or readers – *are*, but what we *see*, and, moreover, because it gives the novel its title, the image that comes first to the reader's mind when he or she thinks of this book. Not only is it phallic in form, but repeatedly connected with men, who seem to have the final control over planning visits to the site, and, it is emphasized, whose heroic job it is to live there alone, with no women. Mrs Ramsay describes the situation of the lighthouse-men to her daughters thus: '"For how would you like to be shut up for a whole month at a time, and possibly more in stormy weather, upon a rock the size of a tennis lawn ... and to have no letters or newspapers, and to see nobody; if you were married, not to see your wife, not to know how your children were ... How would you like that?" she asked, addressing herself particularly to her daughters' (11–12). This is a description of 'gendered spaces' carried to an extreme. Certainly, Mrs Ramsay believes that her daughters should not 'like' living alone in a lighthouse on an island, although it is within the capacity of men to endure or even like it.

As a physical structure, the lighthouse is balanced by the house where almost the entire novel is actually set; symbolically, that image of male life is balanced by the domestic centre of the novel. Taken together, the two structures underline the differences between Mr and Mrs Ramsay, between the ideal and the real, and between the life of the mind and the life of the body. In the first – the major – section of the novel, the trip to the lighthouse is only planned; the dinner actually takes place. Moreover, although this dinner is over early in the novel, it remains central for the characters and the novel itself. The trip to the lighthouse, although it remains an idea throughout the novel, is only undertaken at the end, when time and events have radically transformed the meaning of the outing. In fact, like Mr Ramsay's letter 'R,' the lighthouse is not actually reached. The novel ends just as the boat arrives at the island, with Cam and James poised 'to follow [Mr Ramsay] as he sprang, lightly like a young man, holding his parcel, on to the rock' (308).

As in the case of Mansfield's Mrs Fairfield, we do not know Mrs Ramsay's first name. And, again as with Mrs Fairfield, the maternal and nurturing roles are inextricably intertwined. From the beginning of the novel, Mrs Ramsay is defined not only generally as a mother and a wife, but specifically as a nourisher. Thus, on the first page, her young son James, who is busy cutting a picture of a refrigerator out of a catalogue, seems to feel an unspoken association between his mother and the appliance: from a child's perspective, a potential source of the food his mother puts on the table. He 'endow[s] the picture of a refrigerator, as his mother [speaks], with heavenly bliss' (9). Her promise that he will go to the lighthouse the next day bridges the gap for him between the domestic and the adventurous, the female and the male worlds. The advertisement is transformed, to become imbued, as are his mother's words, with the power of imagination and the anguish of desire.

Early in the novel, the reader is introduced to Mrs Ramsay as the mother of a large family in a scene at the dinner table. Associated with this role of nurturer, emanating from it, is Mrs Ramsay's responsibility to uphold the institution of the family and, within the framework of the Victorian ideology of the family, by extension, civilization itself. In this context, it is worth quoting again a passage first mentioned in chapter 1: 'She was now formidable to behold, and it was only in silence, looking up from their plates, after she had spoken so severely ... that her daughters ... could sport with infidel ideas which they had brewed for themselves of a life different from hers ... as they sat at the table beneath their mother's eyes' (14). The reference to her daughters is important. The table is the place where the expectations of the family are reinforced, and, given their future roles, it is particularly crucial that the girls learn appropriate behaviour in this context. The girls' social conditioning includes not only, presumably, lessons on table manners and the treatment of guests, but also instruction in the appropriate cultural values which underpin everyday behaviour. As in Mrs Ramsay's description of life at the lighthouse, the socialization of her daughters is a key part of her role.

Thus, although she is to some extent a free-thinker in her personal beliefs – she questions the existence of God, for instance – in family and other personal matters, Mrs Ramsay functions as a conservative force, attempting to extend and recreate the structure of the family table. She wants and encourages Paul and Minta to marry; indeed, Lily Briscoe credits her with having engineered their engagement and Paul himself feels 'somehow that she was the person who had made him [propose]. She had made him think he could do anything' (109–10). In 'Prelude,' Linda Burnell remarks that her mother habitually organizes things in pairs, and Mrs Ramsay seems to see people this way. At least momentarily, she even hopes that Lily and William Bankes might marry: 'Everything seemed possible. Everything seemed right' (157). She thinks of encouraging them by sending them on a picnic. A meal without the formal restraints of a dining-room – domesticity in the wild – is her recipe for creating romantic commitment; a situation that resonates with the combined connotations of an intimate, communal structure and something earthier, uncivilized, natural must inevitably lead to marriage.

The story that Mrs Ramsay is reading to James throughout much of the first hundred and twenty pages of the novel reflects her conservatism about domestic life. The Grimms' fairy tale of the fisherman and his wife[18] can be viewed as a sort of morality tale about marriage, greed, and discontent. In section X, as Mrs Ramsay reads the story, she is thinking about her own life, and also about Paul and Minta and whether they will become engaged during their long walk after lunch. The bits of the story quoted in the text form a counterpoint to her thoughts, emphasizing the marital conflict in the tale, and particularly the woman who will not stay in her appropriate place:

> Flounder, flounder, in the sea,
> Come, I pray thee, here to me;
> For my wife, good Ilsabil,
> Wills not as I'd have her will. (87)

The tale ends with the status quo reestablished, thereby upholding the rightness of Mrs Ramsay's view of the world and emphasizing the moral to the child James. However, although Paul and Minta do come back engaged, their marriage will not follow the terms of Mrs Ramsay's lesson. Lily Briscoe thinks, at the end of the novel, that '[s]he would feel a little triumphant, telling Mrs Ramsay that the marriage had not been a success' (260).

Throughout the first section of the novel, Mrs Ramsay also knits socks for the lighthouse keeper's son – an insertion of the domestic and the feminine into that male world. But her knitting is also a metaphor for her roles as a wife: hostess, server of meals, lover, mother – each represented in the passage below by a particular room in the house. Mrs Ramsay is well aware that her ordered housekeeping creates an environment where her husband can thrive:

> It was sympathy [her husband] wanted, to be assured of his genius, first of all, and then to be taken within the circle of life, warmed and soothed, to have his senses restored to him, his barrenness made fertile, and all the rooms of the house made full of life – the drawing-room; behind the drawing-room the kitchen; above the kitchen the bedrooms; and beyond them the nurseries; they must be furnished, they must be filled with life ... Flashing her needles, confident, upright, she created drawing-room and kitchen, set them all aglow; bade him take his ease there, go in and out, enjoy himself. (59)

The above passage suggests that Mrs Ramsay's role goes far beyond mere 'sympathy' and reassurance. Through the metaphor of knitting, the novel claims that she actually creates the house, not building it with boards, nails, and plaster, but transforming the bare structure into a set of rooms with purposes and meaning. Her husband is 'barren,' not only incapable of giving life, but needing his own life given to him. He may literally provide the house, but only she can put life in it. Her support of Mr Ramsay's work in turn allows her a feeling of security and validates her notion of men's place in the economic and political world and her sense of security in that larger world: '[S]he let it uphold her and sustain her, this admirable fabric of the masculine intelligence, which ran up and down, crossed this way and that, like iron girders spanning the swaying fabric, upholding the world, so that she could trust herself to it utterly' (159). This androcentric view of the structure of civilization is, however, illusory; the novel suggests that it is really the domestic constructions created by women that allow the male intellect to function at all. Woolf's valorizing of Mrs Ramsay's work is, to some extent, congruent with the Victorian perspective that the home is ultimately the foundation of the British Empire. The novel, however, by looking more closely not only at the actual import of domestic work epitomized by the dinner but also at its meaning for the woman who performs the work, goes far beyond the ideological co-optation of the domestic for the purpose of upholding the status quo.

At the centre of this domestic world, then, the dinner in the first section reverberates throughout the novel. Even though there are servants, providing dinner is still Mrs Ramsay's job. Thus, during dinner, she is emphatically in control, having chosen the menu, worrying about whether the main dish will be overcooked, organizing the table and the guests, wondering where the stragglers are, dishing out soup, giving orders to the maid throughout the meal, overseeing the flow of conversation. But this central dinner does more than characterize Mrs Ramsay and define her role in the family. It is also significant to the other characters both as individuals and as a group. The process of gathering together is impressive. When dinner is ready,

> the great clangour of the gong announced solemnly, authoritatively, that all those scattered about, in attics, in bedrooms, on little perches of their own, reading, writing, putting the last smooth to their hair, fastening dresses, must leave all that, and the little odds and ends on their washing-tables and dressing-tables, and the novels on the bed-tables, and the diaries which were so private, and assemble in the dining-room for dinner. (124–5)

The very architecture of the house emphasizes the centrality of the dining-room. The dinner-bell pre-empts all other activities, demanding that everyone participate in the communality of the table. All the guests in the various rooms with their independent functions – rooms which exist because of Mrs Ramsay in the first place – now bow to her call to assemble. Although they may be unaware of it, the diners, and indeed the entire house, are celebrating her.

A combination of many ingredients makes up the main dish of the meal, the *boeuf en daube*, a 'confusion of savoury brown and yellow meats and ... bay leaves and ... wine' (151). This *mélange* characterizes the dinner party guests too. From people who, an hour before, were reading, writing, painting, dressing, thinking, they have all become diners. In their coming together, individuals lose their isolation and the company becomes more than the sum of its parts. It is because she, egoistically, perhaps, wants everyone to be joined in this totality, and William Bankes generally resists being incorporated into the group, that Mrs Ramsay says, '"I have triumphed tonight," meaning that for once Mr Bankes had agreed to dine with them and not run off to his own lodging where his man cooked vegetables properly' (111). Bankes himself later adds to Mrs Ramsay's victory by referring to the *boeuf en daube* as 'a triumph' (151), and thus vindicating Mrs Ramsay's belief in the rightness of the dinner table.

It is only after the candles are brought in that the dinner party fully becomes what Mrs Ramsay intends it to be: a world unto itself. The outside ceases to exist and becomes only a distorted reflection of the dining-room. Everyone is in Mrs Ramsay's world, as indeed they want to be, or want her to make them be:

> Now all the candles were lit up, and the faces on both sides of the table were brought nearer by the candle light, and composed, as they had not been in the twilight, into a party round a table, for the night was now shut off by panes of glass, which, far from giving any accurate view of the outside world, rippled it so strangely that here, inside the room, seemed to be order and dry land; there, outside, a reflection in which things wavered and vanished waterily.
>
> Some change at once went through them all, as if this had really happened, and they were all conscious of making a party together in a hollow, on an island; had their common cause against that fluidity out there. (146–7)

The table and its candles become another sort of lighthouse, with, in a sense, a similar function of allowing people to find a safe haven. The two sets of lights can be imagined reflecting each other and communicating across the water: the lighthouse blinking out in the fog, and the answering flicker of the dining-room candles. It is as if the people at dinner are on an island, just as the people at the lighthouse are; the wavering reflection of the candles in the windows even suggests that they are surrounded by water, 'that fluidity out there.'

Eight candles are lit – one for each child, presumably – and it is these that make the table a whole: 'after the first stoop the flames stood upright and drew with them into visibility the long table entire, and in the middle a yellow and purple dish of fruit' (146). The dish, integral to the wholeness of the table, is Rose's arrangement: clearly she is one of her mother's heirs. Reminiscent of the fruit bowl in Mansfield's 'Bliss,' this centrepiece is not purely aesthetic; the fruit is also meant to be eaten. But, as the meal draws to a close, Mrs Ramsay, having fed everyone, prefers its artistic aspect. It is all that is left of the dinner – her work of art – and she finds herself 'keeping guard over the dish of fruit (without realising it) jealously, hoping that nobody would touch it' (163). She refuses a pear (again, the particular reference to a pear is a reminder of 'Bliss'), not wanting to spoil the arrangement. Yet, eventually, a piece of fruit is eaten, just as the spell of wholeness will be broken, the dinner finished and the children grown.

For all this forging of community, however, the individuals are nonetheless important at the dinner, as is the complexity of their interactions and interrelationships. Thus, around the table, people are noticing each other, criticizing, admiring, attracting, envying, playing out or resisting various social roles, thinking about their own concerns, wishing they were elsewhere, or glad to be at the table. For part of the meal, William Bankes chafes at the party and thinks that 'it is a terrible waste of time ... How trifling it all is, how boring it all is ... compared with the other thing – work' (134). But the 'code of behaviour' (137), known by most of the diners, if resisted by some, restrains such impatience, like the convention that, 'when there is a strife of tongues, at some meeting ... speaking French imposes some order, some uniformity' (135–6). Thus, despite the differences, through the common customs of social decorum, the successful party develops its own common discourse or *langage*.

It is not only men who resist the communion of the table. The dinner also emphasizes the, at first, apparently irreconcilable conflict for Lily Briscoe between her self-definition as an artist – an issue which the next chapter will consider more thoroughly – and what she perceives as the very different role of a woman; for, although highly ambivalent about this ability, she is indeed capable of the same traditional woman's role in relation to men that Mrs Ramsay plays:

> There is a code of behaviour, she knew, whose seventh article (it may be) says that on occasions of this sort it behoves the woman, whatever her own occupation may be, to go to the help of the young man opposite so that he may expose and relieve the thigh bones, the ribs, of his vanity, of his urgent desire to assert himself; as indeed it is their duty, she reflected, in her old maidenly fairness, to help us, suppose the Tube were to burst into flames. (137)

Dinner not only reinforces, but generates and imposes the social code, even if an individual does not fully believe in it. In William Bankes's case, it is the code of table behaviour that is at issue; for Lily, it is a larger social code – always overseen by women – in which the two sexes are mutually responsible for the smooth functioning of society.

Since structure and balance are of utmost importance to Lily in her painting, she seems to understand intuitively that such is also true for Mrs Ramsay in her dinner party. Thus, in response to an unspoken plea from her hostess, Lily placates Charles Tansley, helps to dissipate his anger and to make him comfortable, and thus to keep him within the group: 'of course for the hundred and fiftieth time Lily Briscoe had to renounce the experiment – what happens if one is not nice to that young man there – and be nice' (139). Her identity as an artist, in fact, inspires her in her task, for once she sees the solution to her technical problem, 'her spirits rose so high at the thought of painting tomorrow that she laughed out loud at what Mr Tansley was saying. Let him talk all night if he liked it' (140). She accepts the role of assistant hostess because she knows that it is a temporary one, secondary to her real interest, which ironically permits her both to rise above the social fray, and to participate in it.

Later, in the final section of the novel, she will experience a similar conflict in relation to Mr Ramsay.[19] In the latter example, she is at first resentful of his demands, but finally, and then almost desperately, wants to accommodate his need: 'For she felt a sudden emptiness; a frustration. Her feeling had come too late; there it was ready; but he no longer needed it. He had become a very distinguished, elderly man, who had no need of her whatsoever. She felt snubbed' (231). Near the end of the novel, on the way to the lighthouse, Cam, as well, is strongly tempted to give in to her father's insistent demands and be kind to him, even if this means breaking her pact with her brother against what they see as their father's oppression. In these latter two instances, the novel shows something irresistibly appealing, even compelling, if not exactly satisfying for women in reaching out to meet a man's needs for comfort or assurance.

If Lily, like Mrs Ramsay, sees some of the interpersonal complexities of the dinner table, her perceptiveness is portrayed as a female quality. The men have their own very particular attitudes about dinner. Thus, Mr Ramsay wants the meal to move along and does not hide his annoyance when Augustus Carmichael asks for more soup:[20] 'He hated people wallowing in food ... He hated everything dragging on for hours like this' (144). Charles Tansley, like William Bankes, dislikes dinner parties; both men would prefer to be eating in their rooms – quickly and efficiently. Yet they like Mrs Ramsay, even love her, and are willing to be seduced by her feminine vision of the meal. Earlier in the day, Mr Ramsay remembers wandering happily through the countryside as a young man, with just a biscuit in his pocket, stopping at a pub for dinner. Later in the novel, after he has become an old man, his daughter Cam sees that '[n]ow he was happy, eating bread and cheese with these fishermen'; and James, 'watching him slice his cheese into thin yellow sheets with his penknife,' thinks that '[h]e would have liked to live in a cottage and lounge about in the harbour spitting with the other old men' (304). Yet, during his marriage, in the years between youth and old age, Mr Ramsay very much wants his life to be structured by his wife. He expects those separate roles, those separate spaces which some of Mansfield's more modern characters may reject or resist, yet at the same time long for: 'he liked men to work like that, and women to keep house, and sit beside sleeping children indoors, while men were drowned, out there in a storm. So James could tell, so Cam could tell' (245). Mr Ramsay may not want to see himself as a participant in the feminine and the domestic, yet he wants it to surround him.

Part of Woolf's ambivalence about the traditional female role is expressed by Mrs Ramsay herself. Perhaps, on an abstract level, 'the hostess stands for the life force, dissolving differences' (Conradi 436), but we see somewhat more complexity in the character of Mrs Ramsay: she is not merely a representative of the female 'realm ... [which] enshrines the lost wholeness of life' (Conradi 434). Although she has created the dinner and brought together the dinner guests, she questions the meaning of having done so and the significance of all that dinner represents – a manifestation of what her husband dislikes and perhaps fears as her 'pessimistic' (91) side – even while she goes through the motions, even while she believes in it all. She recognizes and even has doubts about her compulsion to get people to marry and to reproduce, and about the rightness of having herself forced life upon eight people, of having 'said to all these children, You shall go through it all' (92). At the beginning of section XVII, immediately following the description of everyone assembling, at the same time as she tries to organize everyone in the appropriate seats, Mrs Ramsay thinks, 'But what have I done with my life? ... taking her place at the head of the table and looking down the table at all the plates making white circles on it ... She had a sense of being past everything, through everything, out of everything, as she helped the soup, as if there was an eddy – there – and one could be in it, or one could be out of it, and she was out of it' (125).

This is partly a case of start-of-the-party jitters, which Clarissa Dalloway, like nearly every hostess, shares. It is also in part Mrs Ramsay's own fatigue. Just as her attention to her husband is presented as exhausting at the start of the novel, so is the task of hostess: 'They all sat separate. And the whole of the effort of merging and flowing and creating rested on her' (126). But her questioning also derives from her understanding that creating a dinner is both everything and nothing. If, as I will argue in the next chapter, dinner is a creative inspiration for Lily Briscoe, cooking or organizing dinner is a creative activity in its own right. Eating is a biological necessity; but if everything works, if all the many parts come together – from the cooking of the main course, to the serving of the soup and the placing of the guests – the dinner may create, at least temporarily, a sense of meaning or structure. This feeling of meaning would be impossible for most of the characters to put into words. But although intangible, its necessity is assumed – unconsciously by the guests and family and consciously by Mrs Ramsay.

However exhausting, Mrs Ramsay's role as creator of structure and meaning is certainly successful. Indeed, when Mrs Ramsay leaves the dining-room, Lily is aware that 'directly she went a sort of disintegration set in' (168). After dinner, Mrs Ramsay continues the same nurturing and structuring role when she goes upstairs to tuck in her two youngest children – and also to mediate between them, allay their fears, and see that each one's needs are met. She does more than say good night; she arranges their world for them, including their dreams. Afterwards, declining a walk to the beach with some of the others, she sits with her husband, not to converse, because he doesn't want to speak, but to be there with him, to form the context of his evening, as she knows he wants her to do. After the central punctuating event of dinner, she is still in charge of the widening ripples within the family, and she slowly eases the day toward the pseudo-death of sleep. In this sense, she is in charge of time, as she is of the creation, reproduction, and maintenance of life.

After Mrs Ramsay's death, the novel almost seems to have ended, to have become an afterthought or epilogue of what Mrs Ramsay started: the now-adolescent youngest children's trip to the lighthouse, under very different circumstances; Lily Briscoe finishing her painting; and, pervasively, the subcurrent of the aftermath of war. Following the poetic rendering of wartime and change in 'Time Passes,' the third section, 'The Lighthouse,' is definitely situated after the fall. Significantly, the place of mealtimes in the motherless family is different. James refers to his father's sometimes sitting silent at the head of the table throughout dinner. In the final section of the novel, it is breakfast that is emphasized, and the sandwich lunch on the way to the lighthouse. Breakfast may possibly have also been informal in Mrs Ramsay's day, but it was not described. Here, Lily's breakfast consists of drinking coffee alone at the table, watching the preparations for the trip to the lighthouse. Everything is somehow familiar to her, yet not at all the same:

> Now she was awake, at her old place at the breakfast table, but alone ... And Cam was not ready and James was not ready and Nancy had forgotten to order the sandwiches and Mr. Ramsay had lost his temper and banged out of the room ...
>
> Nancy had vanished. There he was, marching up and down the terrace in a rage. One seemed to hear doors slamming and voices calling all over the house. Now Nancy burst in, and asked, looking round the room, in a queer half dazed, half desperate way, 'What does one send to the Lighthouse?' as if she were forcing herself to do what she despaired of ever being able to do ... But this morning everything seemed so extraordinarily queer that a question like Nancy's ... opened doors in one's mind that went banging and swinging to and fro and made one keep asking, in a stupefied gape, What does one send? What does one do? Why is one sitting here, after all?
>
> Sitting alone ... among the clean cups at the long table, she felt cut off from other people, and able only to go on watching, asking, wondering. The house, the place, the morning, all seemed strangers to her. She had no attachment here, she felt, no relations with it ...' (217–18)

The architecture itself seems to miss Mrs Ramsay. The house, like the household, is disordered and disorganized, out of control. Doors bang literally and metaphorically, as if they themselves do not know where they lead. And indeed, there is no emotional, structural, or domestic centre. In all the rushing about, the dining-room is no longer the focal point. The rooms are finally just an assortment of spaces, with no inherent meaning. Nobody knows what to do. Lily wonders if she should get herself some more coffee, as Nancy wonders what to send to the lighthouse.

Yet, despite the chaotically banging doors, the house still stands, imbued with at least some remnant of Mrs Ramsay's spirit. 'Time Passes,' the middle section of *To the Lighthouse*, is about war and change, yet the house on its own, in the absence of the Ramsays and their guests, is the important presence. 'Time Passes' answers the question of what is a kitchen table – or a whole house – when no one is there. It is through the house and the down-to-earth domestic practicality of Mrs McNab that we learn about major events: the war, and the deaths of Andrew, Mrs Ramsay, and Prue, the heir to her mother's maternity. Thus a female and domestic vision is reinforced. Despite the passage of time, and the tragedy and cataclysm occurring outside its walls, the house, although somewhat decayed, is still there ten years after the Ramsays have left it. In this sense, it is *only* the domestic that, in fact, endures with any certainty.

If *To the Lighthouse* is, in part, a paean to the traditional woman, the multi-levelled importance of women's role as hostess and creator of dinner is also affirmed, if sometimes ambivalently, in the other works discussed in this chapter. In these texts, the architecture of domestic space reflects and expresses the centrality of dining and of women's role as hostess, whether played out in the private or public realm or both, and whether successful or not. What is new here is that the perspective of the hostess or provider of the meal plays a controlling role in the piece of fiction. Moreover, the importance of the work of creating a dinner or another social event is validated. In *To the Lighthouse*, the significance of dinner is rivalled only by that of art; certainly both are presented as more meaningful than Mr Ramsay's attempt to reach 'R' in his philosophy.

When she looks through the stained glass of the dining-room window at the start of 'Prelude,' Kezia sees a fragmented world, in different colours and pieces depending on the pane of glass through which she looks. The vision from this dining-room is disconcerting, as it shifts her perception of reality, yet it is magical too. This scene suggests that the opportunity for imagination still exists in the dining-room; perhaps, sometimes, for some women, this opportunity can be the saving grace. Certainly, as the next chapter will argue, for the women authors whose works are discussed here, the dining-room and the work associated with it are at the basis of their art.

7

The Art of Domesticity

Creativity and Meals

If the early twentieth-century period saw various changes in women's roles within both the family structure and traditional forms of sociability, one response to these changes was through art. The links between creativity and the serving of meals are evident in both *To the Lighthouse* and *Mrs. Dalloway*, where organizing a dinner or a party is represented as an essentially creative activity. In a larger sense, however, for both fictional characters and the writer herself, preparing the meal is an especially important metaphor for artistic work. Some early twentieth-century fiction portrays the work of the woman artist as actually emerging from women's domestic lives; in other words, despite what the common view of household drudgery might suggest, domesticity is presented not only as potentially creative in itself, not only as a metaphor for the work of art, but also as a creative inspiration for the developing artist. Specifically, in some works of fiction, the serving and preparation of dinner or other meals provide an impetus for creativity for one or more characters; even for the artist who defines herself as having moved beyond the domestic sphere, the work surrounding food may retain a profound creative resonance.

In a number of texts, including Kate Chopin's *The Awakening*, Mansfield's 'Prelude' and other New Zealand stories, and *To the Lighthouse*, the fictional woman artist struggles with, learns from, and/or is inspired by the domestic context. Mansfield presents the domestic world as part of the soil from which Kezia Burnell's artistic sensibility may grow, and Woolf's Lily Briscoe is quite conscious of her debt to the domestic. The domestic vision may also inform the content and structure of the entire work, as if, in creating a work of fiction, the writer is serving us a meal; indeed, from the reader's perspective, the novel, novella, or story may present itself as an invitation to dine. The relationship between the writer, the reader, the work of fiction, and the serving of food may be developed in a number of ways: first, the whole work may literally be about a meal or meals; second, much – even all – of the novel may be structured around the serving of meals; third, the writer may explore her own art through the relationship of the work of the fictional artist to the chores – and the delights – of preparing meals.

The relationship of the writer to meals is part of a larger question confronting the woman modernist: whether, in order to become an artist, it was more important, in Woolf's terms, to 'think back through our mothers' (*Room* 76), or to reject all that 'our mothers' stood for by killing 'the Angel in the House,' as Woolf defines her in 'Professions for Women.' Attempting to reconcile women's traditional role with modern expectations presented a dilemma that was difficult to resolve and that was at least as likely to lead to ambivalence or confusion as to synthesis. Woolf's posing these problems is, of course, symptomatic of her time and her highly self-conscious literary generation. Actively engaged in questioning their relationship to artistic as well as other traditions, modernists saw themselves as having broken with history, and, after 1914, history as having broken with them. The rupture may have been particularly profound, if not always liberating, for women, some of whom tried to brush away any lingering nostalgia for the old order, including family structures as well as social, political, and artistic institutions. If, arguably for writers of both sexes, 'one of the organising principles of the *avant-garde* writing of the period was centred on a new examination of gender, its origins and its instability,' it is certain that 'women writers were analysing themselves with great attention to discover if, and if so *how*, they were other than they had been portrayed' (Fullbrook 12).

While the notion of the 'new woman' was, in the end, reduced to a stereotype and an advertising icon (Marchand 179–88), in fact many women writers and artists, like other women, did reject their own pasts: Edith Wharton moved to France; Kathleen Beauchamp left New Zealand and changed her name; Virginia and Vanessa Stephen escaped the paternal home at Hyde Park Gate into a self-conscious bohemianism. And, in one way or another, they all rebelled against standard sexual relationships. In *To the Lighthouse*, as Margaret Homans points out (277–8), such refusals are suggested when Minta Doyle, on her way to the vacation that will lead to her engagement, leaves *Middlemarch* on the train, and later loses her grandmother's brooch during the walk on the beach when Paul Rayley proposes marriage.[1] In these complicated, if unconscious, acts of carelessness, both literary and biological fore-mothers are sacrificed[2] – in Minta's case for love and what eventually turns out to be a new kind of marriage: openly adulterous but apparently friendly.

Thus, in early twentieth-century fiction, women writers frequently depicted their women characters in the process of reinventing themselves. Such transformations may occur on the largely superficial level of their donning the social masks often worn by Mansfield's characters – an affectation reminiscent of some characters' obsession with clothes and manners in Wharton's work – as well as on a deeper, more agonizing level. The process of creating or recreating the self becomes their narrative. For example, when Janie returns home at the beginning of Hurston's *Their Eyes Were Watching God*, her overalls and her long, loose hair are grist for the town gossips. From her own perspective and that of the novel, her appearance sums up the choices which she has made in her life and the person she has become as a result. It is the story of these choices that forms the substance of the novel.

Since women have been linked to the home both historically and ideologically, the possibilities for their exploring new notions of themselves in the twentieth century would of necessity have arisen from or in reaction against the domestic centre. For a woman to create or recreate herself without somehow dealing with the domestic part of life would have been nearly impossible; even though – or, rather, because – it is a site of contention, the traditional role had to be resolved. As a result, the focus on domestic and maternal responsibilities in the work of many women writers of the early twentieth century is a crucial one: not only as a component in the presentation of character or setting, but in the exploration of creativity, in depictions of the struggle of the artist, and in the structure of the text itself. The prevalence of the two contradictory views of the mother that Woolf suggests may result in a textual ambivalence or ambiguity reflected in the portrayal of various aspects of the domestic, but especially in the serving of dinner, one of the most obvious responsibilities of a mother, as of women in general. As the traditional role is transformed into art, the central domestic activities of preparing, serving, sharing, or providing a meal become key to the very essence of various works of fiction. The potential for transforming this everyday work into art is one way in which it may have been possible to 'think back through our mothers if we are women' (*Room* 76), and at the same time to reject the role of 'Angel in the House.'

A Domestic Language

The domestic content or orientation of women's writing may have been one factor – among others, to be sure, both socio-economic and ideological – in the ongoing exclusion of women from literary circles and publications. Homans's analysis that '[t]he literal is ambiguous for women writers because women's potentially more positive view of it collides with its devaluation by our culture' (*Bearing the Word* 5) is consistent with Huyssen's assertion that 'the repudiation of *Trivial-literatur* has always been one of the constitutive features of a modernist aesthetic intent on distancing itself and its products from the trivialities and banalities of everyday life' (47). In other words, critical definitions of male modernism may have excluded women's writing from the realm of high art in part, at least, because of what content was defined as acceptable for art. Indeed, Huyssen sees the 'avoid[ance of] any contamination with mass culture and with the signifying systems of everyday life' (54) as one of the basic characteristics of the mainstream modernist movement. The everyday, the literal, the domestic – all of these become associated with a second-rate art. Woolf concurs that this critical bias in constructing literary canons has been a problem for women writers: 'it is the masculine values that prevail ... This is an important book, the critic assumes, because it deals with war. This is an insignificant book because it deals with the feelings of women in a drawing-room. A scene in a battlefield is more important than a scene in a shop – everywhere and much more subtly the difference of value persists' (*Room* 74).

Certainly Joyce, Eliot, and other male modernists portray ordinary domestic life, and, in so doing, validate the everyday experience of ordinary people as the subject of art. However, women modernist writers who closely link the essence of their work with women's common domestic roles, particularly those centred around the dinner table, bring another perspective. The fact that the gender of the writer and the server of the meal is the same adds an important dimension to their fiction. In particular, such literary works demonstrate not only the importance of women's relationship with meals but also the peculiarly creative power of this relationship. In books where dinners are central, our position as readers at the table will be very important to our experience of the fictional world.

The process of cooking may organize a literary work or function as a metaphor for the work. But more than this, the preparing, serving, and eating of a meal, as well as the life surrounding and defined by these activities, may be the entire subject or the most crucial component of a piece of fiction. The notion of the text as meal is a notable, if not exactly frequent, literary conceit. In such a case, where the text is the meal and the meal the text, the writer herself becomes the server of both the book and the dinner. The metaphor of the novel as meal can be extended to suggest that the tasks of the writer, like those of the cook, require her to look both inward and outward. Cooking, like writing, may be a solitary, introspective act, based on a personal relationship with one's tools, ideas, and raw materials. But usually one cooks or writes for others as well as for oneself; ultimately as the novel is published, circulated, and read, and the meal served and eaten. Further, like literature, cooking transforms both its raw materials and, potentially, people's lives. In such texts, where dinners provide the structure or the content of the work, the social, cultural, and spiritual importance of meals discussed in chapter 1 is evident. Both a creative and a nurturing act, the provision of a meal is a – perhaps *the* – crucial moment in the fictional world and, moreover, key to the structure of the work of fiction itself. To return to a mid-twentieth-century example mentioned in an earlier chapter, the cook in Dinesen's 'Babette's Feast' emerges as not only the central figure, but, in a sense, the author of the work, as her dinner transforms the small town and the relationships among its people, linking them with the larger world and with the historical events that she has experienced. The dishes she prepares have spiritual, even quasi-magical qualities. Dinner also becomes key in expressing emotional life, and Babette the great artist who can bring emotions to the fore. Although it takes place at the end of the story, the dinner is the subject as well as the culmination of the work; such is its power that it defines the work of fiction, just as it transforms and redefines the entire context of the small Norwegian town and the lives of the villagers.[3]

Like Water for Chocolate, a recent novel by Laura Esquivel, is a good example of a work of fiction which is completely about meals. Not only is the book organized around meals, its *subject* is the preparation and serving of a series of meals. These dinners are completely intertwined with the lives of the family whose history the novel traces; the preparation and consumption of food are not merely parallel but integral to the other events of the novel. Meals resonate in ways which can only be described as magical and miraculous, as well as pleasurable. Moreover, the reader is drawn into the creative process of the work: each chapter begins with a recipe for a dish which will be central to that chapter, as if inviting the reader to participate in the novel by cooking its meals herself.

Even where the whole work is not completely about food, a meal or meals may be so crucial to the novel both structurally and thematically that the reader may feel herself present at the writer's table. For instance, in Amy Tan's *The Joy Luck Club*, the reader participates in the *mah jong* parties hosted by a group of aging Chinese-American women. The food served at these social events is not only a device for recounting the stories of the four women and their families, it is a key factor in the friendship among the women and defines their link with Chinese history and culture. Moreover, the food served throughout the novel, in every generation, illuminates both the relationships between individual mothers and daughters and the passing down of female tradition throughout history.

In the modernist period, we have seen that the party – the public expression of the more intimate celebratory meal at its centre – which takes place at the end of *Mrs. Dalloway* structures and informs not only the activities of Clarissa's day, as she prepares for the party, but all the events of the novel, even, in a sense, for Septimus and Rezia Warren Smith, who are unaware of the gathering. Another modernist work, Zora Neale Hurston's *Their Eyes Were Watching God*, is structured entirely as an after-dinner tale, and offers a particularly good example of the traditional relationship between eating and storytelling. The novel opens with what feels like a ritual dinner and a ritual tale. Meals are mentioned in passing throughout the novel as part of Janie's everyday life and, especially, as descriptors of men's and women's roles and indications of degrees of closeness and conviviality. But the meal at the start of the novel is particularly significant as both the introduction to and the culmination of Janie's story. After her third husband's death, and having returned home from her adventures with him, Janie tells her story to her friend Pheoby, and therefore to the reader, only after Pheoby has made dinner for her and she has eaten. It is a reciprocal relationship. Just as a good eater can inspire a good cook, so 'Pheoby's hungry listening helped Janie to tell her story' (23). Indeed the need to tell one's story is presented as second only to the need for food, and the desire to listen as a natural human impulse: 'They sat there in the fresh young darkness close together. Pheoby eager to feel and do through Janie, but hating to show her zest for fear it might be thought mere curiosity. Janie full of that oldest human longing – self-revelation.

Pheoby held her tongue for a long time, but she couldn't help moving her feet. So Janie spoke' (18). The reader identifies with the server of dinner in this case; like Pheoby, we are impatient to hear Janie's story. Once Janie begins to speak, however, the roles are reversed, and it is as if she is serving *us* a rich meal.

Janie's narrative makes up the entire novel, except for the first chapter and part of the final chapter. Yet only the first two pages of her story are written in the first person. After this, the novel slips into an omniscient narration; in effect, Janie becomes the novelist, her story transformed into the novel. It is particularly appropriate that the activities of cooking and eating dinner introduce her tale, first of all because Janie's life is largely measured by her role as wife in three marriages, each of which represents a further step both in her maturity and in Hurston's development of her character. In a sense, her life has been a multi-course meal; her most recent marriage to the aptly named 'Tea Cake' suggests the dessert. On the day of her return, instead of playing the roles of cook and server herself, she eats a dinner that has been cooked for her, an appropriate consummation to her experiences as a wife. Seen from another perspective, Pheoby's motherly kindness rounds out the story that begins with the loss of Janie's own mother. In any case, Pheoby is the catalyst, for the novel comes to be solely as the result of her serving dinner; she provides not only the meal, but the occasion and the audience for the narrative.

A critical portrayal of domestic experience from the woman's point of view, then, is not only a major component of the art of many modernist women writers, but the apparent inspiration for their work; this is perhaps the most important way in which such writers might be perceived as thinking through their mothers. It is important to recognize that the role of language in this transformation of everyday experience into art is not neutral; in some works a distinctive discourse arises from the portrayal of domestic life, not only proposing an enhanced appreciation of everyday experience, but creating a crucial link between domesticity and art. Virginia Woolf argues that, even in the nineteenth century, women novelists were alienated from standard syntax: '[p]erhaps the first thing [they] would find, setting pen to paper, was that there was no common sentence ready for [their] use' (*Room* 76). She posits further that this sense of alienation extends to literary forms: if '[t]here is no reason to think that the form of the epic or of the poetic play suits a woman ... who shall say that even now "the novel" ... is rightly shaped for her use?' (*Room* 77). Perhaps one answer to Woolf's comments is that the creative energy of the kitchen and the rest of the domestic world might animate a work of fiction, feminizing literary language and form to better fit women writers – and, perhaps, readers.

Certainly, an experimental approach to language formed part of the questioning of identity and tradition for many modernist writers of both sexes: new ideas called for a new language in which to express them, and the overturning of traditional forms was part of what Kaplan calls modernism's defining 'revolt against Victorian fathers' (*KM and the Origins* 6). However, as Woolf argues, the issue of language may have been particularly complex for women writers, whose relationship to the modernist break with literary traditions was quite different from that of men. Thus, even from a feminist perspective, there might be some validity in traditional critics' having excluded women – other than, usually, Woolf – from the modernist canon. Rather than arguing for women's inclusion, Shari Benstock, for one, suggests a parallel and perhaps ambivalent female modernism: '[W]omen writers of this period and place both mimed and undermined Modernist principles, and we have yet to discover whether the "Modernist Mime" constituted an enforcement of the patriarchal poetic law or a skillful subversion of it' ('Expatriate Modernism' 29).[4]

The task of defining a separate category of female modernism is, if possible, even more slippery than that of defining modernism in general.[5] But however they are classified, a number of women writing at the turn of the twentieth century certainly strove to tear down the edifice of traditional fiction, playing with both language and form in very innovative ways. Although there are problems implicit in an essentialist definition of women's language, such a language has sometimes been seen as in itself the most important aspect of female modernism. Thus, Clare Hanson points to those writers 'who, seeing language as inherently oppressive and male-centred, aimed to challenge it, and who saw the forms of *fiction* too as potentially restrictive and gender-bound. The work of [May] Sinclair, [Dorothy] Richardson and Gertrude Stein ... offers a particularly rich field for the study of the relations between gender, language and literary form' (18). One way of 'thinking through our mothers,' then, might have been to transform literary discourse by discovering and using their language and, in the process, redefining form as well. But, although modernist women writers certainly experimented, it is difficult to state that they were actively engaged in writing their mothers' language. If an essential feminine language exists, its literary application may be problematic; as usually defined, the maternal language is preverbal, certainly not written.[6] In fact, as Homans observes, the very notion of female language may be in conflict with the cultural definition of literature:

> [W]omen's memory of and wish to reproduce the nonsymbolic language they shared with the mother takes the form of a literal language that looks like ... an embrace of the very position to which male theory condemns the feminine. These differing versions of – or differing valuations of – the literal will collide with each other and especially with women writers' wish to write in the symbolic order where literature has traditionally taken place. (*Bearing the Word* 32)

An attempt to rediscover and use such language could marginalize the woman writer even more, thus upholding the status quo of the literary establishment. Homans notes (*Bearing the Word* 22) that the historical sanctions against women writing have in fact made women more likely to try to write as men, as evidenced by the nineteenth-century practice of adopting a male *nom de plume*.

It is not surprising, then, that in *A Room of One's Own*, as Rosenman points out (103–7), Woolf's position on female language is contradictory: she seems loath to abandon the traditional completely, and, although she calls for the development of a 'feminine' language, she also vacillates on the question of whether it is desirable to use such language, and even on whether it exists.[7] If Lytton Strachey calls Woolf 'the inventor of a new prose style, & the creator of a new version of the sentence' (McNeillie 4:xvi), Hanson notes (18) that both Woolf and Mansfield were at best ambivalent about Dorothy Richardson's quite conscious attempts to write a new women's language. In Woolf's 1919 *TLS* review of *The Tunnel*, for instance, she seems uncomfortable with Richardson's experiment, if reluctant to criticize it directly.[8] However, Woolf finally concludes that '*The Tunnel* is better in its failure than most books in their success' (3:12), and, in a 1923 review of Richardson's *Revolving Lights*, she seems to appreciate Richardson's having 'invented, or, if she has not invented, developed and applied to her own uses, a sentence which we might call the psychological sentence of the feminine gender. It is of a more elastic fibre than the old, capable of stretching to the extreme, of suspending the frailest particles, of enveloping the vaguest shapes' (3:367).

If female language is difficult to define, a feminine style might be more plausible. Some of Mansfield's innovative techniques in the short story genre have been categorized as female by a number of critics.[9] Her use of ellipses, for instance – which, in different contexts, might suggest an infinite openness, a refusal to state or acknowledge something, a quality of uncertainty, or a lack of concentration characterized by thoughts lost or trailing off – has been viewed as feminine. She avoids a solidly defined subject position, frequently using a shifting narrator and a generally fluid narrative perspective – the stylistic counterparts of her conception 'of self as multiple, shifting, non-consecutive, without essence, and perhaps unknowable' (Fullbrook 17).[10] Mansfield's work had a great influence on Woolf's own stylistic and formal innovations; in the end, however, to make a strong argument that such technical experiments are by definition 'female' would be difficult and perhaps of little value.

In describing the discourse of characters, on the other hand, the notion of feminine language is very useful, and a number of writers have tried to capture it. Homans makes a cogent argument for the occurrence of such language in *To the Lighthouse*, particularly in the bedtime conversation between Cam and her mother. She points out that this language is quite different from that used by Mrs Ramsay with her son:

> ... there is no gap at all between Mrs. Ramsay's words and her bodily presence for her daughter ... This is what I mean by a literal language shared between mother and daughter: a language of presence in which the presence or absence of referents in the ordinary sense is quite unimportant ... Woolf defines as distinctly female the pleasure Cam and Mrs Ramsay share in the rhythm and feel of words, which ... derives from and constitutes a myth of a daughter's never having lost the literal language she shared with her mother. (*Bearing the Word* 17–18)

Mrs Ramsay's facility at non-verbal communication – and Woolf insists upon this quality – is related to this ease with 'literal language.' We see a particularly good example of it at the dinner table, where, in her function as hostess, Mrs Ramsay conveys to her husband her disapproval of his impatience with Augustus Carmichael and to Lily a plea for her help with Charles Tansley. (Another version of female communication of silent but strong disapproval – in this case expressed by the guests – occurs at the farewell dinner party for Ellen Olenska in *The Age of Innocence*.) Later, with her husband in his study, she silently responds to his need, and communicates to him her understanding, without his being fully conscious of her doing so. Gayatri Spivak sees this facility as a significant characteristic not only of her public life as a hostess, wife, and mother, but of her personal, interior life as well: 'she relies little on language, especially language in marriage. Her privileged moments ... are when words disappear, or when the inanimate world reflects her' (32). Although, as Spivak notes, there is a disjunction between the sometimes pessimistic inner person and the woman who gives comfort and love apparently unstintingly to her family and guests, the deep-seated suspicion of language is a characteristic of both.

Other writers also portray very acutely a particular verbal and non-verbal interaction between women that is quite different from the usual verbal exchange among men or between men and women: 'a communal voice that erases female boundaries' (Moran, *Word of Mouth* 106). Specifically, I have already called attention to interactions between Linda and Mrs Fairfield in 'Prelude,' and among Linda, Mrs Fairfield, and Beryl in 'At the Bay.' In Chopin's *The Awakening* there are some scenes in which communication between Adèle Ratignolle and Edna Pontellier goes beyond words to a level of shared understanding that the text itself acknowledges as female. The same is true of the companionship between Janie and Pheoby in the opening and closing sections of *Their Eyes Were Watching God*. Patricia Moran sees this language as powerful. Writing about Mansfield, she refers to 'the singularity and potential subversiveness of a female language that inheres, not in meaning, but in sound' (*Word of Mouth* 106). It is worth noting that in each of the above cases, this communication occurs in a domestic setting: while minding children, sewing, doing housework, cooking, or eating together. If a particular feminine language exists within a text, then, it often describes and arises from women's shared domestic experiences.

The most striking example of a modernist work in which a new language arises from the domestic realm is Gertrude Stein's *Tender Buttons*. It is worth taking note of this work, at least briefly, even though, since it is usually classified as a poem rather than a piece of fiction, it is somewhat outside the purview of this study. Shari Benstock sees Stein's deconstruction of both gender and language as so radical that it excludes her work as a good example of 'feminine writing' (*Textualizing the Feminine* xxvii). However, this comment only serves to point out a problem in the project of setting narrow definitions of 'women's writing.' *Tender Buttons* is perhaps the purest example of a text which is presented as a meal. One section of the poem is entirely concerned with food. This section presents a meal, or, rather, several meals, as Stein cooks and serves a bubbling, if sometimes odd, assortment of dishes. The experimental nature of Stein's language is tempered by her subject matter: the most prosaic of foodstuffs, along with other ordinary items, are presented in a highly associative, imaginative, even bizarre way. Despite the sometimes startling incongruity of the individual images and juxtapositions of images – 'egg ear nuts' (55) is one of many possible examples, chosen randomly and impossible to read out of context – the subject matter of the piece keeps it grounded in the everyday and lends it a warm, social, welcoming nature. The interaction between language and food transforms both.

The poem celebrates not only the experience of eating, but also that of preparing and even naming items of food. Although the piece opens with a list of the food items, meals, and associated words which will become the sections of the poem, the food in *Tender Buttons* is not merely a shopping list or inventory; certainly not raw, it is worked, prepared, served. The section entitled 'Roastbeef,' for instance, seems to explore every aspect of its subject. The poem is very domestic in its loving attention to food, yet at the same time questions traditional domestic organization. Margueritte Murphy argues that Stein uses the language and form of contemporary cookbooks, but then overturns the 'authoritative discourse of the conventional woman's world' (389).[11] In fact, the poem challenges the trend toward culinary homogeneity. No recipes are given, no methods or procedures for cooking prescribed. Standard discourse is undermined: normal sentence structure is absent, or if present, leads in surprising directions; words are put together for their sound as much as for their meaning; usual definitions of logic are questioned. The writing is open-ended; although some of the references are private, the reader is invited to succumb to the resonance of the language and participate in and enjoy the poem – and the meals – in her own way, along with the poet. Sometimes meals are described, and sometimes they emerge from the contiguity of various dishes, but the arrangement of courses is not fully developed and there are odd combinations. Much of the sorting out of the various foods, recipes, and dishes is left up to the reader, as if she or he is a participating cook. Pleasure, surprise, and delight seem to be the motivating factors in putting food together and in suggesting the relationships of food to other everyday objects. Indeed, every aspect of food is relished fully – including the sound of the names of foods. The feel of the words on the tongue replicates the enjoyment of actually eating. The pleasures of language and of eating are blended, as the poem is read and devoured.

Thus, this piece of writing is not only a celebration of the domestic, but a liberation of the domestic into a new manifestation. And this joy in food is – literally – presented as art. Both meals and language are deconstructed and reconstructed along other lines. *Tender Buttons* is a meal which breaks free of domestic constraints at the same time as the poem's attention to food makes it highly domestic; the piece calls into question normal approaches to language and standard literary form through its precise focus on words and its contagious enjoyment of language. *Tender Buttons* makes it seem eminently possible for a woman to be both a cook and a writer.

The Structure of Dinners in *The Awakening*

Although with quite a different effect, dinners also provide a structure for Kate Chopin's *The Awakening*, an early or proto-modernist work. The novella is structured by a series of meals, a framework which, as in Hurston's novel, is particularly appropriate to the life story of a married woman. However, in this work we are kept at a distance; the reader is never allowed to sit and enjoy these meals, as they remain problematic both for the novel and for Edna Pontellier, the main character. The significance of the series of dinners in the novella is multi-layered. Dinners punctuate the plot, allowing revelations, marking turning points, and opening new phases in the novella. Upon this structure is also built an examination of many issues frequently associated with food and meals in literature: family and social life, gender roles, pleasure and the erotic, boredom and routine. Dinners also narrate Edna's attempt to find a creative voice. Her struggle to radically change her life – to replace the domestic role imposed by her marriage with a personal and domestic life of her own choosing – is parallelled by her relationship to art: painting, music, and, implicit in her redefinition of herself, story-telling.

The structuring function of dinners is particularly important in this novella because of the nature of Edna's crisis: in marking the progress of her 'awakening,' the recurring dinners not only form a scaffolding for the novella, but at the same time represent the social structure within which the novel takes place. Neither the text nor the writer can escape or transcend this confining structure. Thus Edna fails to throw off her fetters completely, her story ultimately succumbs to societal expectations, the novella yields to conventional morality, and her rebellion leads to death.[12]

In this turn-of-the-century work, then, both the nature and the outcome of the link between the domestic and the creative are particularly problematic. The novella demonstrates the difficulties faced by women in finding a language and a way of reconciling their creative potential with their social roles and personal history; but, significantly, the difficulties are not resolved. Marianne DeKoven, who explicitly defines *The Awakening* as an early modernist work, argues that it must be understood as functioning in terms of a 'double modernist structure' ('Gendered Doubleness' 24), a structure, on several levels, of often contradictory doubles. For instance, the opening scene is punctuated by two caged birds – a parrot and a mockingbird – on either side of a door; throughout the novella, the sea is consistently presented as both soothing and dangerous; and, most important, both Chopin and Edna see her liberation from marriage as ultimately double-edged. Because it is the negative that prevails, Edna's potential creativity is never really developed and her freedom is self-destructive. The novella's tentative vision of incipient links between domesticity and creativity remains nebulous; if, as I will argue, *To the Lighthouse* leaves the reader hoping for a reconciliation between the two, they ultimately remain antagonistic here.

Meals are also presented in two ways in the novella: as beckoning, erotic, sensual, liberating, and as a part of the patriarchal structure which Edna is trying to escape. In other words, the physical enjoyment of eating has been distorted by the social and domestic structure; thus, for a woman, in this novella, dinner usually means service, not pleasure. No alternative structure to the patriarchal is seriously suggested, although one is hinted at in the community of women on Grand Isle. But this community is a temporary one, limited to the summer months. Moreover, its very existence is determined by the men back in the city: it is amorphous and, by unstated agreement as well as economic and social necessity, would be untenable on its own without the sanction of the men. Significantly, the weekday society of Grand Isle is defined by the absent husbands as asexual, although certainly sensual. The housewife is not supposed to be sexual: glowing and radiant, perhaps, like Edna's friend Adèle, and attractive to men, but not erotic in any conscious or assertive way.[13] The women's flirtations with Robert Lebrun and, presumably, other unattached men who for some reason temporarily inhabit the borderlands of the male world are innocuous for all who accept the implicit constraints of the assumed structure. Thus, for the husbands at work in the city during the week, the women, children, and occasional young man on their own at Grand Isle do not represent a threat, but provide a sort of voyeuristic fantasy.

For Edna, both freedom and confinement are expressed in terms of dinner. Dinners may symbolize the erotic or represent housewifely duties, the two poles between which she is caught. At various times, Edna is shown to take a real sensuous pleasure in eating, but she rejects the female roles associated with food. Although women are generally responsible for seeing that the meals are served, they are not truly in control of dinners, which, throughout most of the novella, are presented as an integral part of the patriarchal mode. Thus, Edna's role as a wife is frequently expressed in terms of food. Her husband eats at the club when he is annoyed with her. On the other hand, he provides her with treats as if she were a spoiled child. During the women's vacation at Grand Isle, he sends her boxes 'filled with *friandises*, with luscious and toothsome bits – the finest of fruits, *pâtés*, a rare bottle or two, delicious syrups, and bonbons in abundance ... the ladies, selecting with dainty and discriminating fingers and a little greedily, all declared that Mr. Pontellier was the best husband in the world. Mrs Pontellier was forced to admit that she knew of none better' (9). These are all treats, luxuries, trifles – nothing particularly nourishing – as if rewards for her service as a wife. Moreover, Léonce's gifts of food are a public statement; appreciated by all the other women, his gifts demonstrate to them his qualities as a man and a husband. The presents also hint at a patronizing quality in Léonce's relationship with his wife, and a superficiality in his perception of what he needs to do to make her happy. In fact, the passage quoted above suggests that Edna has some doubts about her husband and his offerings of food. '[T]he ladies' seem to appreciate Léonce's gifts more than she does; she is, indeed, 'forced' to indicate her esteem for him.

Although she does what is required, Edna holds herself back from fully defining herself as a wife and a mother in the way that her peers do. We are told that, despite her apparently conventional marriage, Edna is not 'a mother-woman ... They were women who idolized their children, worshiped their husbands, and esteemed it a holy privilege to efface themselves as individuals and grow wings as ministering angels' (10). Similarly, the fact that she is often late to lunch and dinner at Grand Isle suggests a rebellion against the traditional meal-imposed structures of the day. It seems as though food, or more likely the rituals and structure surrounding food, are irrelevant to her. This habit of lateness, this hanging back, fits with her desultory manner, her languidness, what Dr Mandelet later describes as her 'listless' quality (92). But her apparent apathy, her lack of energy or interest in life, only emerges when she is in her role as a wife. When she falls asleep during an outing to another island, she awakens as if it is a whole new world and 'our people from Grand Isle disappear[ed] from the earth' (49). Preceded by what Gilbert and Gubar (2:106) point out is a ceremonial partaking of bread and wine, the meal she shares with Robert Lebrun at the Chênière is the first meal in the novella which feels real to the reader. If not described in great detail, it is nonetheless very tangible, and Edna eats it with pleasure:

> [Robert] stirred the smoldering ashes till the broiled fowl began to sizzle afresh. He served her with no mean repast, dripping the coffee anew and sharing it with her. Madame Antoine had cooked little else than the mullets, but while Edna slept Robert had foraged the island. He was childishly gratified to discover her appetite, and to see the relish with which she ate the food which he had procured for her. (50)

While Edna is vacationing at Grand Isle, she is not responsible for dinners; indeed, in the case of the dinner with Robert, *he* serves *her*. But back in the city, she returns to her usual duties as Léonce's wife. When Léonce discovers, at dinner one evening, that Edna has not been home to receive callers, he responds by complaining about the meal and criticizing her for not adequately supervising the cook. The roles of society hostess and domestic meal-provider are linked, and she is not being a good wife in either sense:

> She was somewhat familiar with such scenes. They had often made her very unhappy. On a few previous occasions she had been completely deprived of any desire to finish her dinner. Sometimes she had gone into the kitchen to administer a tardy rebuke to the cook. Once she went to her room and studied the cookbook during an entire evening, finally writing out a menu for the week ...
> But that evening Edna finished her dinner alone, with forced deliberation. (68)

Although this recurrent scene is an old one, Edna's reaction to it is new. Criticized as the server of food, she has begun to focus on herself as an eater. Eating has begun to be linked to Edna's 'awakening.'

Edna's growing aversion to marriage gives her a new perspective when she dines with the Ratignolles. Although 'it was ... a delicious repast, simple, choice, and in every way satisfying' (74), the dinner depresses her, perhaps, as DeKoven suggests, because of her friend's deferring to her husband throughout the meal (*Rich and Strange* 144). In any case, '[t]he little glimpse of domestic harmony which had been offered her, gave her no regret, no longing. It was not a condition of life which fitted her, and she could see in it but an appalling and hopeless ennui' (74). Shortly afterwards, the status of dinner as a patriarchal institution is made particularly clear at the meal where Edna is confronted by all the male authorities in her life: her husband, her father, and the old family doctor whom Léonce has consulted about Edna and invited in order that he might observe her.

If Edna rejects these particular manifestations of dinner, however, she does not reject food itself. In fact, Edna's enjoyment of eating seems to grow. When Léonce goes to New York on business, Edna takes pleasure in dining alone:

> The candelabra, with a few candles in the centre of the table, gave all the light she needed. Outside the circle of light in which she sat, the large dining-room looked solemn and shadowy. The cook, placed upon her mettle, served a delicious repast – a luscious tenderloin broiled *à point*. The wine tasted good; the *marron glacé* seemed to be just what she wanted. It was so pleasant, too, to dine in a comfortable *peignoir*. (96)

Edna's enjoyment of the meal is quickened by a feeling of independence and the absence of the usual domestic habits and formalities. It is also connected with sexual attraction. A few pages later Edna is again described as hungry: after a dinner at the Highcamps with Alcée Arobin, she has a midnight snack of cheese, crackers, and a beer. Raiding the kitchen was not something she would have done as the wife of Léonce Pontellier; as Edna, she has an appetite – for what, she hardly knows as yet, but she 'regretted that she had not made Arobin stay a half hour to talk over the horses with her. She counted the money she had won. But there was nothing else to do, so she went to bed, and tossed there for hours in a sort of monotonous agitation' (99).

If part of Edna's hoped-for liberation is expressed as sexual desire, another part manifests itself in her interest in the arts. The occasions of music and storytelling which run through the text always evoke passionate emotion in her. Her falling in love with Robert is associated with feelings aroused by Mademoiselle Reisz's concerts at Grand Isle;[14]

this association continues in New Orleans, where she visits Mademoiselle Reisz's apartment, after the first time, largely to hear news of Robert. The storytelling sequence following the dinner with her husband, her father, and Dr Mandelet demonstrates the connection for her between emotion and imagination. Under the 'beneficent influence' (92) of dinner, claret, and champagne, each person tells a story, like Janie in *Their Eyes Were Watching God*, following the tradition of after-dinner storytelling. Léonce Pontellier reminisces about his youth, and the colonel about his war experiences; the doctor relates a rather moralistic anecdote about a woman who almost leaves her marriage. Edna's tale of runaway lovers is not very original, yet 'every glowing word seemed real to those who listened' (93). Very different in its intensity and evocativeness from the stories told by the men, Edna's narrative blurs the line between truth and fiction. For the men, telling a story means reminiscing, recounting history, or moralizing; for Edna, it invokes emotional truth.

However, Edna's attempt at rebirth is expressed particularly in her painting. When she gives up receiving visitors on Tuesdays, she paints. As a hobby, painting is not unusual; it seems to be normal in the novella for housewives to dabble in the arts, but only as long as they do not take the pastime too seriously. Thus, Léonce says, 'It seems to me the utmost folly for a woman at the head of a household, and the mother of children, to spend in an atelier days which would be better employed contriving for the comfort of her family ... There's Madame Ratignolle; because she keeps up her music, she doesn't let everything else go to chaos' (75). It is easy to dismiss Edna's painting as a hobby; indeed, the novella itself seems to share the general view of housewife-artists with little real talent. But for a time, Edna takes her painting quite seriously. Although highly critical of her own work, she sells a few sketches. Indeed, a dealer, whom she tells that she might be going abroad to study in Paris, finds her work good enough to commission 'some Parisian studies to reach him in time for the holiday trade in December' (137).

Edna's attraction to the artist's life is at the basis of her friendship with Mademoiselle Reisz. The poverty-stricken spinster pianist explicitly links art with liberation from the quotidian, telling Edna that 'to succeed, the artist must have the courageous soul ... The brave soul. The soul that dares and defies' (84). Her advice is similar for the rebel: after Edna has formed the plan of leaving her husband's house and has admitted her love for Robert, Mademoiselle Reisz cautions her, 'The bird that would soar above the level plain of tradition and prejudice must have strong wings' (110). But liberation can become deprivation;

Mademoiselle Reisz herself apparently leads a very earth-bound life, partly described in terms of her eating habits. Her apartment is 'cheerless and dingy' (104), and furnished with 'a gasoline stove on which she cooked her meals when disinclined to descend to the neighboring restaurant' (81). Her feeling of deprivation and the lack of pleasure in her life are evident at Edna's party, where '[a]ll her interest seemed to be centered upon the delicacies placed before her' (117). Mademoiselle Reisz is at the other feminine pole from Madame Ratignolle, the good and fecund wife, whose interest in music remains within acceptable bounds. But she is also stunted, in her own way, and her life is at least as unappealing as that of a wife. Edna's two friends represent the essence of her dilemma: in the society of the novella, both positions – that of the artist and that of the housewife – would seem to require giving up too much. Synthesis of the two is apparently impossible.

All the previous meals in the novella are really *hors d'oeuvres* leading up to the dinner which marks Edna's leaving the house she has shared with her husband for a small house around the corner and an attempt to create a domestic centre that is her own, a *ménage à une*. In this case, serving the meal is not a wifely duty. Rather, the dinner party is a celebration of herself as an independent woman: it is completely *her* party, in honour of her moving and, appropriately, of her birthday as well. Everything is rich and perfect. As the hostess, Edna holds herself regally and feels the full power of that role. No longer playing the hostess for her husband, Edna has created the party for herself and for the people she has chosen to invite; she has assembled everyone who is important in her life, with the notable exception of Adèle Ratignolle, who is nearing the end of a pregnancy.

The dinner is characterized by the kind of high-society trappings that Undine Spragg so envied in the opening chapters of *The Custom of the Country*. The dishes Edna serves are not emphasized, but the table itself is described in opulent terms:

> There was something extremely gorgeous about the appearance of the table, an effect of splendor conveyed by a cover of pale yellow satin under strips of lace-work. There were wax candles, in massive brass candelabra, burning softly under yellow silk shades; full, fragrant roses, yellow and red, abounded. There were silver and gold, as she had said there would be, and crystal which glittered like the gems which the women wore. (115)

But although the format of the dinner is such as would generally announce one's having 'arrived' in society, in fact, the meal rather marks Edna's farewell to social institutions. If not a parody, the party is certainly an ironical and critical reflection of itself, for, in this celebration, Edna is, in fact, rejecting that life in which such parties can occur. Indeed, she intends to leave for her own rented house directly after dinner.

In its visual detail, the description of the dinner table suggests a painting, emphasizing not only Edna's interest in that art, but her attempt to change her life creatively. Some of the guests join in the aesthetic aspect of the evening. Mrs Highcamp places on Victor Lebrun's head a multi-coloured garland of roses, which, '[a]s if a magician's wand had touched him ... transformed him into a vision of Oriental beauty' (118). When she also drapes him in silk, he lapses into silence and becomes a 'picture' (119), startlingly beautiful to the others. But, verging on the decadent and orgiastic, this image is not what Edna seeks to create. Breaking a glass in her agitation, and the spell of the dinner as well, she finally makes him stop posing when he begins to sing his brother's song, 'Ah, si tu savais ...' (120), because it seems to parody love, and, perhaps, to mock her feelings for Robert. As Gilbert and Gubar note about the after-dinner story Edna told earlier in the novella, Victor's posing 'betrays desire into the banalities of conventional romance' (2:108).

If a piece of fiction can be presented as a dinner, Gilbert and Gubar see Edna's dinner as, itself, a narration, and, moreover, 'the best, the most authentically self-defining, "story" she can tell' (2:108). But it is a complicated story, and defines her life in ways that she does not intend. Although the dinner is a symbolic turning point and is meant to be a celebration, ironically, it also emphasizes her close connections with the men of her family. The party starts with a cocktail invented by her father, and in her hair she wears diamonds sent from New York as a birthday gift by her husband, who has scrambled to concoct a public excuse for her moving out of his house. The party – extravagant, rich, on the verge of ostentatious – must also represent the final expenditure of her husband's money. Given her plans to support herself on a combination of an inheritance from her mother 'which [her] father sends [her] by driblets' (105), race winnings, and the sale of sketches, she will likely not entertain on this scale again. Indeed, Gilbert and Gubar also see this meal as a 'Last Supper' before her eventual betrayal and 'inevitable crucifixion' (2:108).

As the hostess, Edna is described as 'the one who rules, who looks on, who stands alone' (118), and this ultimate loneliness is the price of being the queen. Thus the dinner party is followed by depression, a feeling of anticlimax: once having declared herself free, what is she really free to do? Even the little house does not liberate her completely. Certainly, part of Edna's struggle is to be free sexually, but in relationships with men she is placed, if not exactly back in her old situation, then in other uncomfortable positions. Thus, even though she feels 'disheartened' (121) and wishes to be left alone, she allows Arobin to seduce her on the night of the party. Small dinners punctuate her further encounters with both Arobin and Robert, but, in general, the meals themselves are merely backdrops. Chapter 34, when Robert comes to dinner, begins 'The dining room was very small' (133), implying intimacy, but potentially claustrophobia as well. Chopin calls it a 'dinner of ordinary quality, except for the few delicacies which [Edna] had sent out to purchase' (133). Robert talks of women he knew in Mexico, but makes it clear, by departing when Arobin arrives, that the double standard applies. Arobin also eats in her dining room (138) a few days later, but her affair with him is fast becoming a symptom of her growing cynicism: 'There was no despondency when she fell asleep that night; nor was there hope when she awoke in the morning' (138).

However, Edna's chance meeting with Robert in a suburban garden café where she is eating dinner recalls the day at the Chênière Caminada. Away from the city, nearly secret, walled but outdoors, the café suggests safety and simplicity, as well as what Harbison calls 'a first notion of a garden ... a closed place set apart, protected, privileged, with different rules and styles of life inside and outside' (5–6). Presided over by Catiche, a 'mulatresse' (138), who, like her old cat, naps in the fresh air when she is not preparing fresh, simple food, it also seems like female territory, Edna's territory: 'I almost live here' (139), she says. Her encounter with Robert – the first in some time and awkward at the start – leads to an exchange of kisses and confidences when they return to the 'pigeon-house.' But if Edna's love for Robert is part of her radical attempt at liberation from marriage, Robert's love is highly conventional. Thus, back at her house and away from the magical garden, his 'face [grows] a little white' (143) when she says to him, 'You have been a very, very foolish boy, wasting your time dreaming of impossible things when you speak of Mr. Pontellier setting me free! I am no longer one of Mr. Pontellier's possessions to dispose of or not. I give myself where I choose. If he were to say, "Here, Robert, take her and be happy; she is yours, I should laugh at you both"' (142–3). When the consummation of their affair is interrupted by Adèle's going into labour, Robert begs her not to leave. Yet he is really not willing to love her on the free terms she has outlined, and her absence gives him time to regain control of the situation by writing a manly and correct note: 'Good-by – because I love you' (148).

Edna never quite finds the content of the freedom to which she aspires; ultimately, it seems impossible for her to exist outside of men's hegemony and standard social structures. She may want to be an active subject, but has difficulty imagining herself into that position. Edna's suicide, which follows closely upon her attendance at Adèle's child-birth, seems very much tied up with issues of motherhood, with her own roles as both daughter and mother. In what suggests a female version of the Oedipal archetype, Woolf says of the symbolic 'Angel,' 'had I not killed her she would have killed me' (*Room* 151); in *The Awakening*, Edna resolves this dilemma by suicide. The sea, described as soothing and enveloping, has been viewed by some critics as a conventional maternal image, and Edna's death in the ocean a return to the womb; she is, in fact, naked when she takes her final swim:

> ... for the first time in her life she stood naked in the open air, at the mercy of the sun, the breeze that beat upon her, and the waves that invited her.
>
> How strange and awful it seemed to stand naked under the sky! How delicious! She felt like some new-born creature, opening its eyes in a familiar world that it had never known. (152)

For Edna, there is no liberation in 'thinking back through her mother.' Despite her love for her own two children, motherhood is part of the domestic institution she detests. At one point in the novel, Léonce voices his suspicion that Edna's father may have driven her mother to an early death. Ironically, Edna's inability to escape the patriarchal structures which encircle her and pervade the world of the novella means repeating the fate of her own mother; she gives up on her own awakening.

The emphasis on dinner when Edna returns to Grand Isle just before her death underlines the importance of meals to the novella. Since the text implies that Edna's suicide is planned, it seems odd, at first glance, that she discusses in some detail with Victor and Mariequita what she wants for dinner, who will cook it, whether she has time for a swim before dinner, and so forth. She says that she is hungry and would like fish for dinner – a reference, perhaps, to her impending death by drowning – but repeats in a thoughtful, even slightly self-deprecating way that they should not do 'anything extra' (150, 151). Certainly, it is not unusual for people on the verge of suicide to continue with their everyday lives until the last moment, but in this case the emphasis on dinner is particularly pertinent in terms of both Edna's habits and the novella's structure. As a wife, a mother, and a lover, Edna has led a life punctuated by meals. Indeed, her reputation seems to have become linked with food: in this last scene, Mariequita thinks of her, rather hyperbolically, as the 'woman who gave the most sumptuous dinners in America, and who had all the men in New Orleans at her feet' (150). If meals have structured Edna's days, indeed her life, they have also organized the novella, and this meal that will never be is the final punctuation mark. Edna dies within her usual daily domestic framework, with dinner planned, finally escaping this structure for good by swimming out to sea. No one will enjoy the meal that is being cooked. Chopin withholds the last dinner from the reader as well as from Edna; Edna does not eat, and the reader too is left disappointed and unsatisfied. The uneaten dinner remains as an expression of Edna's absence.

The Artist's Vision

For Edna Pontellier, the series of dinners structuring both the novella and her life creates an enclosure from which she cannot escape. If she finally fails in her attempts to transcend domestic constraints and to nurture the artist in herself, it is because she finds that the oppressive limitations of the domestic world extend outside her marriage as well. There is a sense that Chopin has abandoned her, or has refused to alter a world which is stacked against her. In other works, however, the writer, reinterpreting the domestic world through her own artistic vision, explores ways for the characters to do so as well. In the Burnell stories and in *To the Lighthouse*, Mansfield and Woolf situate the source of the fictional artist's inspiration in the kitchen, the dining-room, and domestic life in general. Although not so freely and ecstatically as Stein does, Mansfield and Woolf each outline the relationship between the work of art and the dinner table, in effect making a link between their own work and that of their non-literary foremothers, and in the process, reinterpreting both women's traditional work and the work of creating fiction.

Although certainly conflicted, Katherine Mansfield's Burnell stories explore the roots of creativity. The emphasis on the dining-room, already noted in 'Prelude,' does not necessarily imply an oppressive structure, but may, rather, establish a creative centre which is as nourishing to the artist as the food being served. In so far as they focus on the child Kezia, the stories emphasize the hopeful, the potential, the ideal. The domestic is both criticized and celebrated; however, the potential exists for daughters to learn from their mothers and foremothers, and the links between creativity and domesticity, although ambivalent, are clearly present.

The portrait of the artist as a young girl is that of Kezia, the middle Burnell daughter. I argued in chapter 6 that Kezia and her sisters are apprentice women, learning to behave according to the cultural ideals of womanhood. But, although she is often presented as just one of the children, Kezia also stands out from her sisters as the most conscious, observant, imaginative, and thoughtful – the potential artist. Along with her sister Lottie, she opens 'Prelude' and, alone, closes it. In the first section of that story she looks through the dining-room window and sees the world transformed, as her sister and the objects in the garden take on the colours of the stained glass. But there is more here than just changes in colour; her imagination carries her away:

> Kezia liked to stand so before the window. She liked the feeling of the cold shining glass against her hot palms, and she liked to watch the funny white tops that came on her fingers when she pressed them hard against the pane. As she stood there, the day flickered out and dark came. With the dark crept the wind snuffling and howling. The windows of the empty house shook, a creaking came from the walls and floors, a piece of loose iron on the roof banged forlornly. Kezia was suddenly quite, quite still, with wide open eyes and knees pressed together. She was frightened. She wanted to call Lottie and to go on calling all the while she ran downstairs and out of the house. But IT was just behind her, waiting at the door, at the head of the stairs, at the bottom of the stairs, hiding in the passage, ready to dart out at the back door. (15)

There are other points in the stories where Kezia stands out as well. In the children's game in 'At the Bay,' Saralyn Daly (87) sees Kezia's insistence on being a bee, despite the argument of one of the other children – presumably her sister – that a bee is not a real animal, as a creative rebellion against rules and roles. In 'Prelude,' Kezia tells her more conventional sister Isabel, 'I hate playing ladies' (43). Again, in 'Prelude,' it is Kezia who has the strongest reaction to the duck's being killed, as if she is more able than the others to imagine the feelings of another creature. Her response is also perhaps aesthetic: ducks ought to have heads, and it is repugnant to see one running about headless. Yet, in her distraction by Pat's earring – 'Do they come on and off?' (47) she asks – she also seems capable of using her experience to interpret the world, in this case to explore the notion that some actions can be undone, others not.

Kezia ends 'Prelude' by playing with and gently undercutting and mocking her Aunt Beryl's self-absorbed obsession with her appearance, and, with it, traditional femininity. Having gone to call her aunt to lunch, Kezia remains alone for a few minutes in Beryl's room, fascinated by the dressing table and the accoutrements of female beauty: bedroom equivalents of the kitchen utensils and products used by Mrs Fairfield in another manifestation of women's role. When Beryl leaves, Kezia experiments with her toiletries, playfully putting the lid of the cold cream jar on the ear of her stuffed cat, which she positions, as Beryl was positioned, in front of the mirror. When the toy falls off the dressing table and the lid flies through the air, she is, like any child, afraid of being punished; but she also seems to feel the strong symbolic importance in this apparently insignificant object. Although it is not damaged, she feels it to be:

> for Kezia it had broken the moment it flew through the air, and she picked it up, hot all over, and put it back on the dressing-table.
>
> Then she tiptoed away, far too quickly and airily ... (60; ellipsis in original)

Kezia is influenced by both her mother and her grandmother, and it is this dual lineage that moulds her consciousness. Her link with her mother lies in sharing an imaginative, if sometimes rather frightening perception of the everyday world. There is a suggestion in 'Prelude' that, because Linda has not fully surrendered to the demands of adult life, she has not lost the imagination of childhood, and is still capable of dreams, of creativity. Indeed, she has the capacity to see the world as imaginatively as Kezia does, although sometimes with a more sinister cast. She seems to find ordinary physical reality uncertain and unpredictable; for Linda, as for Kezia, '[t]hings had a habit of coming alive' (27).[15] Linda daydreams of escape from mundane household existence; the aloe becomes the ship which will take her away. She imagines

> that she was caught up out of the cold water into the ship with the lifted oars and the budding mast. Now the oars fell striking quickly, quickly.

They rowed far away over the top of the garden trees, the paddocks and the dark bush beyond. Ah, she heard herself cry: 'Faster! Faster!' to those who were rowing.

How much more real this dream was than that they should go back to the house where the sleeping children lay and where Stanley and Beryl played cribbage (53).

She also imagines that the aloe is her swelling body, but strong and equipped with thorns and claws. Interestingly, Kezia's only moment alone with her mother in all the Burnell stories is when they look at the aloe together; this has been viewed as the scene where the mother passes along her creative vision to her daughter. Patricia Moran, calling attention to the critical controversy about whether Kezia's role model is her mother or her grandmother, argues that Linda's refusal to participate in the typical life of women inspires Kezia in her creativity (*Word of Mouth* 111–12). But if Kezia is the artist as a young girl, Linda's creative potential has never been fulfilled: her creativity, if it exists, is merely part of her disquiet; she is not, after all, an artist.

I find it, then, a misreading of the stories to deny Kezia's grandmother paramount importance. The child's very close relationship to Mrs Fairfield forms the foundation for her growing up. Certainly, Kezia learns from her grandmother. In 'At the Bay,' for instance, the discussion of her Uncle William's death – and the resulting tickling fight over whether or not she and her grandmother will also die – introduces her to the profoundly contradictory notion of the magnitude and ordinariness of life and mortality. But this is more than just a case of intergenerational closeness; Mrs Fairfield's influence on Kezia is directly domestic. Moran proposes that 'Kezia's emulation of Mrs Fairfield's domestic artistry results in a transformation of nature into culture that reenacts the old woman's transformation of the fruit into jam' (*Word of Mouth* 112), citing as particularly significant examples the several occasions when Kezia, playing with her food at the table, transforms it into something else: '[I]n "Prelude," she makes a piece of bread "a dear little sort of gate" by eating a bite of it; in "At the Bay" she changes porridge into a landscape: "She had only dug a river down the middle of her porridge, filled it, and was eating the banks away"' (*Word of Mouth* 112). Moran sees this influence as a negative and anti-creative force in the girl's life: 'Kezia's emulation of Mrs Fairfield ... raises doubt about the efficacy of the magna mater as artistic model, for, as the representative and priestess of nature, Mrs Fairfield is not a model of the speaking subject or writer' (*Word of Mouth* 112). However, the fact of Kezia's grandmother being house-bound and completely oriented to the domestic does not rule out a creative influence. On the contrary, as Rosenman says in her analysis of *A Room of One's Own*:

> Ancestors do more than simply provide technical models for aspiring writers or symbolize particular aesthetic philosophies – indeed, they may do nothing of the sort, for they may not even be writers. Instead, this female tradition – with distinct values, attitudes, and even modes of selfhood – sustains a woman writing in a male world, giving her a kind of affirmation of identity like that which a mother ideally gives to her child ... If providing nurturance rather than literary models is the central function of the foremother, it does not matter whether she writes at all ... (85)

Mansfield's language affirms a link between the housewifely and the artistic domains. Symbolically, Mrs Fairfield is associated with light, particularly when she is with the children. When Lottie and Kezia arrive at the new house, their first view of it includes '[s]omeone ... walking through the empty rooms carrying a lamp' (18). The 'someone' is their grandmother, who hands the lamp over to Kezia in a solemn, quasi-religious gesture:

> 'Kezia,' said the grandmother, 'can I trust you to carry the lamp?'
> 'Yes, my granma.'
> The old woman bent down and gave the bright breathing thing into her hands ... (18)

Clearly her grandmother's heir, Kezia herself is also associated with light. When the grandmother guides the children to bed with a candle, Kezia asks, 'Aren't you going to leave me a candle?' (21). And in 'The Doll's House,' a story in which Mrs Fairfield does not appear, it is the lamp on the dining-room table of the miniature house that Kezia likes so much: '"The lamp's best of all," cried Kezia. She thought Isabel wasn't making half enough of the little lamp' (387). Across class lines, she shares her appreciation with 'our Else,' one of the pariah Kelvey girls, who, after having been chased from the Burnells' yard by Aunt Beryl, whispers to her sister, 'I seen the little lamp' (391).

Thus Kezia is inspired by her grandmother and the image of the lamp associated with her grandmother. It is significant that the doll's house lamp is on the dining-room table. The imagery implies that the role of the provider of meals is potentially a creative one. Linda's rejection of that role in fact may stymie her creativity. Daly sees Mrs Fairfield as exemplifying order (58); viewed from this perspective, Linda's experience of the world may remain inexpressible, chaotic, even frightening to her, in part because her refusals have not granted her an alternative life, but, rather, a passive acquiescence in the usual family and social structures.

The implications of Linda's refusals are ambiguous at best. Linda sees maternity, like the entire domestic role, not as creative, but merely as burdensome. Viewed one way, Linda is protesting the constraints and imperatives of her body, which seem to prevent her from ever doing anything but reproducing; viewed another way, she is repressing whatever pleasure and creativity might be experienced or expressed through her body. Rosenman notes a similar ambivalence in Woolf about whether women find their creative voice through their physical being or by transcending it: 'Woolf must insist on [the body's] reality, both to retrieve women from Victorian stereotypes of purity and to undo women's oppression. At the same time, however, the body remains haunted by disability and danger, and Woolf longs to escape from its complications' (111). Thus, although Jane Marcus argues that a denial of the body may be 'a strategy of power for the woman mystic or artist' ('The Niece of a Nun'),[16] Woolf, in both *A Room of One's Own* and *Three Guineas*, links taboos against women's writing with those against women's sexuality. As Moran says, 'It is this consciousness of impropriety that most often thwarts women writers in Woolf's texts; women internalize paternal proscriptions and then become censors of their own speech' (*Word of Mouth* 73).

Although there is no suggestion that Linda Burnell has literary aspirations, her struggle may nonetheless echo that of the woman writer, a more complex version of the narrator's ambivalent stance in some of the *German Pension* stories. Homans notes the conventional but nevertheless crucial metaphoric relationship between maternity and the creative act, especially the act of writing.[17] On the other hand, if maternal language is non-symbolic language, the very state of maternity might seem to preclude active participation in language. Thus a daughter who wants to write might refuse to become a mother herself; after all, a baby is not figurative.[18] Linda seems to find the worst of both worlds, however: in limiting her experience of motherhood to the biological fundamentals, she is, at least until the birth of her son in 'At the Bay,' all the more defined by her body and her role as a wife, haunted by the spectre of pregnancy and trapped by her situation.

In *A Room of One's Own*, Woolf describes in detail the bland and minimal fare served to students at women's colleges as compared with the sumptuous meals at 'Oxbridge.' The difference has both physical and spiritual implications, and her point is that women must be adequately nourished in both senses in order to achieve their creative and intellectual potential. The fact that Linda denies herself nourishment as part of the denial of her body implicates her in her own impotence. Kezia's essentially having two role models, then, may liberate her to the possibility of becoming a more complete woman. Perhaps she will not spend her life as her mother has, reacting against expectations by repressing herself to a point of near-total passivity.

If Mansfield gives Kezia two mothers, each with a different relationship to domestic structures, Woolf suggests a somewhat similar resolution to the problem of the woman artist in *To the Lighthouse*, by splitting the creative woman in two. In the characters of Lily Briscoe and Mrs Ramsay, art and celibacy, on the one hand, and domesticity, marriage, and fecundity, on the other, are at the same time contrasted and linked. Reverberating in each other, the two apparent antitheses become complementary creative poles. Despite the fact that Lily and Mrs Ramsay are opposites, there is a special understanding, a special communication between them. A woman who has not taken on Mrs Ramsay's role as a wife and the mother of a family, and who has ambivalent feelings about not having done so, Lily is still inspired as an artist by these roles. They seem to be an aesthetic source for her, a necessary base from which to work.

The connection between the two women is multifaceted. First, beyond the obvious relationship of hostess and guest, there is the subtler link between model and painter. As she sits knitting and playing with her child, Mrs Ramsay is aware, if only sporadically, that Lily is painting her, and reminds herself that 'she was supposed to be keeping her head as much in the same position as possible for Lily's picture' (29). This connection between subject and painter – as between character and writer – exists even though Mrs Ramsay neither sees the finished work nor even evinces an interest in the canvas-in-progress. However, Mrs Ramsay is not simply a convenient model, but provides a subject for Lily's painting in a larger sense: Mrs Ramsay and James do not exactly 'sit' for her, but continue their normal domestic routine, symbolically framed by the drawing-room window. It is the whole situation that Lily paints, including the bond between mother and son, and their physical and emotional relationship to the house. Lily is painting domesticity. Attempting to explain to William Bankes, who is expecting something like a representationalist portrait or landscape, why, in her painting, Mrs Ramsay and James have become a purple triangle, Lily tells him that it is not their 'likeness' she is trying to capture: 'But the picture was not of them, she said. Or, not in his sense. There were other senses too in which one might reverence them. By a shadow here and a light there, for instance. Her tribute took that form if, as she vaguely supposed, a picture must be a tribute' (81).

Mrs Ramsay provides Lily with inspiration on more than one level. If Mrs Ramsay has several spiritual daughters, Lily is the most important, and, at the novel's central dinner-table scene, Lily's responses to the meal are particularly emphasized. Lily's work is nourished by Mrs Ramsay's dinner table: the *actual* table, in contrast to the abstract notion of a kitchen table that Andrew Ramsay uses to explain to her Mr Ramsay's philosophy. For Lily, a lot happens at dinner. Earlier, I noted the wordless communication between Lily and Mrs Ramsay during the meal. It is not only the bond with her hostess, however, but the whole ambiance of Mrs Ramsay's dinner which inspires Lily. Even the dinner table itself, as a setting, a physical object, and a reference point, helps her to define herself as a painter and to clarify a particular problem in her work-in-progress:

> She remembered, all of a sudden as if she had found a treasure, that she had her work. In a flash she saw her picture, and thought, Yes, I shall put the tree further in the middle; then I shall avoid that awkward space. That's what I shall do. That's what has been puzzling me. She took up the salt cellar and put it down again on a flower in pattern in the table-cloth, so as to remind herself to move the tree. (128)

It is as if the painting, somehow inspired by dining, becomes an after-dinner story. Indeed, since the painting is not, in fact, finished until the last section of the novel, the remainder of the novel *is* that after-dinner story.

Perhaps Lily inspires Mrs Ramsay as well. Although she thinks that 'one could not take her painting very seriously' (29), Mrs Ramsay appreciates Lily's independence: 'There was in Lily a thread of something; a flare of something; something of her own which Mrs. Ramsay liked very much indeed, but no man would, she feared' (157). Despite her urge to pair people up, Mrs Ramsay appreciates the quality in Lily that resists pairing: 'she was an independent little creature, and Mrs. Ramsay liked her for it' (29). Of the two young women guests at the dinner table, Minta, because of her engagement, seems likely to continue Mrs Ramsay's sort of life and therefore to be her favourite. The fact that her married name – Rayley – will be so similar to Mrs Ramsay's reinforces this sense of affinity. But Lily too is her heir, in a more important sense. Comparing her to the radiant, newly paired Minta, Mrs Ramsay thinks that 'at forty Lily will be the better' (157).

The contrast between Minta and Lily echoes that between two of the Ramsay daughters, Prue and Cam. In the first section of the novel, Prue, on her way to marriage and a family, is clearly very like her mother. But Prue dies in childbirth, an event which suggests, perhaps, the demise of the traditional domesticity that Mrs Ramsay lived, and which leaves Cam, the second youngest child, at first described as 'wild and fierce' (36), as the most important Ramsay daughter in the last section of the novel. Eating sandwiches with her brother and father, and imagining herself to be embarked on a great adventure, Cam is the only female in the boat on the way to the lighthouse, and much of that trip is seen from her viewpoint. She not only provides one of the major narrative perspectives on the end of the novel, but participates, for her mother, in the trip to the lighthouse and the closure that it brings about.

Our first view of Lily is from Mrs Ramsay's perspective, as she watches Lily painting herself and James. Unlike Mr Ramsay – who, according to his near-sighted wife, 'never looked at things' (108), despite his 'long-sighted eyes' (307) – the two women are observers, in this scene of each other. It is perhaps because Lily is an observer that she is an artist, and vice versa. She is particularly keenly aware of people, their relationships and interactions, and especially of love and marriage – states she expects never to experience herself. Thus, at dinner, a profound awareness of the simplicity, complexity, and ambiguity of love descends upon her, as she watches the Ramsays and the soon-to-be Rayleys. Silently observing that 'there is nothing more tedious, puerile, and inhumane than this; yet it is also beautiful and necessary,' she returns her attention to the table. In an amusing juxtaposition, Lily returns from her ruminations to Bankes's comments on 'that liquid the English call coffee' (155), part of his discussion with Mrs Ramsay about the horrors of English cooking. The everyday banality of coffee, and bad coffee at that – presented as the response to her thoughts about love – punctures Lily's seriousness, but also suggests the tedium of shared meals that is, as well, a part of love.

Lily is the Kezia of this novel, but she is already an artist. We do not know for certain that she is a better or more successful artist than Edna

Pontellier, only that both she herself and the novel in which she is a character take her work more seriously. Lily explicitly sees her painting as an alternative to a traditional marriage and family life. Yet the one canvas that we see her painting is inspired by Mrs Ramsay and seems to encompass all of domesticity. Painting is, of course, very different from writing, yet in *To the Lighthouse*, Lily represents the artist in general, as if she is both Virginia, the writer, and Vanessa, the painter. The two arts are linked by Charles Tansley's reported comment, 'Women can't write, women can't paint' (130). Lily proves him wrong on both counts; in a very real sense, she is painting the novel. Her painting, begun in the first section of the novel, is finished, with the novel, on the last page: 'She looked at the steps; they were empty; she looked at her canvas; it was blurred. With a sudden intensity, as if she saw it clear for a second, she drew a line there, in the centre. It was done; it was finished. Yes, she though, laying down her brush in extreme fatigue, I have had my vision' (310).

If, together, the painting and the plan to visit the lighthouse form the starting inspiration of the novel, the line in the centre is the finishing stroke of the painting and, the island having been reached almost simultaneously, the last line of the novel as well. Together, the two achievements complete the 'vision' of the novel, in the sense both of finishing it and of making it whole. In a striking conflation of media, the painting is about the novel, and the novel is about the painting; the time it takes for the painting to be finished comprises the novel, and the subject of the painting is the subject of the novel. The painting is never fully described – we know only that it includes a purple triangular shape and a line in the centre – yet the novel unveils the painting to us by preserving its vision in writing.

Lily's art emerges from a domestic life which perhaps cannot exist in more modern times and in modern marriages like Minta and Paul's. Although, or perhaps because, she herself does not have children, Lily is the inheritor, and charged with preserving this domestic vision through art; perhaps one must be an outsider to that life to do so. As she tells Mr Bankes, Lily cannot and does not wish to reproduce Mrs Ramsay and James on her canvas, but, rather, tries to capture the essence of her subject: 'rapture' (74), perhaps, which she sees Mrs Ramsay inspiring in others; or a sense of '[h]ow life, from being made up of little separate incidents which one lived one by one, became curled and whole like a wave which bore one up with it and threw one down with it, there, with a dash on the beach' (73); or her own frustration at the impossibility of being one with Mrs Ramsay and gaining access to her apparent source of wisdom, 'for it was not knowledge but unity that she desired ... nothing that could be written in any language known to men, but intimacy itself, which is knowledge' (79).

Just as the title of the novel emphasizes the intention to go to the lighthouse rather than the actual attainment of that goal, the novel is also more about the process of Lily's painting than the painting itself as an object or a commodity. Unlike Mr Ramsay, who desperately wants to be recognized during his lifetime and to have his philosophy endure after his death, Lily is aware that her achievement may be short-lived: 'It would be hung in the attics, she thought; it would be destroyed. But what did that matter? she asked herself, taking up her brush again' (309–10). For her, the act of creation itself is important. In this sense, Lily's work is parallel to Mrs Ramsay's, for the process of her painting recollects that of cooking a dinner, which is meant to disappear. However, if the latter effort, by definition, always results in a transitory creation, it is nonetheless an essentially creative act with a potentially creative effect; in fact, it is perhaps its close association with mortality that gives the meal its power. Thus the cook in 'Babette's Feast,' for instance, is presented as an artist as great as any, and in the painting/ novel *To the Lighthouse*, the artistry of the cook/wife/mother is also preserved and celebrated.

If the tenuous nature of art that Lily accepts reflects both the fragility of human life and the ephemeral satisfaction of domestic work, it is, nevertheless, only through art that a vision or a life can be understood and have even a chance of being preserved. There is a sense in which domestic work also seems to transcend time. Like other housework, preparing meals is eternal not only in that it may seem a never-ending chore to a particular woman, but also because it is a constant of human experience and existence. This sense of immortality is emphasized in part II of *To the Lighthouse*, where it is not Mr Ramsay's philosophy about the meaning of a table but Mrs McNab's work that holds both the house and the novel together through time, death, and war. Mrs Ramsay, her short-sightedness suggesting an attention to detail which forms a contrast to her husband's focus on the horizon, represents not so much that trivial work – this belongs to another class – but the timelessness of the domestic realm in a general sense and specifically of the work done by the mother/nurturer/provider of food/organizer of the dinner table. Thus, even after her death, Mrs Ramsay continues to inspire Lily's painting, and the novel continues to be about her. According to Spivak's 'grammatical allegory,' if Mrs Ramsay is the subject of the first section of the novel, in the third section 'the painting predicates her' (30).

The fact that it is Lily and Cam, rather than Minta and Prue, who become the important female characters in 'The Lighthouse,' the third part of the novel, indicates a change in the role of women. Yet the 'wedge of darkness' (96) with which Mrs Ramsay identifies herself near the beginning of the novel is still present at the end: 'Suddenly the window at which [Lily] was looking was whitened by some light stuff behind it. At last then somebody had come into the drawing-room; somebody was sitting in the chair ... [W]hoever it was had settled by some stroke of luck so as to throw an odd-shaped triangular shadow over the step' (299). Ultimately, of course, the understanding that the modern woman artist may have for Mrs Ramsay does not resolve the predicaments of modernity suffered by women like Edna Pontellier or Linda Burnell. And, indeed, Lily's artistic vision is not always clear; in fact, she finishes her painting in a leap of faith, 'as if she saw it clear for a second,' although in fact her sight is 'blurred.' Still, her offering is a step. At least through the language of art, a reconciliation of the two views of the mother is possible. Woolf certainly rejects the Victorian valorization of the domestic realm as a cornerstone of the Empire; yet, through Lily, she suggests a new validation of the work of the mother and portrays another dimension of women's work that, potentially, might even be subversive of bourgeois culture. Serving the meal is affirmed as something female, but in a different and admirable way: a form of communication, of expression, it proposes a new artistic language, and, indeed, is posited as a crucial component of female art.

To the Lighthouse is not exactly a meal in itself in the sense that other works may be. Yet, in so far as her creative work emerges from the dinner of 'The Window' and is inspired by the entire domestic realm which that dinner represents, Lily transforms the meal into a painting, which also becomes, in effect, the novel. In *To the Lighthouse*, the unspoken language emanating from the dinner table is translated into the language of art; the reader thus shares in both the pleasure of eating and the pleasure of reading. At the end of the novel, the reader has been satisfied, not only by the meal which occurred ten years earlier, but by the recuperation and perpetuation of the vision of that meal in Lily's painting. Completed almost synchronously with the Ramsays' boat reaching the island where the lighthouse stands, the painting seems to reconcile male and female, past and future, permanence and transiency, as well as art and cooking. *To the Lighthouse*, then, represents Lily's version of the meal in two ways: both in celebrating and perpetuating that vision of Mrs Ramsay defined by the dinner party of 'The Window,' and in suggesting what Lily can do instead of preparing a literal meal. Contrary to Charles Tansley's view, creating a work of art is shown to be another kind of women's work.

Conclusion

She wrote a poem on the milk bill

Mina Loy, 'The Effectual Marriage'

Our reading of literature in this study has occurred at the conjunction of an understanding of the power and imaginative resonance of dinner and a more prosaic perspective on meals as part of women's domestic work. Virginia Woolf's notion of the 'room of one's own' became a sort of rallying cry in the twentieth century for several generations of women. However, women have always had a room of their own: the kitchen or the dining-room. The literature discussed in this study explores women's attempts to move out of these spaces into the rest of the house, at the same time as it grapples with the power of these rooms: the power to impose and ratify conservative social values, to bind and hold back individual women; but a power also characterized by generosity, openness, sociability, and, most significantly, a strong creative force. I have argued that some modernist women writers recognize the domestic labour of preparing and serving a meal by giving it a central place in their fiction, thus, perhaps, suggesting the important role that the kitchen and the dinner table have played in their own writing. In the modernist period, meals have a special place for women writers, and, arguably, for women readers as well.

This study began with the assumption that a dinner communicates a great deal; that, in fact, the cluster of customs, habits, and rituals surrounding the preparation, serving, and eating of a meal can be considered a language, and the dinner itself a text which speaks directly to the diners, the hostess, and, in the case of a fictional dinner, to the reader.

We are familiar from earliest childhood with meals as texts of our lives; biologically, psychologically, culturally, imaginatively, we already know how to read the meal. Thus we are prepared for dinner as both a metaphor and the subject of a literary text. As chapter 1 notes, it is not just the raw and the cooked that are juxtaposed when we talk about a meal, but the conjunction of the body and the imagination, the physical and the spiritual, desire and intellect, loneliness and a sense of belonging, the individual and the social. When food is prepared, changes occur: the transformation of raw materials into a meal, the transformation of individuals into a community of the table, occasionally the transformation of ordinary, everyday reality into something extraordinary. On the other hand, even this basic sense of the community of the meal does not always exist. In Mansfield's stories, the appeal of commensality is sometimes resisted; at other times it is just not there. Yet the notion of sociability is always hovering around the dinner table, even as a phantom in the absence of the real thing.

I have noted that, for women writers, the link between the modern and 'Modernism' included a whole set of issues that were far less immediately relevant for their *confrères* and that are reflected in their work. Thus, for instance, in Edith Wharton's novels, disquiet about social change is reflected in a conservative and defensive set of manners and rituals surrounding meals. In the early twentieth century, even those women who welcomed change experienced some confusion and even ambivalence. As noted in chapter 2, the supposedly improved and enthusiastically modern approaches to cooking and housekeeping were, in many ways, fundamentally conservative. Similarly, the possibility of liberation from the kitchen was to some degree illusory, or at least less than straightforward: Katherine Mansfield's bohemian disregard for bourgeois standards, for instance, did not free her from the obligation to get tea ready. Moreover, the cost of modernity was a loss of both traditional power and traditional security. Custom and ritual help to maintain a sense of oneself and of one's place in the world, setting out key parameters and guidelines of behaviour that smooth social interaction, and providing a basis for direction and decisions. Moreover, since women often control the everyday application of custom, it can be a source of power for them. Thus, as discussed in terms of Mansfield's stories, the loss of tradition is a significant one for women.

Yet in the early twentieth century there was no going back. As various writers of the time record, women's traditional role within the family and the home – caught up in a process of far-reaching social change – was not only becoming untenable, but was, in fact, disappearing. Thus, when Lily Briscoe returns to Scotland at the end of *To the Lighthouse*, she feels alone, at first, and cast adrift; everything seems 'chaotic ... unreal' (219) without Mrs Ramsay's benignly controlling presence. The point is that even if Lily or Nancy or Cam *wanted* to fill Mrs Ramsay's role, none of them knows how. As a result, the sandwiches are not ready and no one knows what to send to the lighthouse. Near the end of the ten-year period of 'Time Passes,' Mrs McNab complains that '[a]ll of a sudden ... one of the young ladies wrote: would she get this done; would she get that done; all in a hurry' (209). Unlike Mrs Ramsay, who, because she understood Mrs McNab's work, would never have written in this way, the letter-writer seemingly does not know what is involved in these domestic demands.

In works of literature of the period, there are no easy recipes, no step-by-step instructions on how to deal with change. Everyday life is far more complicated than formulae for proper behaviour at table or col-our-coded meals. As I have pointed out, however, fictional dinners at least raise the problems and sometimes even suggest possibilities for synthesizing the old and the new. Fictional perspectives on women as either hostesses or guests or both set out the larger dilemmas for women in general and for the woman artist in particular. If some works of fiction specifically take up the woman artist's relationship to dinner, in a larger sense, this relationship is always at issue, for, whether or not an artist-character figures in the piece of fiction, all the writers considered here are exploring their own stance in relation to the dining-room. *To the Lighthouse* points out – as do other works to a lesser degree – a similarity between the transformations in perception that occur around the dinner table and through a work of art; indeed, in some cases, the possibility of literature seems to arise from the meal.

It is worth noting that hunger – the lack or absence of a meal – may also be a potent metaphor associated with art or the artist. In various works of literature, the inability or refusal to eat has been presented as part of a general existential *angst*; moreover, as suggested earlier, a denial of the body may be read as homage to a particular notion of uncompromised artistic purity. Although some of Mansfield's stories certainly depict the hunger of poverty and homelessness, or suggest a sense of anorexia and a general attitude of detachment from the dinner table, the metaphor of hunger may be particularly important in the fiction of male writers, who are cut off from the tradition of serving food, and whose work, like that of Mr Ramsay, may assume a disjunction between everyday reality and the creative life of the mind. This hypothesis raises larger questions for another study to explore; however, it is certainly true that the examples of the literary cliché of the starving writer that come immediately to mind are from books by male writers. Thus, Paul Auster describes the dilemma of the nameless protagonist in Knut Hamsun's 1890 novel, *Hunger*: 'The process is inescapable: he must eat in order to write. But if he does not write, he will not eat. And if he cannot eat, he cannot write. He cannot write' (9). Kafka takes the metaphor a long step farther. His 'hunger artist,' in raising starvation to an art, redefines himself as a totally spiritual or intellectual being and pushes the limits of art in a direction which denies the body. At first it seems possible for him to create art at a level which is, by its very definition, above basic needs; ultimately, however, he does not rise above the ordinary, but in fact becomes less than human. Ending his career and his life in a menagerie, he is even lower than a side-show freak; ironically, by rejecting his physical nature, he becomes an animal.

Given the links I have posited between the work of the artist and domestic labour, my study concurs with Virginia Blum that '[a]rt is labor, rooted in a process of material production, rooted in the body of the artist which art plunders for the very metaphors that presumably exceed corporal exigencies' (71). Like the meal placed on the table, a piece of fiction is finally the creation of a physical person moving her hand across a piece of paper, her fingers on a keyboard. Although Kafka's artist plunders – indeed destroys – his body for his art, it is in the service of denying that the artist is necessarily grounded in the physical body and in everyday life. In the work of the women writers considered in this study, on the other hand, an active engagement with food – or, at least, a profound and perhaps intuitive understanding of that engagement – is crucial: the role of cook or hostess goes beyond metaphoric importance to become, in fact, a necessary foundation for writing. A link with art is suggested in the willingness of the cook to immerse herself in the physical, to grapple with the material world in order to create something which is ephemeral yet significant, and, possibly, of lasting importance.

Homans notes that the phrase 'it was finished' is used only twice in *To the Lighthouse*: when Lily Briscoe completes her painting and when Mrs McNab finishes cleaning the house (*Critical Essays* 6), a clear and deliberate link between domestic work and art. Yet there are limits to this connection. I have referred at various points in this study to serving the meal as one kind of domestic work; however, in some ways, it is quite different from other household chores. It is the only task that ultimately includes the whole family; it is nourishing, creative, and social. Only cooking becomes a metaphor for art; the book can be seen as a dinner, but certainly not as a scrubbed floor. Like other women's work, the process of cooking is not a finite and self-contained task. Indeed Mrs Ramsay keeps on working once her dinner is on the table, and the dinner itself does not end definitively, but rather peters out slowly: 'And directly she went a sort of disintegration set in; they wavered about, went different ways' (168). However, if Mrs Ramsay's work has no clear end, it is not only because there is always another meal to put on the table, but also because the dinner continues to resonate across the years. In this fictional portrayal, then, we can appreciate the exhausting toil that serving dinner demands, yet, because of the potentially multi-levelled creativity of the table, cooking becomes more than just a tedious task, and does not leave us with a sense of being bogged down in the boredom of the domestic. Throughout this study we have seen women struggling against domesticity; yet, as chapter 7 argues, an appreciation of the creativity which resonates from the dining-room and kitchen can liberate the fictional character, the writer, and the reader to claim art as women's domain, and in so doing, both to offer and to accept the book as a meal. The kitchen table is not merely a figment of the philosopher's mind, but as the woman writer knows, it exists, and, is, in fact, central, even when no one is there to perceive it. And always, the table suggests that people will sit around it, just as dinner implies that someone will eat, and a book that someone will read.

Notes

1: *Hors d'Oeuvres*

1 It is not my purpose here to present a detailed literature review of sociological and anthropological texts; this has been done by others. Roy Wood
   (3), in his own critical summary of recent work on food and anthropology,
   cites in particular Murcott's 'Sociological and Social Anthropological
   Approaches to Food and Eating' (*World Review of Nutrition and Dietetics*
   55 (1988): 1–40), and Mennell, Murcott, and van Otterloo.
2 Wood is paraphrasing Beardsworth and Keil here. These two notions of
   culture and biology represent a methodological controversy in anthropology: whether to base one's work in cultural theory or material reality. Like
   Beardsworth and Keil, Wood attempts to reconcile the two approaches.
3 It should be noted here that Lévi-Strauss's emphasis on the notion of
   dualism has been criticized by a number of anthropologists as simplistic
   and over-generalized. The dynamic tension of opposites can be, nevertheless, a useful way of talking about the important transformations involved
   in cooking.
4 Later writers, influenced by Lévi-Strauss, have made similar points about
   food and civilization, but see the connection as symbolic rather than
   causal. For example, Anne Murcott argues: 'Metaphorically, the transformation of "natural" food-stuffs into the "cultural" products of the table
   parallels other general processes whereby the material world is worked on
   and incorporated into the human domain. It thus can stand for the many
   different ways in which the world of culture – of meanings, values and
   human work – is created and sustained in the face of an alien, non-human
   universe (the jungle, the desert, "the world"). At the same time, food
   furnishes a direct link – metonymically – between the cultural and the
   biological: ingested and processed, it thus spans the two spheres' (11).

5 Some European examples are well known: the British calling the Germans 'krauts' and the French 'frogs' (Mennell, Murcott, and van Otterloo 117). Similarly, the Cree called the Inuit 'Esquimaux' or 'meat-eaters' (Farb and Armelagos 97).

6 It is worth noting that some of Frank Lloyd Wright's dining-room furniture designed in the early 1900s – high-backed chairs and a table with built-in lights at the corners – was specifically meant to give diners a feeling of enclosure around the table.

2: The Angel in the Kitchen

1 Hermione Lee points out that, after the death of their mother, Woolf's half-sister Stella Duckworth and, after Stella's marriage, her sister Vanessa were in charge of supervising the basement kitchen. Thus Woolf would have understood from personal experience that, even in her class, serving meals was women's work.

2 Dorothy Parker notwithstanding, it has been a cliché throughout the twentieth century that women journalists begin their careers in the society or food pages of a newspaper.

3 Virginia Woolf, in 'Mr. Bennett and Mrs. Brown,' places this break, 'arbitrar[il]y,' in 1910. Interestingly, she cites transformations in 'the character of one's cook' as a 'homely illustration' (320) of the change.

4 According to Christine Frederick's *Household Engineering*, in 1910, only 8 per cent of American homes employed permanent servants.

5 Shapiro also makes this point (219).

6 Lemenorel, Mintz, and Mennell have all made this point; Roy Wood, however, maintains that these claims are exaggerated, and that there is little evidence that the family meal is really disappearing.

7 Many people have, of course, discussed the growth of individualism as an important factor in recent history. Elias sees an increasing, although illusory, sense of the self as an autonomous actor. And Douglas notes that 'the individual had once been seen as a partially autonomous subunit, gaining full significance from his part in a hierarchical whole. In contemporary philosophizing he has become a separate, self-justified unit, locked in individual exchanges with other such self-seeking, rational beings' (*Food in the Social Order* 6).

8 Invented in about 1850, the gas stove had come into wide use by the mid-1920s (Hooker); other nineteenth-century domestic inventions followed similar trajectories.

9 Irene also sometimes passes for white, at, for instance, the rooftop tea-room where she encounters Clare for the first time in many years.

10 It might be interesting to investigate whether the Martha Stewart phenomenon plays a similar role today.

11 A few examples: *Good Form for Women: A Guide to Conduct and Dress on All Occasions* (1907); *Social Usage and Etiquette: A Book of Manners for Every Day* (1904); *A Dictionary of Etiquette: A Guide to Polite Usage for All Social Functions* (1904); and *Correct Social Usage: A Course of Instruction in Good Form, Style and Deportment, Being also an Authoritative Work of Ready Reference, Covering All Essentials of Good Manners* (1904).

12 My favourite title, from 1922, is *Perfect Behavior*, tantalizingly subtitled 'A Guide for Ladies and Gentlemen in All Social Crises.' A good number of etiquette books are explicitly addressed to both sexes: two examples are the 1889 book, *The Home Manual: Everybody's Guide in Social, Domestic, and Business Life*, and the 1914 title, *Good Form for All Occasions: A Manual of Manners, Dress and Entertainment for Both Men and Women*.

13 Siegfried Giedion, writing in the 1940s, suggests that, with the 'servantless household' firmly entrenched after the First World War (620), houses with a more open design became fashionable, because woman wished to feel less isolated in the kitchen. In any case, even today, the equipment, size, and layout of the dining and kitchen areas continue to be an index to social standing and to modernity.

3: In with the In-Crowd

1 It is worth noting in this context that the British *Who's Who* was first published in 1897. The New York *Social Register* was begun in 1887 and the list of the Four Hundred first published in the *New York Times* in 1892. F. Rhinelander Jones, whose name appears on the list, is presumably Wharton's brother Freddy.

2 In the following passage, Leonore Davidoff sums up the impact of these changes in England, and especially the increased structuring of social life, which, she argues, resulted: '[T]he shift from a society where patronage and familial or client relationship were the norm to a system where individual achievement was rewarded with great wealth and power, was bewildering to those living through the change. Increased geographical mobility through better transport also disrupted received notions of social placing. In contradistinction to those chaotic new developments, the rules of Society and the confining of social life to private homes made possible the minute regulation of personal daily life. It also made possible the evaluation and placing of newcomers in the social landscape' (17).

3 This scene of evening activity is somewhat reminiscent of the passage in *Mrs. Dalloway* where Peter, on his way to Clarissa's party, watches people

leave their houses for the evening. However, the latter scene is far more anonymous, urban and festive, as well as evocative of a larger world: 'Doors were being opened ... women came; men waited for them, with their coats blowing open, and the motor started. Everybody was going out. What with these doors being opened, and the descent and the start, it seemed as if the whole of London were embarking in little boats moored to the bank, tossing on the waters, as if the whole place were floating off in carnival' (249).

4 It is hard not to write about 'society' as a discrete, almost living entity in *The Age of Innocence*. Some critics have argued that society is indeed the main character in this novel. Gary Lindberg notes, 'Wharton investigates a society as an anthropologist examines a tribe, not as a collection of persons but as a system of sanctions, taboos, customs, and beliefs. This abstract system is, in turn, reified by both author and characters, assuming a personality that corresponds to the moral ambience of the community' (9).

5 The causal association of eating and pregnancy, often manifested in children's misinterpretations, and in some cultures explicitly ritualized, also comes to mind here. This link is manifested in another way in some of Mansfield's work.

4: The Art of Being an Honoured Guest

1 Cynthia Wolff's comments on the roots of this novel in contemporary drama are useful in this context. She notes the theatrical references throughout, comments like Gus Trenor's 'don't talk stage-rot,' and Simon Rosedale's 'it's a farce – a crazy farce' ('Lily Bart and the Drama of Femininity' 75). She also points out that many of the characters are drawn from or against stage stereotypes.

2 Tea is also drunk frequently in Nella Larsen's 1929 novel *Passing*, where an affirmation of middle-class gentility is particularly important.

3 Sidney Mintz's book *Sweetness and Power* chronicles the history not only of sugar but of tea and other foods and beverages associated with sugar. According to Mintz, the social, cultural, and economic importance of tea in England, particularly, during the last few centuries can hardly be overestimated.

4 Some critics have seen Selden as the villain of the novel. Hochman, for instance, calls him a moral coward, and hypocritical in regard to his expectations of Lily and his own physical attraction to her (229). Norris says he 'transform[s] her into a specimen' and 'conduct[s] moral experiments' on her (433).

5 As in *The Age of Innocence*, it seems that everyone knows where everyone
   is. For this exclusive set of New Yorkers, Fifth Avenue is like Main Street in
   a small town.

6 The characteristics of a good guest are still at issue. 'The Art of Being an
   Honored Guest' in the 'Style' section of the 26 November 1995 *New York
   Times* uses a visit of Monaco's Prince Rainier to analyse, light-heartedly,
   the behaviour of the perfect guest. The article poses the question, 'What
   makes a good guest? A century ago, when New York's "Four Hundred"
   were the only people invited to private balls, the rules were well understood ... They've been changing ever since.' Prince Rainier provides one
   model: 'He was, first of all, polite to a staff member. He was enthusiastic.
   He held up his end of the conversation. And most importantly, he was
   flexible. He took things in stride' (51). Apparently, one can still turn to
   royalty for inspiration.

7 *The Rise of Silas Lapham* presents a rather humorous account of the anxiety
   of the newly wealthy about entertaining: 'Up to a certain period Mrs.
   Lapham had the ladies of her neighborhood in to tea, as her mother had
   done in the country in her younger days. Lapham's idea of hospitality was
   still to bring a heavy-buying customer home to pot-luck; neither of them
   imagined dinners' (23). Mrs Lapham might well have been a potential
   reader for the books on entertaining mentioned in chapter 2.

5: 'Hungry Roaming'

1 Felski bases her argument on Gail Finney's 1989 study, *Women in Modern
   Drama: Freud, Feminism, and European Theater at the Turn of the Century*.

2 On the other hand, children in some novels of the 1920s seem to have no
   reality; children in *The Great Gatsby*, for instance, and in Carl Van Vechten's
   Parties are treated as dolls by both their parents and the writer.

3 Although she never returned to New Zealand, Katherine Mansfield never
   felt fully accepted in England either. Quoting from her journals, Gardner
   McFall reports that 'Mansfield considered herself the "little Colonial
   walking in the London garden patch – allowed to look perhaps, but not to
   linger"' (54).

4 Felski sees Berman's definition of modernity as specifically male; however,
   the 'creative destruction and constant transformation unleashed by the
   logic of capitalist development' (Felski, *Gender of Modernity* 2) surely had
   an impact on women as well, and certainly applies to modernist depictions of women and their relationship to the home.

5 The modernist emphasis on questions of identity is reflected, for instance,

in Mansfield's interest in the motif of masks and the notion of multiple selves.

6 Patricia Waugh argues that '[i]n modernist fiction the struggle for personal autonomy can be continued only through *opposition* to existing social institutions and conventions. This struggle necessarily involves individual alienation and often ends with mental dissolution' (10). Waugh's argument is perhaps oversimplified. 'Personal autonomy' is not the clearly definable state she seems to imply. Also, while 'mental dissolution' may seem imminent in *Nightwood*, this is not a very common situation in modernist fiction. Generally, 'individual alienation' is both far more mundane and more subtly pervasive.

7 Mary Burgan's *Illness, Gender, and Writing: The Case of Katherine Mansfield* and Patricia Moran's 'Unholy Meanings: Maternity, Creativity, and Orality in Katherine Mansfield' are examples of recent influential criticism almost completely based in Mansfield's life. Ruth Parkin-Gounelas quite rightly sees problems in the fact that 'all female writing has traditionally been decoded as autobiographical' (*Fictions of the Female Self* 5) and notes in particular 'the unwillingness of readers to separate the popular myths of [Mansfield's biography] from the characters in [her] fiction' (24). In Mansfield's case, this critical approach has sometimes reduced her work to a question of neurosis, leading to her 'being read as a "case" rather than as a writer' (Fullbrook 4).

8 Excerpt from a 1913 letter from Katherine Mansfield to John Middleton Murry (O'Sullivan and Scott 1:125–6; misspellings and first and third ellipsis in original).

9 This question certainly poses itself for the characters within the story, but may also pertain to the writer's relationship with her own work. In an interesting essay on Mary Wilkins Freeman, Virginia Blum suggests that the pervasive poverty faced by Freeman's characters, and their resulting obsession with money, is reflected in an anxiety about food. Like Freeman, Mansfield wrote many of her stories because of an immediate need for money, a fact that Blum sees as significant both in Freeman's work and in her attitudes toward literary value.

10 This relaxation of class demarcations can also be seen in depictions of public transport, another site where classes mix. Except for those in the highest stratum of society, everyone takes the bus, from Mansfield's Rosabel, a hat-shop clerk, to Woolf's Elizabeth Dalloway. But beneath the semblance of equality, class distinctions remain. In *Mrs. Dalloway*, the upper-class Clarissa mingles with the Bond Street crowds; yet her shopping errands remain firmly rooted in her class, their purpose to prepare for

the party that she will be hosting as the wife of a member of Parliament. Mrs Dalloway's attention, like that of the other shoppers and strollers, is seized by a passing limousine; but, for readers of the novel, she is distinguished from the crowd by the fact that the prime minister – quite possibly the passenger in the car – will be a guest at her party.

11 Flowers appear frequently in Mansfield's stories, and are often associated with food as well as with femaleness. Unfortunately, a full discussion of their importance is beyond the scope of this study.

12 Mansfield later disavowed this early collection, and resisted having it reprinted. Certainly, the stories are immature, somewhat clumsy, and dwell rather heavily on pre-First World War stereotypes of Germans. Still, as a number of recent critics – Patricia Moran, C. A. Hankin, and others – have pointed out, the collection is quite important in the context of her whole work, and is particularly linked to her New Zealand stories.

13 Mansfield herself spent time at a spa in 1909. While there, she suffered a miscarriage. Presumably her pregnancy was the reason for her being there in the first place.

14 Fullbrook argues that 'At Lehmann's' joins 'images of male assault, female desire, pain, bewilderment and violence as the important aspects of a typical sexual initiation for women' (58).

15 Alpers believes that V.S. Pritchett was responding to this characteristic of Mansfield's work when 'he declared that the sense of a country, the sense of the "unseen character," was ... weak in her writing' (*The Life of KM* 346).

16 Moran follows the line of thought traced by Elaine Showalter in *The Female Malady*: 'Disgust with meat was a common phenomenon among Victorian girls; a carnivorous diet was associated with sexual precocity' (129).

17 The earrings distract Kezia from the duck's death, but also raise for her the issue of gender, and particularly the relationship between biological gender and its usual surface symbols. Here, as elsewhere in the story, essential gender differences are, at the same time, both alluded to and questioned.

18 Bynum explores the symbolic value of food for medieval women: 'Like body, food must be broken and spilled forth in order to give life. Macerated by teeth before it can be assimilated to give life, food mirrors and recapitulates both sacrifice and service ... Women's bodies, in the acts of lactation and of giving birth, were analogous both to ordinary food and to the body of Christ, as it died on the cross and gave birth to salvation' (30).

19 Obviously, there are many factors involved in tracking statistics on eating disorders, not least of which is the reliability of diagnosis and reporting of the syndrome. Perlick and Silverstein report, 'At the beginning of the 20th

century, disordered eating among females did not appear to be common; however, it increased dramatically, reaching possible epidemic proportions in the 1920s, as evidenced in an emergency meeting of the American Medical Association' (80).

20 '[T]he key to the development of [anorexia] is feeling ambivalent about one's own gender' (Perlick and Silverstein 89).

21 Linda's dual response to gender might fit what Parkin-Gounelas refers to in terms of the woman writer as 'the discourse of the hysteric': in other words, 'a simultaneous refusal of, yet submission to, femininity as it is constructed under patriarchy' ('KM Reading Other Women' 45). Parkin-Gounelas credits Julia Kristeva as the originator of this notion.

22 Bynum also refers to 'the mother-daughter relationship' as key in the treatment of anorectics (202).

23 Linda's dilemma can be seen as an inheritance of the nineteenth-century fictional tradition, in which '"the only choices available to a female protagonist are frequently revealed as negative ones: a stifling and repressive marriage or a form of withdrawal into inwardness which frequently concludes in self-destruction"' (Felski, *Beyond Feminist Aesthetics* 124; quoted in Kaplan, *KM and the Origins* 87).

6: Through the Dining-Room Window

1 Spain argues that 'nonindustrial societies in which the division of labour is associated with spatial proximity of the sexes tend to have lower levels of gender stratification and higher status for women' (91).

2 Sarah Sandley takes this word from Mansfield's journals and uses it loosely to mean a sort of epiphany. Mansfield called it a '"moment of suspension. ... In that moment ... the whole life of the soul is contained"' (Sandley 71). Sandley also suggests a difference between male and female perceptions of time, reading the release of the women from Stanley's presence as liberation from 'a chronological series of nows, ruled by the clock' into 'a discontinuous time of half-thoughts, daydreams, fantasies, and remembrances' (88).

3 Although 'The Doll's House' certainly evolved out of Mansfield's childhood and is connected to other New Zealand stories, it is hard not to think of Ibsen as well. Library records in Wellington show that Mansfield's reading of 'some Ibsen' (Alpers, *Life of KM* 50) goes back to her adolescence.

4 Fullbrook also makes this point (122).

5 Indeed in this instance, as in a number of others, it is difficult to ignore Mansfield's probable influence on Woolf.

6 'On the one hand, Woolf felt a deep nostalgia for the security and emotional intensity the nuclear family had provided; on the other, she was
implacably hostile to the fundamental assumptions and practices of
nineteenth-century domestic life' (Zwerdling 175). Clearly, this ambivalence is based in Woolf's conflicted memories of her mother, Julia Stephen,
the model for Mrs Ramsay.

7 Moran enumerates an 'astounding number of resemblances' (*Word of
Mouth* 67) between Clarissa and Mansfield's Bertha in 'Bliss,' including a
'prefer[ence] for a companionate marriage' (68) and a partly repressed
attraction to women.

8 Clarissa's outing is balanced by the party itself, which takes up approximately the *last* forty-five pages of the novel.

9 Zwerdling reminds us that, if some critics – and Clarissa herself – refer to
'her ability to merge different worlds and create a feeling of integration. ...
Clarissa's integration is horizontal, not vertical' (127).

10 In Zwerdling's terms, this passage describes 'a way of life that seems part
of some eternal order, functioning without apparent friction or even
choice' (126).

11 I am reminded of Christie Logan's 'By their garbage shall ye know them'
in Margaret Laurence's *The Diviners* (32).

12 The curtains are the sole furnishings described – several times – either as a
backdrop for conversation or blowing in the open window, as if magically
infusing energy into the party: 'Gently the yellow curtain with all the birds
of Paradise blew out and it seemed as if there were a flight of wings into
the room, right out, then sucked back' (256).

13 Lady Bruton, 'derived from the eighteenth century' (264), a minor character in the novel, uses luncheons to wield influence in her own right, inviting to her table men whose help she needs in promoting her latest cause.

14 This is not a new phenomenon. In her study of hospitality in early modern
England, Felicity Heal notes that 'as peers and gentry shifted to London to
pursue office as well as fashion ... the calculus of reward became a more
important element in entertaining' (402).

15 Already changed by the war, London has now been transformed to a
modern consumer economy; in the new post-war world there is a bom-
bardment of commodities. Despite the military name, the Army and Navy
Stores sell consumer goods, indeed very feminine consumer goods: Elizabeth Dalloway and Doris Kilman have tea there, and buy petticoats.
Instead of dropping bombs, an airplane advertises a product, tracing its
name in the sky.

16 Ames and other critics have commented thoroughly on this part on the

novel, where, thinking about the window through which Septimus jumped, Clarissa looks through her own window at an old woman framed in another window across the courtyard: a mirror image of Clarissa, her other *alter ego*, representing old age, the alternative to Septimus's premature death.

17 A gendered relationship to the world is also suggested in *Mrs. Dalloway*, where Septimus must concentrate hard on ordinary domestic objects in order to maintain the sense of reality that his wife never questions: 'And so, gathering courage, he looked at the sideboard; the plate of bananas; the engraving of Queen Victoria and the Prince Consort; at the mantelpiece, with the jar of roses. None of these things moved. All were still; all were real' (215).

18 Günter Grass's *The Flounder* forms an interesting contrast to the original tale.

19 Hermione Lee, in her biography of Woolf, suggests a basis for this scene in Leslie Stephen's emotional demands on his stepdaughter, Stella Duckworth, after his wife's death, and on Vanessa after Stella died (136–7; 146).

20 Zwerdling quotes Mrs Beeton on this behaviour: '"It is generally established as a rule" ... "not to ask for soup or fish twice, as, in so doing, part of the company may be kept waiting too long for the second course"' (160).

7: The Art of Domesticity

1 Gilbert and Gubar also mention the significance of the lost brooch (3:30).

2 Homans points out that Woolf did not like the last volume of *Middlemarch* (278). Nevertheless Woolf considered Eliot one of the great writers, and published several pieces on her work. In 1919, the centenary of Eliot's birth, she wrote a long essay for *TLS*, later revised and reprinted in *The Common Reader*; in 1921, a brief article for the *Daily Herald*; and in 1926, a review of Eliot's collected letters in *Nation and Atheneum*.

3 The recent film *Big Night* is similar in its structure, with the planning and preparation of an elaborate feast making up much of the script, and the dinner itself the culmination of the work. In fact, all the recent works of fiction mentioned here have been made into films. Elaborate meals seem to provide excellent cinematic possibilities.

4 Kaplan reminds us, 'it is still necessary to restate the fact that until recently the academic critical tradition generally ignored the presence, let alone the overwhelming significance, of women writers – *as women* – in the creation of the [modernist] movement' (6). She goes on to note, however, that a more liberal definition of modernism than was used by, especially, the

New Critics, might be more useful than a project of creating a whole new modernism (*KM and the Origins* 7).

5 For instance, Benstock's quasi-definition of female modernist writing as 'a genderized writing that situates itself creatively, politically, and psychologically within a certain space and time' ('Expatriate Modernism' 29) is far too general to be either meaningful or useful.

6 In the Lacanian terms generally used to define such language, the feminine is associated with the literal; the text, on the other hand, represents a step beyond the literal to the figurative, the imaginative, the intellectual, the abstract. It is both a cause and an effect of this view of language that women are always 'the other' in male culture. De Beauvoir's notion of women's collusion in this position is crucial: '"one is not born, but rather becomes, a woman" by accepting definition as object rather than seizing one's exigent individuality as subject' (Fullbrook 6).

   Writing the mother's language, then, is not a straightforward proposition. Homans's summary of this question is particularly useful. First, the woman writer must redefine maternal language to insist on her own identity as a subject. Moreover, if the son's gradual detachment from the mother makes 'language both necessary and possible' (*Bearing the Word* 13) for him, the question of the literal and the figurative is more complex for the daughter. On one level, since she is female, she continues to identify with the female parent and thus does not have to abandon the mother for the father as a model. But on another level, the girl child is as abandoned as her brother is: as Irigaray notes, both sexes are thrown into the symbolic order at the moment when the umbilical cord is cut (Homans, *Bearing the Word* 24).

7 Woolf herself calls these 'difficult questions ... I must leave them, if only because they stimulate me to wander from my subject into trackless forests where I shall be lost and, very likely, devoured by wild beasts' (*Room* 78).

8 Woolf calls Richardson's 'a method that demands attention, as a door whose handle we wrench ineffectively calls our attention to the fact that it is locked' (McNeillie 3:10), and carries her ambivalence a step farther in observing: 'That Miss Richardson gets so far as to achieve a sense of reality far greater than that produced by the ordinary means is undoubted. But then, which reality is it, the superficial or the profound?' (3:11).

9 Kaplan takes a different approach, arguing that 'Mansfield frequently takes the culturally defined characteristics of "feminine" style as the object of satire. Mansfield *sees through* the stylistic devices to their origins in women's oppression or self-delusion' (*KM and the Origins* 159).

10 The beginning of 'At the Bay' provides one example of Mansfield's fluid

method of narration. An anonymous perspective, perhaps that of an early-rising cottager, written in the second person, merges into those of the flock of sheep, dog, and shepherd who appear around a bend in the road and slowly pass by. The narration – like a children's story – allows the reader directly into the thoughts of the Burnells' cat and, indirectly, those of the shepherd's dog before reverting to a more conventional omniscient narrative voice as the flock disappears again (205–7).

11 Murphy and many others have noted 'the lesbian component' (384) of the poem, which subverts the usual image of the audience for cookbooks: the wife in the conventional heterosexual family.

12 Some critics have insisted on the end of the novella as a liberation. For instance, Gilbert and Gubar say that 'Edna swims ... not into death but back into her own life, back into the imaginative openness of her childhood' (2:109). However, without moving to a completely symbolic level, it is difficult to see how drowning herself can be considered a positive outcome in Edna's case.

13 I am reminded of the standard advertising images of women already beginning to develop at the turn of the century. Writing about the 1920s, Marchand notes that the high-fashion, sophisticated image of the modern female consumer was altered to create a 'softer' picture of the housewife and mother (181).

14 Mademoiselle Reisz plays Chopin. The pun suggests the author's taking credit for awakening Edna (I am indebted to Jay Bochner for calling this *jeu de mots* to my attention).

15 Mrs Ramsay, as well, in *To the Lighthouse*, perceives things imaginatively; however, she does not experience an antagonistic relationship with the physical world, but rather a blurring of boundaries between the self and the world: 'It was odd, she thought, how if one was alone, one leant to inanimate things; trees, streams, flowers; felt they expressed one; felt they became one; felt they knew one, in a sense were one' (97). For Mrs Ramsay this conscious identification with the natural world is not frightening or threatening, merely an acknowledgment of a truth that she lives.

In a similar vein, Mansfield wrote to her friend Dorothy Brett: 'When I pass the apple stalls I cannot help stopping and staring until I feel that I, myself, am changing into an apple too – and that at any moment I may produce an apple, miraculously, out of my own being ... When I write about ducks I swear that I am a white duck ... This whole process ... is so thrilling that I can hardly breathe ... There follows the moment when you are *more* duck, *more* apple ... than any of these objects could ever possibly be, and so you *create* them anew. ...' (Hanson 28–9; final ellipsis in original).

16 'The Niece of a Nun: Virginia Woolf, Caroline Stephen, and the Cloistered Imagination' is reprinted in Marcus, *Virginia Woolf and the Languages of Patriarchy* 118; also quoted in Moran, *Word of Mouth* 72.

17 Susan Stanford Friedman's 'Creativity and the Childbirth Metaphor: Gender Difference in Literary Discourse' presents an overview of various literary examples of this link.

18 On a less theoretical level, it has, of course, been a truism that successful, creative, artistic women do not have children, as children interfere with time of one's own, as well as with a 'room of one's own,' and both the energy and the social permission to be obsessed with one's work or one's art. Woolf notes in *A Room of One's Own* that Austen, the Brontës, and Eliot were all childless. Chopin, on the other hand, had six children.

Works Cited

Alpers, Antony. *The Life of Katherine Mansfield*. New York: Viking Press, 1980.
– *The Stories of Katherine Mansfield*. Auckland: Oxford University Press, 1984.
Ames, Christopher. *The Life of the Party: Festive Vision in Modern Fiction*. Athens and London: University of Georgia Press, 1991.
Auster, Paul. *The Art of Hunger: Essays, Prefaces, Inverviews*. Los Angeles: Sun and Moon Press, 1991.
Aurell, Martin, Olivier Dumoulin, and Françoise Thelamon, eds. *La Sociabilité à table: commensalité et convivialité à travers les ages*. Rouen: l'Université de Rouen, 1992.
Bakhtin, Mikhail. *Rabelais and His World*. Trans. Hélène Iswolsky. Bloomington and Indianapolis: Indiana University Press, 1984.
Barthes, Roland 'Toward a Psychosociology of Contemporary Food Consumption.' Trans. Elborg Forster. *Annales, E.S.C.* 16 (September–October 1961): 977–86. Rpt. in *Food and Drink in History*. Ed. Robert Forster and Orest Ranum. Baltimore and London: Johns Hopkins University Press, 1979. 166–73.
Beardsworth, Alan, and Teresa Keil. 'Putting the Menu on the Agenda.' *Sociology*. 24.1 (1990): 139–51.
Bell, Millicent, ed. *The Cambridge Companion to Edith Wharton*. Cambridge: Cambridge University Press, 1995.
Benstock, Shari. 'Expatriate Modernism: Writing on the Cultural Rim.' *Women's Writing in Exile*. Ed. Mary Lynn Broe and Angela Ingram. Chapel Hill: University of North Carolina Press, 1989. 19–40.
– *Textualizing the Feminine*. Norman and London: University of Oklahoma Press, 1991.
Berman, Marshall. *All That Is Solid Melts into Air: The Experience of Modernity*. New York: Simon and Schuster, 1982.

Blum, Virginia L. 'Mary Wilkins Freeman and the Taste of Necessity.' *American Literature* 65.1 (1993): 69–94.

Bowlby, Rachel. 'Walking, Women and Writing.' *New Feminist Discourses: Critical Essays on Theories and Texts.* Ed. Isobel Armstrong. London: Routledge, 1992. 26–47. Rpt. in *Feminist Destinations and Further Essays.* Ed. Rachel Bowlby. Edinburgh: Edinburgh University Press, 1997.

Bruch, Hilda. *The Golden Cage: The Enigma of Anorexia Nervosa.* 1978. New York: Vintage Books, 1979.

Burgan, Mary. *Illness, Gender, and Writing: The Case of Katherine Mansfield.* Baltimore and London: Johns Hopkins University Press, 1994.

Burnett, John. *Plenty and Want: A Social History of Diet in England from 1815 to the Present Day.* 1966. 3rd ed. London and New York: Routledge, 1989.

Bynum, Caroline Walker. *Holy Feast and Holy Fast: The Religious Significance of Food to Medieval Women.* Berkeley and Los Angeles: University of California Press, 1987.

Chaline, J.P., and C. Vincent. 'Convivialité, commensalité: de la cohésion sociale à la civilisation des moeurs.' Aurell et al. 253–62.

Chopin, Kate. *The Awakening and Selected Short Stories.* 1899. Toronto, New York, London: Bantam, 1981.

Clark, Clifford E. 'The Vision of the Dining Room: Plan Book Dreams and Middle-Class Realities.' Grover 142–72.

Conradi, Peter. 'The Metaphysical Hostess: The Cult of Personal Relations in the Modern English Novel.' *ELH* 48.2 (1981): 427–53.

Daly, Saralyn R. *Katherine Mansfield.* New York: Twayne Publishers, 1994.

Davidoff, Leonore. *The Best Circles: Society, Etiquette and the Season.* London: Croom Helm, 1973.

DeKoven, Marianne. 'Gendered Doubleness and the "Origins" of Modernist Form.' *Tulsa Studies in Women's Literature* 8.1 (Spring 1989): 19–42.

– *Rich and Strange: Gender, History, Modernism.* Princeton: Princeton University Press, 1991.

Douglas, Mary, ed. *Constructive Drinking: Perspectives on Drink from Anthropology.* Cambridge: Cambridge University Press, 1987.

– *Food in the Social Order: Studies of Food and Festivities in Three American Communities.* New York: Russell Sage Foundation, 1984

Elias, Norbert. *The Civilizing Process.* Trans. Edmund Jephcott. New York: Urizen Books, 1978. Trans. of *Über den Prozess der Zivilisation.* Basel: 1939.

Ewen, Stuart. *Captains of Consciousness.* New York: McGraw-Hill, 1976.

Farb, Peter, and George Armelagos. *Consuming Passions.* Boston: Houghton Mifflin Company, 1980.

Felski, Rita. *Beyond Feminist Aesthetics.* United Kingdom: Hutchinson Radius, 1989.

– *The Gender of Modernity*. Cambridge: Harvard University Press, 1995.

Finkelstein, Joanne. *Dining Out: A Sociology of Modern Manners*. Cambridge: Polity Press, 1989.

Frederick, Christine. *Household Engineering: Scientific Management in the Home*. Chicago: American School of Home Economics, 1923.

Friedman, Susan Stanford. 'Creativity and the Childbirth Metaphor: Gender Difference in Literary Discourse.' *Feminist Studies* 13.1 (Spring 1987): 49–82.

Fryer, Judith. *Felicitous Space: The Imaginative Structures of Edith Wharton and Willa Cather*. Chapel Hill and London: University of North Carolina Press, 1986.

Fullbrook, Kate. *Katherine Mansfield*. Bloomington and Indianapolis: Indiana University Press, 1986.

Giedion, Siegfried. *Mechanization Takes Command: A Contribution to Anonymous History*. 1948. New York: W.W. Norton and Company, 1969.

Gilbert, Sandra M., and Susan Gubar. *Letters from the Front*. New Haven: Yale University Press, 1994. Vol. 3 of *No Man's Land: The Place of the Woman Writer in the Twentieth Century*. 3 vols. 1988–94.

Gilbert, Sandra M., and Susan Gubar. *Sexchanges*. New Haven: Yale University Press, 1989. Vol. 2 of *No Man's Land: The Place of the Woman Writer in the Twentieth Century*.

Gilman, Charlotte Perkins. *The Home: Its Work and Influence*. 1903. Urbana: University of Illinois Press, 1972.

Godden, Richard. *Fictions of Capital: The American Novel from James to Mailer*. Cambridge: Cambridge University Press, 1990.

Grover, Kathryn, ed. *Dining in America 1850–1900*. Amherst. University of Massachusetts Press, 1987.

Gusfield, Joseph R. 'Passage to Play: Rituals of Drinking Time in American Society.' Douglas, *Constructive Drinking* 73–90.

Hanson, Clare, ed. *The Critical Writings of Katherine Mansfield*. London: Macmillan Press, 1987.

Hanson, Clare, and Andrew Gurr. *Katherine Mansfield*. New York: St Martin's Press, 1981.

Harbison, Robert. *Eccentric Spaces*. New York: Alfred A. Knopf, 1977.

Hardy, Thomas. *Tess of the d'Urbervilles*. 1891. Harmondsworth: Penguin Books, 1985.

Harris, Marvin. *Good to Eat: Riddles of Food and Culture*. New York: Simon and Schuster, 1985.

Heal, Felicity. *Hospitality in Early Modern England*. Oxford: Clarendon Press, 1990.

Hobsbawm, E.J. *The Age of Empire 1875–1914*. 1987. London: Sphere Books, 1989.

Hobsbawm, Eric, and Terence Ranger, eds. *The Invention of Tradition*. Cambridge: Cambridge University Press, 1983.

Hochman, Barbara. '*The Awakening* and *The House of Mirth*.' *The Cambridge Companion to American Realism and Naturalism*. Ed. Donald Pizer. Cambridge: Cambridge University Press, 1995. 211–35.

Homans, Margaret. *Bearing the Word: Language and Female Experience in Nineteenth-Century Women's Writing*. Chicago: University of Chicago Press, 1989.

Homans, Margaret, ed. *Virginia Woolf: A Collection of Critical Essays*. Englewood Cliffs, NJ: Prentice Hall, 1993.

Hooker, Richard J. *Food and Drink in America*. Indianapolis and New York: The Bobbs-Merrill Company, 1989.

Howells, William Dean. *The Rise of Silas Lapham*. 1885. New York and London: W.W. Norton and Company, 1982.

Hurston, Zora Neale. *Their Eyes Were Watching God*. 1937. Urbana and Chicago: University of Illinois Press, 1978.

Huyssen, Andreas. *After the Great Divide*. Bloomington and Indianapolis: Indiana University Press, 1986.

Jeanneret, Michel. *Des mets et des mots*. Paris: Librairie José Corti, 1987.

Kaplan, Sydney Janet. *Katherine Mansfield and the Origins of Modernist Fiction*. Ithaca and London: Cornell University Press, 1991.

Knights, Pamela. 'Forms of Disembodiment: The Social Subject in *The Age of Innocence*.' Bell 20–46.

Larsen, Nella. *An Intimation of Things Distant: The Collected Fiction of Nella Larsen*. New York: Doubleday, 1992.

Laurence, Margaret. *The Diviners*. Toronto: McClelland and Stewart, 1974.

Lee, Hermione. *Virginia Woolf*. London: Chatto and Windus, 1996.

Lemenorel, Alain. 'Fonction symbolique, fonction sociale: l'aliment et la table à l'époque contemporaine.' Aurell et al. 359–68.

Levenstein, Harvey. 'The "Servant Problem" and American Cookery.' *Revue française d'études américaines* no. 27–8 (February 1986): 127–37.

Lévi-Strauss, Claude. *Le Cru et le cuit*. Paris: Plon, 1964.

Lindberg, Gary H. *Edith Wharton and the Novel of Manners*. Charlottesville: University Press of Virginia, 1975.

Lipovetsky, Gilles. *The Empire of Fashion: Dressing Modern Democracy*. Trans. Catherine Porter. Princeton: Princeton University Press, 1994. Trans. of *L'Empire de l'éphémère*. Paris: Gallimard, 1987.

Litvak, Joseph. *Strange Gourmets: Sophistication, Theory, and the Novel*. Durham and London: Duke University Press, 1997.

Loy, Mina. *The Lost Lunar Baedeker: Poems of Mina Loy*. Ed. Roger L. Conover. New York: Farrar Straus Giroux, 1996.

Mansfield, Katherine. *The Collected Stories of Katherine Mansfield.* Constable, 1945. London: Penguin Books, 1981.

Marchand, Roland. *Advertising the American Dream: Making Way for Modernity.* Berkeley and Los Angeles: University of California Press, 1986.

Marcus, Jane. *Virginia Woolf and the Languages of Patriarchy.* Bloomington and Indianapolis: Indiana University Press, 1987.

Marin, Louis. *Food for Thought.* Trans. Mette Hjort. Baltimore and London: Johns Hopkins University Press, 1989.

Maslow, Abraham H. *Motivation and Personality.* 1954. 2nd ed. New York, Evanston, and London: Harper and Row, 1970.

McFall, Gardner. 'Katherine Mansfield and the Honourable Dorothy Brett: A Correspondence of Artists.' Robinson 53–69.

McNeillie, Andrew, ed. *The Essays of Virginia Woolf.* London: Hogarth Press, 1986–94. 4 vols.

Mennell, Stephen. *All Manners of Food: Eating and Taste in England and France from the Middle Ages to the Present.* Oxford: Basil Blackwell, 1985.

Mennell, Stephen, Anne Murcott, and Anneke H. van Otterloo. *The Sociology of Food: Eating, Diet and Culture.* London: Sage Publications, 1992.

Mintz, Sidney W. *Sweetness and Power: The Place of Sugar in Modern History.* New York: Viking Penguin, 1985.

– *Tasting Food, Tasting Freedom: Excursions into Eating, Culture, and the Past.* Boston: Beacon Press, 1996

Moran, Patricia. 'Unholy Meanings: Maternity, Creativity, and Orality in Katherine Mansfield.' *Feminist Studies* 17.1 (Spring 1991): 105–25.

– *Word of Mouth. Body Language in Katherine Mansfield and Virginia Woolf.* Charlottesville and London: University Press of Virginia, 1996.

Murcott, Anne. *The Sociology of Food and Eating: Essays on the Sociological Significance of Food.* Aldershot, Hants.: Gower, 1983.

Murphy, Margueritte S. '"Familiar Strangers": The Household Words of Gertrude Stein's *Tender Buttons.' Contemporary Literature* 32 (1991): 383–402.

Murray, Oswyn, ed. *Sympotica: A Symposium on the 'Symposion.'* Oxford: Clarendon Press, 1990.

Nathan, Rhoda B. *Katherine Mansfield.* New York: Continuum Publishing Company, 1988.

Norris, Margot. 'Death by Speculation: Deconstructing *The House of Mirth.' 'The House of Mirth': Complete, Authoritative Text with Biographical and Historical Contexts, Critical History, and Essays from Five Contemporary Critical Perspectives.* Ed. Shari Benstock. New York: St Martin's Press, 1994. 431–46.

O'Sullivan, Vincent, and Margaret Scott, eds. *The Collected Letters of Katherine Mansfield*. Oxford: Clarendon Press, 1984.

Parkin-Gounelas, Ruth. *Fictions of the Female Self: Charlotte Brontë, Olive Schreiner, Katherine Mansfield*. New York: St Martin's Press, 1991.

– 'Katherine Mansfield Reading Other Women: The Personality of the Text.' Robinson 36–52.

– 'Katherine Mansfield's Piece of Pink Wool: Feminine Signification in "The Luftbad."' *Studies in Short Fiction* 27.4 (Fall 1990): 495–507.

Pasquier, Marie-Claire. 'La Cuisine et les mots: morceaux choisis.' *Revue française d'etudes américaines* 27 (February 1986): 37–50.

Perlick, Deborah, and Brett Silverstein. 'Faces of Female Discontent: Depression, Disordered Eating, and Changing Gender Roles.' *Feminist Perspectives on Eating Disorders*. Ed. Patricia Fallon, Melanie A. Katzman, and Susan C. Wooley. New York and London: Guilford Press, 1994. 77–93.

Poole, Roger. *The Unknown Virginia Woolf*. 4th ed. Cambridge and New York: Cambridge University Press, 1995.

Rendall, Jane. *Women in an Industrializing Society: England 1750–1880*. Oxford: Basil Blackwell, 1990.

Robinson, Roger, ed. *Katherine Mansfield: In from the Margin*. Baton Rouge and London: Louisiana State University Press, 1994.

Rosenman, Ellen Bayuk. *A Room of One's Own: Women Writers and the Politics of Creativity*. New York: Twayne Publishers, 1995.

Sandley, Sarah. 'The Middle of the Note: Katherine Mansfield's "Glimpses."' Robinson 70–89.

Schlesinger, Arthur Meier. *Learning How to Behave, a Historical Study of American Etiquette Books*. New York: Macmillan Company, 1946.

Selden, Catherine. 'The Tyranny of the Kitchen.' *North American Review* 157.4 (October 1893): 431–40.

Shapiro, Laura. *Perfection Salad: Women and Cooking at the Turn of the Century*. New York: Farrar, Straus and Giroux, 1986.

Showalter, Elaine. '*The Custom of the Country*: Spragg and the Art of the Deal.' Bell 87–97.

– *The Female Malady: Women, Madness, and English Culture, 1830–1980*. New York: Pantheon Books, 1985.

Simoons, Frederick J. *Eat Not This Flesh: Food Avoidances from Prehistory to the Present*. 2nd ed. Madison: University of Wisconsin Press, 1994.

Spain, Daphne. *Gendered Spaces*. Chapel Hill and London: University of North Carolina Press, 1992.

Spivak, Gayatri Chakravorty. 'Unmaking and Making in *To the Lighthouse*.' *In*

Other Worlds: Essays in Cultural Politics. New York and London: Routledge, 1988. 30–45.

Stein, Gertrude. *Tender Buttons.* 1914. New York: Haskell House Publishers, 1970.

Thelamon, Françoise. 'Sociabilité et conduites alimentaires.' Aurell et al. 9–19.

Tilley, Christopher, ed. *Reading Material Culture.* Oxford: Basil Blackwell, 1990.

Trilling, Lionel. *The Liberal Imagination.* 1950. New York: Anchor Books, 1953.

Veblen, Thorstein. *The Theory of the Leisure Class.* 1899. Boston: Houghton Mifflin Company, 1973.

Visser, Margaret. *The Rituals of Dinner.* Toronto: HarperCollins, 1991.

Waid, Candace. *Edith Wharton's Letters from the Underworld.* Chapel Hill and London: University of North Carolina Press, 1991.

Waugh, Patricia. *Metafiction: The Theory and Practice of Self-Conscious Fiction.* London and New York: Methuen, 1984.

Wharton, Edith. *The Age of Innocence.* 1920. New York: Collier Books, 1993.

– *The Custom of the Country.* 1913. London: Constable, 1941.

– *The House of Mirth.* 1905. New York: Collier Books, 1987.

Wharton, Edith, and Ogden Codman, Jr. *The Decoration of Houses.* 1897. New York: W.W. Norton and Company, 1978.

Williams, Susan R. 'Introduction.' Grover 3–23.

Wolff, Cynthia Griffin. *A Feast of Words: The Triumph of Edith Wharton.* New York: Oxford University Press, 1977.

– 'Lily Bart and the Drama of Femininity.' *American Literary History* 6.1 (Spring 1994): 71–87.

Wood, Roy C. *The Sociology of the Meal.* Edinburgh: Edinburgh University Press, 1995.

Woolf, Virginia. *The Complete Shorter Fiction of Virginia Woolf.* Ed. Susan Dick. 2nd ed. San Diego, New York, and London: Harcourt Brace and Company, 1989.

– *The Death of the Moth and Other Essays.* 1942. London: Hogarth Press, 1947.

– 'Mr. Bennett and Mrs. Brown.' *The Captain's Death Bed.* Ed. Leonard Woolf. London: Hogarth Press, 1950. Rpt. in *Collected Essays,* vol. 1. Ed. Leonard Woolf. London: Hogarth Press, 1966. 319–37.

– *Mrs. Dalloway.* 1925. New York: Harcourt, Brace and World, 1953.

– *A Room of One's Own.* 1928. Harmondsworth: Penguin Books, 1972.

– *Three Guineas.* 1938. New York and London: Harcourt Brace Jovanovich, 1966.

– *To the Lighthouse.* 1927. New York: Harcourt, Brace and World, 1955.

Zwerdling, Alex. *Virginia Woolf and the Real World.* Berkeley, Los Angeles, and London: University of California Press, 1986.

Works Consulted

Atwood, Margaret. *The Edible Woman*. 1969. Toronto: McClelland and Stewart, 1973.

Barnes, Djuna. *Nightwood*. 1937. New York: New Directions, 1961.

Barrett, Eileen, and Patricia Cramer, eds. *Re: Reading, re: Writing, re: Teaching Virginia Woolf: Selected Papers from the Fourth Annual Conference on Virginia Woolf*. New York: Pace University Press, 1995.

Beardsworth, Alan, and Teresa Keil. *Sociology on the Menu: An Invitation to the Study of Food and Society*. London and New York: Routledge, 1997.

Beecher, Catharine. *Treatise on Domestic Economy for the Use of Young Ladies at Home and at School*. 1841. New York: Schocken Books, 1977.

Beecher, Catharine, and Harriet Beecher Stowe. *The American Woman's Home: or Principles of Domestic Science*. 1869. Hartford, Conn.: Stowe-Day Foundation, 1975.

Beeton, Isabella Mary. *The Book of Household Management*. London: S.O. Beeton, 1866.

Bendixen, Alfred, and Annette Zilversmit, eds. *Edith Wharton: New Critical Essays*. New York and London: Garland Publishing, 1992.

Benstock, Shari. *No Gifts from Chance: A Biography of Edith Wharton*. New York: Scribner's, 1994.

– *Women of the Left Bank*. Austin: University of Texas Press, 1986.

Bentley, Nancy 'Edith Wharton and the Science of Manners.' Bell 47–67.

Bernikow, Louise. *Among Women*. New York: Harmony Books, 1980.

Bevan, David, ed. *Literary Gastronomy*. Amsterdam: Editions Rodopi B.V., 1988.

Boddy, Gillian. *Katherine Mansfield: The Woman and the Writer*. Harmondsworth: Penguin Books, 1988.

Booth, Alison. *Greatness Engendered: George Eliot and Virginia Woolf*. Ithaca and London: Cornell University Press, 1992.

Bowlby, Rachel. *Just Looking: Consumer Culture in Dreiser, Gissing and Zola.* New York: Methuen, 1985.

Bowlby, Rachel, ed. *Virginia Woolf.* New York: Longman, 1992.

Boyle, Kay. *The First Lover and Other Stories.* New York: Harrison Smith and Robert Haas, 1933.

Broe, Mary Lynn, and Angela Ingram, eds. *Women's Writing in Exile.* Chapel Hill and London: University of North Carolina Press, 1989.

Brown, James. *Fictional Meals and Their Function in the French Novel.* Toronto: University of Toronto Press, 1984.

Busch, Jane. 'Cooking Competition: Technology on the Domestic Market in the 1930s.' *Technology and Culture* 24 (April 1983): 222–45.

Caughie, Pamela L. *Virginia Woolf and Postmodernism: Literature in Quest and Question of Itself.* Urbana and Chicago: University of Illinois Press, 1991.

Cochrane, Kristy. 'In and Out of Perspective: Katherine Mansfield's Imagery.' *La Nouvelle de Langue Anglaise: The Short Story: In and Out/Dedans, Dehors.* Paris: Publications de la Sorbonne Nouvelle, 1991. 21–31.

Davey, Lynda. 'Sémiotique de l'aliment dans les romans français du XIXe siècle.' Dissertation. Université de Montréal, 1989.

Dinesen, Isak [Karen Blixen]. *Babette's Feast and Other Anecdotes of Destiny.* 1958. New York: Vintage Books, 1988.

Dos Passos, John. *Manhattan Transfer.* 1925. Boston: Houghton Mifflin Company, 1953.

Dreiser, Theodore. *Sister Carrie.* 1900. New York: Signet Classics, 1980.

Dunn, Jane. *A Very Close Conspiracy: Vanessa Bell and Virginia Woolf.* London: Pimlico, 1990.

Erlich, Gloria. *The Sexual Education of Edith Wharton.* Berkeley and Los Angeles: University of California Press, 1992.

Esquivel, Laura. *Like Water for Chocolate.* Trans. Carol Christensen and Thomas Christensen. New York: Doubleday, 1992.

Farmer, Fannie Merritt. *The Boston Cooking-School Cook Book.* 1896. New York: New American Library, 1988.

Fieldhouse, Paul. *Food and Nutrition: Customs and Culture.* Beckenham, Kent: Croom Helm, 1986.

Fitzgerald, F. Scott. *The Great Gatsby.* 1925. New York: Charles Scribner's Sons, 1953.

Gilbert, Sandra M., and Susan Gubar. *The War of the Words.* New Haven: Yale University Press, 1988. Vol. 1 of *No Man's Land: The Place of the Woman Writer in the Twentieth Century.* 3 vols. 1988–94.

Gillespie, Diane F., and Leslie K. Hankins, eds. *Virginia Woolf and the Arts: Selected Papers from the Sixth Annual Conference on Virginia Woolf.* New York: Pace University Press, 1997.

Goodman, Susan. *Edith Wharton's Inner Circle*. Austin: University of Texas Press, 1994.
– *Edith Wharton's Women*. Hanover and London: University Press of New England, 1990.
Goodwin, Sarah Webster. 'Knowing Better: Feminism and Utopian Discourse in *Pride and Prejudice, Villette*, and "Babette's Feast."' *Feminism, Utopia, and Narrative*. Ed. Libby Falk Jones and Sarah Webster Goodwin. Knoxville: University of Tennessee Press, 1990. 1–20.
Goody, Jack. *Cooking, Cuisine and Class: A Study in Comparative Sociology*. Cambridge: Cambridge University Press, 1982.
Grass, Günter. *The Flounder*. Trans. Ralph Manheim. New York: Harcourt, Brace, Jovanovich, 1978.
Hankin, C.A. *Katherine Mansfield and Her Confessional Stories*. New York: St Martin's Press, 1983.
Hanscombe, Gillian, and Virginia L. Smyers, eds. *Writing for Their Lives: The Modernist Women 1910–1940*. Boston: Northeastern University Press, 1988.
Hemingway, Ernest. *The Short Stories of Ernest Hemingway*. 1938. New York: Charles Scribner's Sons, 1966.
Holbrook, David. *Edith Wharton and the Unsatisfactory Man*. New York: St Martin's Press, 1991.
Howard, Maureen. '*The House of Mirth*: The Bachelor and the Baby.' Bell 137–56.
Hussey, Mark, and Vara Neverow-Turk, eds. *Virginia Woolf Miscellanies: Proceedings of the First Annual Conference on Virginia Woolf*. New York: Pace University Press, 1992.
– eds. *Virginia Woolf: Themes and Variations. Selected Papers from the Second Annual Conference on Virginia Woolf*. New York: Pace University Press, 1993.
Joslin, Katherine. *Edith Wharton*. Hampshire and London: Macmillan, 1991.
Joyce, James. *Dubliners*. 1916. Harmondsworth: Penguin Books, 1983.
– *Ulysses*. 1922. New York: Vintage Books, 1961.
Kafka, Franz. *The Metamorphosis, the Penal Colony, and Other Stories*. Trans. Willa and Edwin Muir. 1948. New York: Schocken Books, 1988. Trans. of *Gesammelte Werke, Bd. I, Erzählungen und Kleine Prosa*. New York: Schocken, 1947.
Kaivola, Karen. *All Contraries Confounded: The Lyrical Fiction of Virginia Woolf, Djuna Barnes and Marguerite Duras*. Iowa City: University of Iowa Press, 1991.
Kaplan, Sydney Janet. *Feminist Consciousness in the Modern British Novel*. Urbana and Chicago: University of Illinois Press, 1975.
Kasson, John F. 'Rituals of Dining: Table Manners in Victorian America.' Grover. 114–40.

Kobler, J.F. *Katherine Mansfield: A Study of the Short Fiction*. Boston: Twayne Publishers, 1990.

Laurence, Patricia Ondek. *The Reading of Silence: Virginia Woolf in the English Tradition*. Stanford, Calif.: Stanford University Press, 1991.

Levenstein, Harvey. *Revolution at the Table*. New York: Oxford University Press, 1988.

Loeffelholz. Mary. *Experimental Lives: Women and Literature, 1900–1945*. New York: Twayne Publishers, 1992.

Lupton, Deborah. 'Food, Memory and Meaning.' *Sociological Review* 42 (1994): 675–85.

MacClancy, Jeremy. *Consuming Culture*. New York: Henry Holt and Company, 1992.

Mansfield, Katherine. *The Stories of Katherine Mansfield*. Ed. Antony Alpers. Auckland, Melbourne, and Oxford: Oxford University Press, 1984.

Marcus, Jane. 'Still Practice, A/Wrested Alphabet: Toward a Feminist Aesthetic.' *Tulsa Studies in Women's Literature* 3–4 (1984–5): 79–97.

Marcus, Jane, ed. *New Feminist Essays on Virginia Woolf*. London: Macmillan Press, 1981.

– *Virginia Woolf: A Feminist Slant*. Lincoln and London: University of Nebraska Press, 1983.

Martin, Wendy, ed. *New Essays on 'The Awakening'*. Cambridge and New York: Cambridge University Press, 1988.

Moi, Toril. *Sexual/Textual Politics*. London and New York: Routledge, 1985.

Moore, Henrietta L. *Feminism and Anthropology*. Cambridge: Polity Press, 1988.

– *Space, Text, and Gender*. Cambridge University Press, 1986.

Nathan, Rhoda B., ed. *Critical Essays on Katherine Mansfield*. New York: G.K. Hall and Company, 1993.

Nicholson, Mervyn. 'Food and Power: Homer, Carroll, Atwood and Others.' *Mosaic* 20 (Summer 1987): 37–55.

O'Connor, Mary. 'The Objects of Modernism: Everyday Life in Women's Magazines, Gertrude Stein, and Margaret Watkins.' *American Modernism across the Arts*. Ed. Jay Bochner and Justin D. Edwards, New York: Peter Lang, 1999. 97–123.

Palmer, Arnold. *Movable Feasts*. 1952. Oxford: Oxford University Press, 1984.

Parker, Dorothy. *Here Lies: The Collected Stories of Dorothy Parker*. New York: Literary Guild of America, 1939.

Parloa, Maria. *Home Economics*. New York: Century Company, 1898.

Poovey, Mary. *Uneven Developments: The Ideological Work of Gender in Mid-Victorian England*. Chicago: University of Chicago Press, 1988.

Post, Emily. *Etiquette in Society, in Business, in Politics and at Home*. 14th ed. New York and London: Funk and Wagnalls Company, 1926.

Raphael, Lev. *Edith Wharton's Prisoners of Shame: A New Perspective on Her Neglected Fiction*. New York: St Martin's Press, 1991.

Rhys, Jean. *The Collected Short Stories*. New York and London: W.W. Norton and Company, 1987.

– *Quartet*. London: Deutsch, 1969.

Ruderman, Judith. 'An Invitation to a Dinner Party: Margaret Drabble on Women and Food.' *Margaret Drabble: Golden Realm*. Ed. Dorey Schmidt and Jan Seale. Edinburg, Texas: School of Humanities, Pan American University, 1982. 104–16.

Saxton, Ruth, and Jean Tobin, eds. *Woolf and Lessing: Breaking the Mold*. New York: St Martin's Press, 1994.

Schofield, Mary Anne, ed. *Cooking by the Book: Food in Literature and Culture*. Bowling Green, Ohio: Bowling Green State University Popular Press, 1989.

Scott, Bonnie Kime. *Refiguring Modernism*, vols. 1 and 2. Bloomington and Indianapolis: Indiana University Press, 1995.

Scott, Bonnie Kime, ed. *The Gender of Modernism: A Critical Anthology*. Bloomington and Indianapolis: Indiana University Press, 1990.

Smith, Barbara Herrnstein. *Contingencies of Value: Alternative Perspectives for Critical Theory*. Cambridge: Harvard University Press, 1988.

Spacks, Patricia Meyer. *Gossip*. Chicago and London: University of Chicago Press, 1985.

Squier, Susan M. *Virginia Woolf and London: The Sexual Politics of the City*. Chapel Hill and London. University of North Carolina Press, 1985.

Stead, C.K., ed. *The Letters and Journals of Katherine Mansfield: A Selection*. London: Allen Lane (Penguin Books), 1977.

Szekely, Eva Aniko. *Never Too Thin*. Toronto: Women's Press, 1988.

Tan, Amy. *The Joy Luck Club*. New York: Ballantine Books, 1989.

Tannahill, Reay. *Food in History*. New York: Stein and Day, 1973.

Timm, Uwe. *The Invention of Curried Sausage*. Trans. Leila Vennewitz. New York: New Directions, 1995.

Tobin, Ronald W. *Littérature et gastronomie*. Paris: Biblio 17, 1985.

Tomalin, Claire. *Katherine Mansfield: A Secret Life*. New York: St Martin's Press, 1987.

Tuttleton, James W., Kristen O. Lauer, and Margaret P. Murray, eds. *Edith Wharton: The Contemporary Reviews*. Cambridge and New York: Cambridge University Press, 1992.

Van Vechten, Carl. *Parties: Scenes from Contemporary New York Life*. New York: Knopf, 1930.

Vita-Finzi, Penelope. *Edith Wharton and the Art of Fiction*. New York: St Martin's Press, 1990.

Warde, Alan and Kevin Hetherington. 'English Households and Routine Food Practices: A Research Note.' *Sociological Review* 42 (1994): 758–78.

Waugh, Patricia. *Feminine Fictions: Revisiting the Postmodern*. London and New York: Routledge, 1989.

– *Practising Postmodernism, Reading Modernism*. London: Edward Arnold, 1992.

Wecter, Dixon. *The Saga of American Society: A Record of Social Aspiration 1607–1937*. New York: Charles Scribner's Sons, 1937.

Wharton, Edith. *The Collected Short Stories of Edith Wharton*. Ed. R.W.B Lewis. 2 vols. New York: Scribner, 1968.

Wheeler, Kathleen. *'Modernist' Women Writers and Narrative Art*. New York: New York University Press, 1994.

White, Barbara A. *Edith Wharton: A Study of the Short Fiction*. New York: Twayne Publishers, 1991.

Wolfe, Linda. *The Literary Gourmet: Menus from Masterpieces*. 1962. New York: Simon and Schuster, 1985.

Yeazell, Ruth Bernard. 'The Conspicuous Wasting of Lily Bart.' *ELH* 59 (1992): 713–34.

Index